ALL THE
BISHOPS'
MEN

TOM MOONEY is editor of *The Wexford Echo* group of newspapers. He has reported on the clerical abuse scandal in the Diocese of Ferns since 1990 and was one of two journalists to report the first ever trial of a priest in Ireland charged with sexual assault. A journalist since 1988, he has won a Law Society Media Justice Award and an Amnesty International Media award.

ALL THE
BISHOPS'
MEN

TOM MOONEY

The Collins Press

FIRST PUBLISHED IN 2011 BY
The Collins Press
West Link Park
Doughcloyne
Wilton
Cork

British Library Cataloguing in Publication Data
Mooney, Tom.
    All the bishops' men.
    1. Catholic Church. Diocese of Ferns (Ireland)—
    Clergy—Sexual behavior. 2. Child sexual abuse by
    clergy—Ireland—Wexford (County)
    I. Title
    261.8'3272'088282-dc22

ISBN-13: 978-1-848-89099-2

Typesetting by The Collins Press
Typeset in Bembo 11 on 13 pt
Printed by CPI Cox and Wyman, UK

Interior photographs courtesy of *The Wexford Echo* and Jim Campbell.

Cover photographs courtesy of iStockphoto.

Contents

Foreword   1

1. All the Bishops' Men   9

2. Fr Seán Fortune   24

3. Fr James Doyle   53

4. Canon Martin Clancy   66

5. Fr John Kinsella   76

6. Fr Donal Collins   85

7. Fr James Grennan   106

8. Monsignor Micheal Ledwith   127

9. Canon Law   143

10. Bishop Brendan Comiskey: His Rise and Fall   170

11. Comiskey and the Media   206

Epilogue   221

*Appendix 1: Transcript of interview given by Bishop of Limerick Donal
     Murray on 27 November 2009, following publication of the
     Commission of Investigation report into Child Sex Abuse
     Allegations in the Archdiocese of Dublin (The Murphy Report)
     to Joe Nash on Limerick's Live 95FM.*   249

*Appendix 2: Interview with Colm O'Gorman in December 2003 by
     Brendan Keane. which was published in* The Wexford Echo.   261

Appendix 3: Timeline of Events   272

Bibliography   278

Acknowledgements   282

Foreword

'I am the King's good servant but God's first.'
Sir Thomas Moore

*'The Inquiry wishes to record its revulsion at the extent, severity and
duration of the child sexual abuse allegedly perpetrated on children by
priests acting under the aegis of the Diocese of Ferns.'*
The Ferns Report

On the third Sunday in April 2006, the great and the good – including four Oireachtas members, two Ministers, one MEP, the Mayor of Wexford, the Chairman of the County Council, the County Managers of Wexford and Wicklow, the Garda Chief Superintendent, Cardinal Desmond Connell, seventeen bishops, the Papal Nuncio and representatives from four other religious denominations – convened in St Aidan's Cathedral, Enniscorthy, to witness the ordination to the episcopate of the Bishop of Ferns, Denis Brennan. In their own unique way, the Gardaí, politicians and representatives of the Churches had contributed to the concatenation of events across three decades in Wexford that inevitably led to the dishonourable discharge of Brennan's predecessor, Brendan

Comiskey. Ferns was a diocese in disarray, reeling from the findings of an inquiry the previous October that had examined the handling of over a hundred allegations of child sexual abuse against priests in the diocese from 1966 to 2005. Half of those accused of clerical abuse refused to cooperate.

The Ferns Report exposed the repeated failure and dereliction of duties of those in positions of trust – the Catholic Church and the Gardaí – who did not do nearly enough to stop abusers or take effective measures to protect the young victims. Regulation of priests in Wexford by their bishops was crippled by the absence of accountable governance or by a blind obedience to drawn-out, in-house investigations that inevitably failed to meet the Church's standard of proof necessary to remove a priest from active ministry. And when the Church in Wexford came under fire for shirking its responsibility to vulnerable children, politicians rode to its rescue, bestowing honour upon honour on its prelates, engaging the Fourth Estate, or withdrawing into the shadows whenever a new scandal unfolded. Left to the body politic in Wexford, *The Ferns Report* would have become cardiganed by time, a footnote in a horror story most of the guests at Brennan's ordination as bishop would have wanted to forget, because its 270-odd pages are a lacerating depiction of a collective ineptitude.

No metaphor can convey the emotional destruction of victims at the hands of priests in the diocese, the majority of whom were ordained at St Peter's College Seminary, though the coat of arms of Bishop Brennan – featuring a gold torch – is a genuinely symbolic attempt to shine light on the shadow of shame masking Wexford. 'Today is about persons abused by priests of the diocese: it's about their struggle to be listened to and believed, their ongoing pain and their search for healing,' said Brennan at his ordination as bishop, a theme taken up by Fr Joseph McGrath in his homily. 'The future must be based on all the past. Nothing in our past will be forgotten, ignored, airbrushed out or unrepented of,' he stressed, with the qualification that 'neither will any one experience dominate'.

Four years after his words echoed in St Aidan's Cathedral, that 'one experience' continues to dominate the Catholic Church both at home and abroad. If 2009 was a bleak year for the Irish Church with the publication of *The Ryan Report* and *The Murphy Report* on top of each other, 2010 was horrendous for the Vatican, as the world's media turned on Pope Benedict for his mishandling of abusive priests when he was a cardinal.

The Ferns Inquiry was non-statutory, as recommended by a report of George Birmingham SC to the government, as the Church had indicated that its cooperation would be forthcoming. The Inquiry was chaired by Supreme Court Judge Francis Murphy, assisted by Dr Helen Buckley and Dr Laraine Joyce, and examined a hundred allegations against twenty-one priests – from single complaints against nine priests to twenty-six against one – between 1966 and 2005, at a cost of €1.868m. When allegations were made, Bishop Comiskey believed that the proper response was to remove the priest from active ministry. However, he did not do that. He received allegations against ten living priests but, as protracted and inconclusive consultations got bogged down in nebulous semantics, no priest was made to stand aside during Comiskey's episcopacy and no effective child protection measures were put in place. He put the reputation of the Church before the protection of children. In this he was not alone, a symptom of the general malaise within the Dublin archdiocese from which he came. Comiskey was conscious of the need to protect the reputation of his priests but he failed to recognise the paramount importance of protecting children.

The Ferns Report was published by the Department of Health and Children and laid before the Houses of the Oireachtas.

Words that resonated in Minister Brian Lenihan's response to its findings are 'repeated failure' and 'gross dereliction of duties'. The government referred the report to the Director of Public Prosecutions (DPP) because the Inquiry was of the view that the Garda investigation of allegations made by ten children in Monageer was 'neither adequate nor appropriate'. No proceedings were instigated by the DPP. *The Ferns Report* was an indictment of the totality of the response to clerical abuse in Wexford during the period under investigation. 'With the benefit of hindsight, it is possible to see that the Church authorities, the medical profession and society in general failed to appreciate the horrendous damage which the sexual abuse of children can and does cause,' said the report. Brendan Howlin, Labour Party TD for Wexford, was disarmingly blunt: 'Society went on as normal with such hurt and evil flowing freely beneath the surface.' The Church of Ireland Bishop of Ferns Peter Barrett adopted a conciliatory position: the faithful Catholic clergy and parishioners in Ferns 'must not in any way be associated with grave information at this time of profound distress'. If anything, enough of the faithful were culpable of the bystander effect – they turned a blind eye and did and said nothing. Avril Doyle MEP, who publicly endorsed Comiskey during the tumultuous autumn in the diocese in 1995, accepted 'our society owes a profound and sincere apology to those who suffered so seriously at the hands of men in a position of trust throughout the diocese'.

Undoubtedly, *The Ferns Report* was a watershed in the history of contemporary Ireland. It was intended by the government as a body of work upon which to base legislative reform to end the scourge of child abuse. Barnardos Chief Executive Fergus Finlay sounded a warning that was never fully heeded: an open and informed environment is needed to encourage a willingness to report promptly inappropriate sexual behaviour towards children.

Catholicism, in a country as morally bankrupt and incandescently corrupt as early 21st-century Ireland, is sustained intravenously by the belief that the presence of evil is compatible with faith: one proves the existence of the other. If a flagrant disregard for the welfare of others is a form of evil, the aberrant priests of the Ferns and Dublin dioceses are guilty as charged. Their evil sprang from a callous thoughtlessness, sustained by habituation within an unregulated fish bowl. Should we consider their evil recidivistic? This book is no more and no less than a footnote in the collective memory of clerical abuse in the Diocese of Ferns; but neither a disclosure nor an aide memoire will prevent further abuse today or tomorrow until we grasp that labelling offenders obscures the fact that outwardly they are as unassumingly ordinary as we are, if disconnected from society by a malfunctioning moral compass. 'By distancing ourselves from sexual offenders, we can distance ourselves from that part of us which we do not even wish to acknowledge,' reasoned Dr Eamonn Conway in the book *The Church and Child Sexual Abuse*. Until we decide that prevention is far better than cure, the Church, as Paul Muldoon said in his address at the 2010 Dun Laoghaire poetry festival, is not fit to police itself. Micheál Martin pointed out in 1999 that the concept of the child as a separate individual with rights came late to this country. There is still a long road ahead in putting safe mileage between the abuser and the abused. Lenient sentencing by the courts has not helped. For assaulting a twelve-year-old boy, Fr James Doyle received a three-month sentence at Wexford District Court, which was suspended if he left the diocese. And Doyle did, fleeing unpunished to England where he continued, unsupervised, in ministry. Fr Donal Collins abused his pupils in the 1960s, the 1970s and the 1980s: at Wexford Circuit Court he received a four-year sentence for indecent assault and a two-year term for gross indecency to run concurrently. For good behaviour, he was out after a year.

It has not been said loud enough: the punishment of priests in Ferns never fitted the crime. At the core of this book are ordinary people who did the right thing: the couple in Fethard who alerted a succession of bishops to the criminality of Seán Fortune; the teacher in Monageer who reported the allegations of young girls to the Health Board; the victims of Martin Clancy in Ballindaggin who responded to an appeal by Bishop Eamonn Walsh to come forward and tell their story; the schoolboys abused by Donal Collins who came back as adults to face their abuser in court and the good Gardaí, like Detective Pat Mulcahy, who protected and served victims of abuse, not the Catholic Church. Misconceptions abound about why priests, of all people, should elect to perform the most heinous of acts. The answers are not easy, but certainly the absence of policing of candidates for the seminary at St Peter's College, Wexford, before admission, facilitated the progress of the mentally unsuitable. It is more than reasonable to speculate that seminary life, and being surrounded by young boys attending school day and night, stunted the sexual development of some seminarians. Richard Sipe, who has written extensively about clerical paedophilia, and is convinced that the problem of sexual abuse by Catholic clergy is systemic, has pointed out that in a system as homosocial (exclusively male) as the Church, psychosexually immature men are prone to select sexually immature partners, and abusers become involved with minors under the self-delusion or guise that they are being kind.

Sexual orientation was a source of huge shame for clerical abusers. Both Donal Collins, who advised pupils how to part their hair to avoid an effeminate look (at the side and not in the middle), and Seán Fortune, vehemently denied that they were homosexual, but they focused their sexual fantasies onto teenage boys, with incalculable damage. Dr Attracta Shields, a clinical psychologist, believes that unequal power relationships between men and women perpetuated by institutes and ideologies can create a climate for abuse of power and provide the milieu where child sexual abuse is likely to occur. Observing the trial of Donal Collins from the wings, I had never heard testimony as moving as from the men who stood before their abuser and told in acrid detail the damage he had done. If you have to stifle the reflex yawn when clerical abuse comes up in conversation, consider them.

There is in Wexford a desire for a collective forgetfulness about the catalogue of clerical abuse, much of which cannot be covered in this book because so many priests had their names redacted in *The Ferns Report*: priests like 'Fr Gamma', who left the priesthood after the publication of *The Ferns Report*, and was accused of abusing eleven girls, some as young as eight; 'Fr Delta', who abused young boys at St Peter's in the mid-1960s and was moved to a half-parish in Ferns by Bishop Donal Herlihy without monitoring; and 'Fr Iota', who drove a girl – whom he met at a youth club when she was thirteen – from her school to his rooms at St Peter's College in the early 1970s and abused her over a number of years. She disclosed the abuse to her family doctor who prescribed antidepresssants, which she then used in a suicide attempt. The doctor informed Bishop Herlihy about the abuse and the suicide attempt and 'Fr Iota' was sent to Westminster. Herlihy described the priest in a letter to Cardinal Heenan as 'a gentle refined young man, but has always demanded understanding and sympathy'. Herlihy later recalled 'Fr Iota' to serve in Ferns as a national school chaplain, manager and teacher. In a desperate effort to stop the abuse, the teenage girl, called Pamela in *The Ferns Report*, confided in another priest, 'Fr Kappa', who in turn abused her. She became pregnant by 'Fr Kappa', fled to London but returned to Wexford to have the child. She was one of the first victims to receive compensation – in December 2006 – from the Diocese of Ferns during the episcopacy of Bishop Brennan, whom she described as treating her with 'total dignity'.

Statues honouring the rebellion in 1798 are erected by local authorities throughout Wexford to adorn each new roundabout or bypass, but there is no monument to the boys and girls who made over 100 allegations of clerical abuse to the Ferns Inquiry, nor will there be. The challenge in writing a book like this, for a generation that did not grow up with the daily tittle-tattle of disclosure and revelation, is to avoid the savour of fish served on Monday – not quite fresh. There was something rotten in the Diocese of Ferns, for a long time, and it is a mistake to assume that financial reparation or restitution is the ultimate atonement. It is also a mistake not to exculpate those few priests, sullied by association, who were conscientious in encouraging victims not to remain silent about suspected abuse.

Classifying the abusers is another decade's work: familiarisation with *The Ferns Report* might substantiate a belief that clerical abusers are predominantly homosexual ephebophiles (abusers of young adolescents), but a study in 2002 showed that most acts of sexual abuse by priests in the country were paedophile in nature. Facts and figures may increase the sum of our collective knowledge, but the one common denominator among all the victims chronicled in this book, which does not purport to be a definitive history, is that the system failed them. It is impossible not to be outraged at their treatment by the Church and by society. The words of Dr Eamonn Conway, addressing a conference, Child Abuse: Learning from the Past – Hoping for the Future, organised by the National Conference of Priests of Ireland, might point the way to redemption. 'The Church needs to develop a charter for its own recovery if the Gospel is to be preached today.'

Tom Mooney
Wexford, 2011

1

All the Bishops' Men

'When a long abuse of power is corrected, it is generally replaced by an opposite violence. In the new dispensations, all that was good in what went before is tarred indiscriminately with the bad. This is, to some extent, what is happening in Ireland. The most dramatic change in my lifetime has been the collapse of the Church's absolute power. This has brought freedom and sanity in certain areas of human behaviour after a long suppression – as well as a new intolerance.'
John McGahern, *The Guardian*, 8 April 2006

Dramatis Personae: Fr Donal Collins, Fr James Doyle, Canon Martin Clancy, Fr Seán Fortune, Fr James Grennan, Fr John Kinsella, Monsignor Micheal Ledwith and Bishop Brendan Comiskey.

In the courtyard at the rear of the high crenellated tower of the college, pupils and staff assemble. They organise into a dozen regimental rows, their steps muffled by the soft grass, their backs turned to the tower, which overlooks the parish of Wexford, extending from Farnogue stream to

Drinagh, and from Coolree to the sea, representing in total a union of eleven old parishes. This part of the world is truly God's Acre: eight years after a Roman Catholic seminary was established at Michael Street in the town in 1911, staff and students transferred to Summerhill. It is said the first Christian monastery was established in Taghmon, outside Wexford in AD 597. Legend has it that Wexford is so old that its birth cannot be dated. The foundation of the Diocese of Ferns dates from 598 when Brandubh, King of Uí Cinsealaigh, granted land to Maodhog (St Aidan). At the synod of Rath Breasail in 1111, the boundaries of the diocese were determined.

It is a dry, autumnal day. The senior students, the fifth and the sixth years, form the rear column, about six rows behind the line-up of teachers, twenty-five of whom are lay and all men, attired in shirt and tie and either blazer or jacket, and seventeen priests, most of whom were seminarians at St Peter's College, home to the first chapel designed in Ireland by Augustin Welby Pugin.

It is a busy school on this mild October day in 1982, just weeks before Wexford indulges in its annual international opera festival. Former rector of the seminary and President of the College, Fr Patrick O'Brien, has forty seminarians under his wing. All 570 pupils – 200 boarders – are dapper in light grey or anthracite-black slacks, their arms folded purposefully across the sable blazers. Neither disapprobation nor indiscipline has summoned them to this brief sabbatical from the classroom, but posterity. Each and every one has his place in a group photograph, to be published in a week's time in the local press, upon which will be superimposed *Tibi dabo claves regni caelorum* – the words of Jesus to Peter: 'I will give you the keys to the kingdom of heaven.' It is yet another milestone for St Peter's, the opening of a sports complex, the biggest in Wexford. And flanked by his colleagues, a patient Fr Donal Collins (educated

10

at St Peter's College from 1949 to 1955), who is himself an expert in photography, prepares a wan smile for when the photographer signals his intention to capture the moment.

A career priest he is not, but Collins – quietly and unobtrusively – has done rather well for himself. With the notable exception of a short stint with the Diocese of Westminster, which he enjoyed, Collins has been a Peter's man through and through for two decades. He was chairman of the Priests' Council in Ferns in the 1970s and Spiritual Director of the South Ferns Curia of the Legion of Mary from 1976 for six years. His professional profile (he was the author of textbooks on physics and science and compiled *A Minute a Day* – daily reflections on the gospel) in the autumn of 1982 is on an upward curve. In three years he will be co-opted by the successor to the Bishop of Ferns Donal Herlihy, who lives in a house across the road from the college, to the Administrative Council of St Peter's; in six years he will be appointed principal, after a lengthy process – which is not unusual – by a selection panel, a unanimous choice because no suggestion of impropriety of any kind is brought to its attention.

And all of this, promotion after promotion, must have come as a surprise to Collins, whose penchant for impropriety had got him into a spot of bother in the past. How, he might have wondered, was his escapade with boarders at St Peter's in the 1960s overlooked, or forgotten, and how could the diocese – which had banished him to London for measuring the penises of his pupils – now make him the overseer of the college? Odd that, the absence of files. Rumour once reached Comiskey's predecessor, Donal Herlihy, a seriously devout man whose dreams were in Latin, that Collins was having it off with boarders. Herlihy knew how the Archdiocese of Dublin handled such matters and he offered Collins the choice of a curacy elsewhere in the diocese or a stint in England until he could be recalled.

London town beckoned and Collins was content there, for it was not commonly known among his colleagues that, gifted though he was as a teacher (he was the first in Ireland to receive a Teacher of Physics Award from the Institute of Physics, England), his preference was for parish work. Herlihy could not afford to lose such a gifted pedagogue as Collins and ended his spell spreading the Gospel to the British after two years. The episode with the boarders shelved, Herlihy allowed Collins to teach once more, encouraging his extra-curricular activities with pupils, such as photography and swimming.

He contributes an article on the Young Scientist Exhibition, with which he is heavily involved, to the 1971 college magazine *Petrus* (opposite the first published fiction of future Booker Prize nominated novelist Colm Tóibín, then a fourth-year fledgling writer). Herlihy, who believes priests are ontologically distinct from the laity because they are configured to God, and as such understands that an impropriety is a moral failure, not criminal, and can be redeemed by prayer and forgiveness, or by moving priests like chess pieces from diocese to diocese, performs the opening of the college sports complex in early October 1982. Sitting in the second row, facing him, is Donal Collins. It is not known whether Collins abused a St Peter's boy before or after the school assembled for the photograph, or before or after Herlihy opened the complex, which was attended by the well endowed of Wexford society, for the scant information on the charge sheet presented by the DPP to a crowded but hushed Wexford Circuit Court sixteen years later will read, 'indecent assault on date unknown in October 1982'.

In court, the ageing Collins sits alone, thrown to the wolves by the diocese that had so long cosseted his crimes and misdemeanours. Collins will become one of twenty-one diocesan priests identified in *The Ferns Report*, against whom hundreds of allegations of child sexual abuse were made between

1966 and 2005 in the diocese. Within a random five-year probe by the Ferns Inquiry, ten priests who were at St Peter's came under the spotlight as probable sexual abuse offenders. Among them is a contemporary of Collins, Fr James Doyle (ordained at St Peter's College, 1974), who suffered the distinct ignominy of becoming the first Irish priest to be brought to heel in an Irish court on a sexual-assault-related charge against a minor, in 1990. That distinction alone, which should have opened the eyes of his community to the burgeoning sins of some clergy in its midst, was dismissed at the time as an anomalous deviation by one of the better known priests in Wexford town. His appearance before a judge ought to have set alarm bells ringing, yet few could have anticipated the public support he received, when his transgression with a boy about the same age as the pupils in the primary school he ministered to became headline news. The antipathy to the local media was instantaneous and virulent: it was never demonstrably clear if supporters of Doyle – teachers and fellow priests – objected to the publicity or the audacity to publish, for no priest in Wexford had ever been outed for such a calumny. Naming and shaming was hitherto the preserve of the pulpit.

But the disturbing ephemera of Doyle's psychosis were laid bare in court for all to see. According to his legal team, Doyle was an abuse victim himself, had a chronic drinking problem and was suffering from blackouts, but was nevertheless deployed without monitoring by the Diocese of Ferns to a curacy in Clonard Parish, with access to children in primary schools and teenagers at St Peter's College.

Canon Martin Clancy (ordained at St Peter's College in 1942) had two D-Days in his long life as a priest of Ferns: 6 June 1944, when Allied troops landed on the beaches of Normandy and Clancy served his last day in England in the Diocese of Newcastle before returning to his native Wexford, and the spring day in 1991 when he received a letter out of the blue from his bishop, which repeated the allegation of a woman who said that Clancy had abused her when she was a young girl. Brendan Comiskey had no idea that Clancy had been interfering with young girls since 1965. Clancy fitted the classic description of a paedophile: he had recurrent, intensely sexually arousing fantasies involving the molestation of girls aged thirteen or younger. Confronted by Comiskey's allegation, Clancy decided to reply to his bishop. It was 99 per cent denial, but the 1 per cent admitting wrong was instrumental in exposing the mind of a serial predator who stalked primary school girls in the rural parish of Ballindaggin. Clare, as she was called in *The Ferns Report*, endured abuse by Clancy while attending the local national school. When she told her friends that Clancy had encouraged her to visit the parochial house to learn how to play music, they predicted she would be 'the next one'. She did not know then what they meant, but soon did.

While Clare practised her music, Clancy sat at his writing desk, positioning her between his legs: he would fondle her breasts or rub between her legs. She was twelve. It was Clare who prompted Comiskey to write to Clancy, who replied in some detail after the accusation was brought to his attention. 'At the time she was a good-looking, red-headed youngster, provocative etc, and I clearly remember the last occasion when I momentarily touched her on the upper thigh . . .' A meeting followed between Comiskey and Clancy but the priest suspected his bishop was not proficient at managing miscreants like himself, and though Clancy's carefully massaged correspondence implies a moral vacuity at the core of his character, he did convince Comiskey of his genuineness, and he was switched to an adjacent parish. It was an age-old diocesan solution to an age-old diocesan problem. *The Ferns Report* expressed its concern that the bishop's response did not take into consideration child protection policies in the diocese, that he had not taken his own advice. In 1990, Comiskey had told senior Churchmen about new child abuse guidelines: one was that 'a bishop must relieve the accused priest temporarily of his duties in order to protect other children'. Comiskey interpreted this a year later as moving Clancy three miles down the road, with no restrictions placed on him and no monitoring whatsoever.

Seán Fortune (ordained at St Peter's College in 1979) acquired a wealth of sobriquets. A newspaper report in 1987 first alluded to him as 'Father Goldfinger' and 'King Midas' because of his business acumen; he was known as 'Flapper' to the first-year boarders at St Peter's College whom he supervised, apparently rewarding the pupil who told the dirtiest joke with a bar of chocolate; Brendan Comiskey once called him the Monsignor Horan of the Southeast; within forty-eight hours of his suicide in New Ross in March 1999, a week after he appeared in court to face multiple charges of sexual assault, *The Irish Times* paraphrased a Fethard-on-Sea villager's description of him as 'the greatest liar'. Another said that he had all the deadly sins, except sloth. The process of decanting fiction from fact in the life and death of Seán Fortune begins with the acknowledgement that his extreme disconnection from the reality of his precarious position belied the hidden truth that, on a personal level, he was close to a fatal implosion. His death caught everybody by surprise – his housekeeper, his family, his victims, his caretaker, the Gardaí, the media and the Diocese of Ferns. In one fell swoop he escaped the clutches of justice. Fortune had become a hunted man who, until his detention, had avoided being cornered. He had been running out of excuses and places to hide. He could not have recognised the caricature of him that surfaced in newspaper and magazine articles, and once the DPP pressed charges the media tracked his every movement. In security footage viewed by the Gardaí, Fortune is seen pursuing a group of youths who had continuously attacked his home with stones and bricks and added to his torment like merciless harpies. The headlines his death generated in the Sunday newspapers were in direct proportion to the speed with which accuracy and truth were excised. Under the skin of Fortune was a weather system of complexity: no admission of guilt was ever forthcoming from his black despair. The man described by another priest, a month after his death, as the essence of generosity, is the recusant priest scapegoated by Comiskey, vying desperately to cast himself on the right side of history, in his resignation speech ('I found Fr Fortune virtually impossible to deal with').

As he discovered the toughest of learning curves in a part of the world unfamiliar to him and unfamiliar with him, away from the intellectual razzmatazz of Dublin, Brendan Comiskey slowly came to an awakening that the backwater of Wexford and its vipers' nest of a diocese, with a coterie of degenerate priests who did as they pleased in their small fiefdoms, could only be borne by being less than sober some of the time. Comiskey did not need reminding that there was much more to being Bishop of Ferns than addressing the elderly faithful at Our Lady's Island pilgrimage in late summer or the merry-go-round of confirming thousands of children in spring, but he was unprepared for the fallout from his handling of abuse allegations against the parish priest of Monageer, James Grennan (ordained at St Peter's College in 1958). In rural parishes in the 1980s the priest was seen to have power, and exercised it: in community halls, in schools, in scout troops, on committees, always at the centre of any parochial politburo with a semblance of authority or vigilance, rubbing shoulders with other pillars of society: bankers, councillors and the Gardaí. Grennan was such a priest.

This proximity between people trained in circle-squaring in a crisis was to have tumultuous consequences for young girls preparing for their confirmation in Monageer, when a Garda investigation was undermined from the outset by the clouded judgement of senior police officers in the county, whose misplaced loyalty to the Church shielded the one individual accused of abuse, the parish priest. Half a dozen Gardaí, not all motivated by a shared consideration, descended on Monageer to find out what had happened to the girls in the local church, but the mysterious and unsolved disappearance of their handwritten notes prohibited any prosecution.

The Gardaí, with all their resources, did not move their investigation forward by an inch after it was launched. The correlative and corrosive relationship between the Church and those whose duty is to protect and serve meant that the system the girls and their parents believed in failed them, and failed them badly, with execrable consequences. And sometimes, too, priests believed that the Church failed them.

The world of Fr John Kinsella (ordained at St Peter's College in 1974) fell apart in full view of his rural parish in the spring of 2002: for years he had been battling Comiskey and defending his reputation against a string of allegations that he had abused three youths, beginning shortly after his ordination at St Peter's College. He gave the diocese the same answer that he gave the Gardaí: he was not culpable of abusing anybody. But still the diocese, and in particular his bishop, pursued him relentlessly in the hope that he would do the decent thing and step aside from his ministry. Kinsella would not budge, and he let it be known to anybody listening that if he was forced to go, he would not do so quietly. It did not help his morale when he learned that the diocese's Advisory Panel had encouraged the quizzing of other priests who had worked with him in Enniscorthy and his present parish, The Ballagh, in the expectation that incriminating rumours and innuendo about him would unfold.

The years 1995–1996 were tumultuous in the diocese, with the machinations of Comiskey – calling for a debate on celibacy, taking a sabbatical in America, holding a major press conference on his return – the sole source of an intense scrutiny by the media, which only abated when his detailed and seemingly watertight explanation of his handling of abuse cases at a press briefing appeared to satisfy the baying hordes of journalists rummaging throughout Wexford.

The ceasefire between the bishop and the media, an uneventful lull of six years, except for one week in 1999 after Seán Fortune's suicide, came to a shattering end on 19 March 2002, when a BBC documentary, *Suing the Pope*, about Comiskey's failure to manage Fortune, turned the stomachs of ordinary people in the diocese, who listened to the sons of neighbours recalling their rape at the hands of a priest. Comiskey did not last a month and voluntarily tendered his resignation. Hot on his heels would be John Kinsella, caught up in the avalanche in Ferns that Comiskey's resignation had precipitated. The time for canon law, polite correspondence and declarations of innocence were over. There was a new sheriff in town and it was his way or the highway. Administrator Eamonn Walsh simply ignored the restrictions of canon law that had shackled Comiskey and encouraged Kinsella to go from his ministry. Walsh's line was that the absence of evidence, in the wake of a series of allegations, was not in itself conclusive. Kinsella decided to use the armature of narrative: he had made up his mind to go public. This, for a priest accused of abuse in Ferns, was unprecedented. He said that no findings of wrongdoing were ever made against him but that, in light of the prevailing climate in the diocese after Comiskey's resignation, 'these matters have now been revisited though there has been no new evidence brought to my notice'. With that, Kinsella made up his mind to step down as curate of the Parish of St John the Baptist in The Ballagh, albeit on a temporary basis. That would turn out to be wishful thinking.

When the Vatican rushed to laicise the man it knew as Monsignor Micheal Ledwith (appointed to the seminary staff at St Peter's in 1969), acclaimed as the best President Maynooth College ever had in its official history, days before the publication of *The Ferns Report* in 2005, it was a last-ditch effort to sever ties with someone who was once a celebrated theological adviser to the Holy See. Neither party had cause to regret the divorce. Ledwith's rise through the ranks of the Church was spectacular: he joined the staff of Maynooth in 1971, after two years' teaching at his old school, St Peter's College, on the strength of his doctoral thesis *The Theology of Tradition in Modern Anglicanism*; he was appointed editor of the *Irish Theological Quarterly* in 1975; he became a Vice-President of Maynooth in 1980 and was appointed President in 1985. As befits a man whose intellect and didacticism were the admiration of his contemporaries, Ledwith was revered within the governance circle of Maynooth. Handsome and charming, he enjoyed life to the full but his outgoing nature and material extravagance were interpreted by half a dozen mature students in 1983 as an unacceptably ostentatious display unworthy of a Vice-President of Maynooth. They felt his lavish and worldly lifestyle – he liked travelling, spending his money and going away for weekends to places like Rome to window-shop with certain students – was at odds with the spiritual values of a life dedicated to vows of chastity and poverty, and they decided to do something about the flash and sexually ambiguous Monsignor from Taghmon in County Wexford. The six seminarians set about casting aspersions on Ledwith's character among bishops being canvassed by the

Papal Nuncio for their opinions on the shortlist of candidates for the vacant post of Bishop of Ferns. The seminarians carefully worded their opposition to Ledwith. They did not have a specific incident to bolster their recriminations, but by innuendo and allegations, a portrait was presented of the Vice-President (Maynooth was governed by the statutes of St Patrick's College and was overseen by a President and two Vice-Presidents) as having an improper sexual orientation, i.e. gay. Ledwith defended his reputation resolutely and survived. He was made President of Maynooth in 1986.

Ledwith never became the princeling of Ferns but he did live 'happily ever after' (or, at least, for a while) and served as secretary to three World Synods of Bishops in Rome. But life is not a fairy tale and a far more serious accusation was made by a teenager against Ledwith in 1994, precipitating his resignation as President of Maynooth in less than a year. On this occasion the bishops lined up against him, the Catholic Church was set to forsake him, and the man who might have been a contender for the bishopric of Ferns set out for America to reinvent himself.

Just what Brendan Comiskey (installed as Bishop of Ferns 1984–2002) expected when he first landed in Wexford is anybody's guess: for the laity in the diocese he was a blessing in disguise, a harbinger of modernity. Handsome, articulate and witty, at forty-nine he was a refreshing antidote to the ailing septuagenarian Donal Herlihy, in his mid-fifties when he succeeded Bishop James Staunton (who had died on the morning of President Kennedy's visit to Wexford.) There are parallels between Kennedy and Comiskey: urbane, aesthetically minded, obsessed with the media, educated in America, a record of achievement at a young age – Comiskey was Auxiliary Bishop of Dublin at just forty-four – and both recipients of the Freedom of Wexford, a distinction conferred upon a line of luminaries stretching back to Parnell, whose fall from grace – like Comiskey's – occurred after his name became a byword of opprobrium among a once adoring flock. Comiskey was twenty when he began the first of several academic stints in America, studying philosophy at Jaffrey Center in New Hampshire. Following ordination in his native Monaghan, he taught English and Latin at Damien High School, La Verne, California, and later, after a spell in Rome, he taught Moral Theology at the Washington Theological Union.

Not in a month of Sundays did Comiskey expect his eclectic career to bring him to Wexford, at the time as indistinct as most towns in rural Ireland, with its best writers and artists having left for recognition in Dublin, London or New York. A week before Comiskey's arrival, the Borough Council had given its most famous son, former Tánaiste Brendan Corish, the freedom of the borough. Corish was emblematic of Wexford in the mid 1980s: socialist and conservatively Catholic. Being politically left-leaning did not, however, prevent Wexford from succumbing to Celtic Tiger excesses, when the nouveau riche swelled the ranks of golf clubs new and old and abandoned their urban pads for oversized, pillared mansions in the country, guarded by statues of eagles and equine heads, their children ferried to school in mud-shy new Land Rovers.

Backwater perhaps, but not historically so: defiant and truculent Wexford was sacked by Cromwell and was the capital of the insurrection in 1798, whose most famous personage was a priest. At the turn of the millennium the diocese celebrated 1,400 years of Catholic faith, a history of service and dignity back to St Aidan.

Fernenses laetamini	*(Serene and calm in every breast*
Hic dies est Aedani	*And gladsome is the tongue*
Nostri Patroni Sancti	*That celebrates the joyful feast*
Ergo dedicemus ei	*And chants the festive song*
	Of St Aidan)

This paean to St Aidan in Latin appeared in *The Wexford Independent*, now defunct, in 1845. There was and is a whiff of cordite about the history of Wexford (a famous press conference by Comiskey in February 1996 clashed with the funeral in Gorey of a young IRA member who blew himself up – accidentally – on a London bus).

With his customary enthusiasm and penchant for being drawn to the intelligentsia of a locale (Comiskey was the first Catholic bishop to graduate from Trinity College, Dublin), he set about getting to know Wexford and Wexford reciprocated: it has been said that more people saw the inside of the bishop's house in Comiskey's first five years than in a half a century of service by bishops Browne, Codd, Staunton and Herlihy. Loquacious and erudite, Comiskey was comfortable in most social settings and he was celebrated for his consistency in his dealings with people, irrespective of their background or the occasion. He engendered loyalty without forfeiting commission: a petition was once signed by all Wexford members of the Oireachtas, when suspicions of clerical abuse were rife, that the media back off the bishop until he returned from a sabbatical in America.

Comiskey had a love–hate affair with the media. He could ingratiate himself with journalists, highbrow and lowbrow, broadsheet and tabloid, but while scribes are easily flattered, it ought never to be mistaken for subservience: the *raison d'être* of a good journalist is, to paraphrase diarist Alan Clark, attention to the actuality, and never canapés and sherry in rooms gilded with magnificence. A founding member of the Irish Churches' Council for Television and Radio Affairs, Comiskey helped establish the Christian Media Trust to copper-fasten the diocese's involvement in local radio. A patron of Wexford Festival Opera, he was made a Freeman of Wexford with undue haste – only seven years after his arrival. Poor Bishop Herlihy had been left waiting seventeen years.

Wexford town, with its long winter days of mist, fog and rain, was unlikely to detain the bishop's genetic wanderlust: he travelled to Thailand so often that he came to love the country, though in 1996 he denied a rumour that he had visited the country six times in four years. He became aware of the malicious innuendo sweeping through the diocese when it became known that Thailand was his holiday destination of choice. 'To say that I was on holiday in Bangkok is like saying a person travelling through London on his way to Brighton was, in fact, in Soho,' he said. Thailand, being Thailand, is rarely without misadventure: his passport and personal papers were stolen on a winter trip in 1994. By then, the Comiskey rumour mill was in overdrive and there was no let-up, just the odd ceasefire, brokered by denial after denial. He was adept at deflecting the cauterising scrutiny of the media, such as calling for an end to celibacy and (not for the last time) disappearing overnight, but the accusations, the recriminations and the crescendo excited by the shenanigans of priests like Seán Fortune ensured that the headlines were constant.

A decade into his term in Wexford, the bishop's name frequently appeared in the red tops alongside the lurid – financial irregularity, drinking bouts, sale of Church property, trips abroad and, fatally, clerical paedophilia – and his habit of leaving behind untidy endings left loose threads which the media could not resist tugging. Comiskey has maintained that his regulation of abusive priests in Wexford was crippled by the lack of precedent, but his supervision of these priests incrementally unveils a reluctance to be decisive. Priests like Seán Fortune sensed this and, as Comiskey's word was not binding, they continued behaving recklessly.

2

Fr Seán Fortune

'Draining Times. Something is dying and the experience is ugly.'
Fr Colm Kilcoyne, *Sunday Tribune*, 1999

*'One hopes that Ferns is at least different in one respect: that Seán
Fortune was unique.'*
Catriona Crowe, *The Dublin Review*, 2006

When Donal Herlihy administered Holy Orders to the
deacon kneeling before him, on 27 May 1979, laying
his hands on the younger man's head, the Holy Spirit entered
Seán Fortune and he was immediately set apart from the life
he was born into. The black habiliments, which he wore to the
very end, signalled the death of his old life. Held in awe by an
obedient laity, he was among an ancient order of men who
could confer the Holy Sacrifice and administer the Sacraments
of the Catholic Church. His moment had arrived. Priesthood
for Fortune started out as office and sacrament and became a

means of exploitation. The words of Bishop Donal McKeown to seminarians in 2010 would have had no receptacle in Fortune: 'God makes use of us poor men in order to be, through us, present to all men and women, and to act on their behalf.'

He had joined an organisation desperate for seminarians. It rewarded him with a roof permanently over his wandering self and gave him unfettered access to male teenagers with whom, in his fluctuating moods, he behaved as he pleased, safe in the knowledge that his ordination had practically absolved him from any personal responsibility. Once over the encumbrance of being moved from parish to parish, or being interviewed by psychiatrist after psychiatrist, he understood fully the limitation of Bishop Brendan Comiskey's canonical power and he exploited the Irish Church's servility to Rome. Fortune, whose surname is among the oldest in Wexford but rarely found outside it, was entirely devoted to self-gratification. The 'mental reservation' popularly associated with bishops after *The Murphy Report* can be viewed in its full abundance in Fortune's suicide note. When civil law brings priests and bishops down to earth, they cower behind canonical explanations and either perjure themselves or blame others. Fortune blamed Comiskey: Comiskey blamed Fortune. The Church seen as Goya's Saturn, devouring its own offspring. Psychotherapist Richard Sipe believes there is a very straightforward reason why prelates and clergy are prepared to lie under oath: to avoid scandal and to preserve an image. Fortune, from an early age augmented by the lack of discipline at seminary training at St Peter's and the ineffectiveness of entreaties by his superiors to behave, both before and after he became a priest, acted as if he were answerable only to a higher authority. He was above the civil law that constrained the riff-raff he preached to. More than most, Fortune believed that his ordination had ontologically elevated him above the flock he had committed himself to protecting, that his collar and soutane opened doors and, if you add his bullying and his arrogance into the mix, you have the clerical equivalent of Frankenstein's monster, made in Ferns and soon to be out of control.

'People rely on them [priests] when they are at their most vulnerable, so this gives them enormous cachet, which ideally should breed humility and a sense of privilege, but can, and in some cases obviously does, breed a kind of superiority and arrogance, whereby one might feel oneself to be above the law,' observed author and historian Louise Fuller. After his death, Fortune was immortalised by the media as the poster boy for clerical paedophilia in Ireland. Depicted as the epitome of untrammelled evil in Alison O'Connor's book, *A Message from Heaven: The Life and Crimes of Fr Seán Fortune*, his transmogrification is completed by the BBC documentary *Suing the Pope*. His reach from beyond the grave was decisive, and a bishop's head rolled. *Suing the Pope* became the missing link in the drawn-out denouement of Comiskey's term as Bishop of Ferns: he had no room to manoeuvre and so he walked, but with the media camped outside his front door, he could not resist the temptation to blame Fortune. Was this the same man who delivered a three-page homily at Fortune's funeral in Gorey?

With his nemesis in the grave three years, Comiskey was not in a forgiving mood. His priest was impossible to deal with. Comiskey portrayed himself as a scapegoat and whoever helped him compose his resignation statement did not think it unchristian to speak so ill of the dead. In the final weeks of his life, as Fortune kept reality at bay, the disparity between his perspective and others' was a considerable psychological achievement considering the enormous pressure he was under. He scrambled to his last court appearances supported by crutches. Torrents of invective showered upon him after his awful death: Avril Doyle described him 'as the most evil and manipulative of men, of the cloth or otherwise, that I have ever met in my life, and I don't say that lightly'. 'The worst bad apple in the barrel,' wrote Rev. Norman Ruddock in his memoirs. It was easy and less of a risk legally to pillory Fortune once he was dead, but a consensus emerged that he had the capacity to be psychologically unnerving to those in a position to administer him.

Comiskey, who moved Fortune from one parish to another, even though he knew that wherever he served he brought 'division and pain', received the public endorsement of all of Wexford's Oireachtas members when he was accused of fleeing the diocese to avoid facing up to abuse cases. Not one Wexford politician ever thought it important enough to raise the handling of abusive priests in Ferns in either the Dáil or the Senate. Others did, like David Norris and Micheál Martin. Comiskey in the autumn of 1995 jumped ship for America, with his diocese on the brink of pernicious dissolution, less than seven months after he had publicly praised Fortune, who had just quit his last parish posting, Ballymurn, on 'administrative leave'. 'Bishop's Praise for Departing Ballymurn Curate,' reported the *Wexford People* in a glowing eight-paragraph report, which was a compromise between the hagiographic and the histrionic. The report and the comments by the bishop, who had recently launched a book by Fortune, *Ballymurn 1847–1993, A Pictorial History,* bore no relation to the facts. Fortune had been arrested by Gardaí and questioned about the serial abuse of young men. Nor did his leave banish him from the diocese. In the summer, both Comiskey and Fortune were in Screen Church (just north of Wexford town) to celebrate the silver jubilee of a priest.

Since 1987, the bishop had been decamping a priest about whom he had grave concerns from Wexford to London and back without any proper supervision. A cursory glance at *The*

Ferns Report indicates that Fortune was addicted to abuse and was prepared for all manner of risk to satiate his lust. It is a mystery that he did not come to the attention of the Gardaí before he did, even allowing for the failure of the diocese to pass on abuse allegations. 'Fortune's predatory behaviour,' wrote Diarmaid Ferriter, 'was not stopped until almost twenty years after it started.'

When Fortune died by his own hand in a domicile beneath the grandiosity he had become accustomed to, an RTÉ radio researcher could not find a single person in Wexford to put in a good word for him. Fortune was somebody's son, somebody's brother, somebody's uncle. Colm O'Gorman, with more reason than most to espouse the sentiments of Avril Doyle and Ruddock after Fortune's death, refrained, and was a solitary voice in the bleakness. 'Yesterday I wept for him. He was a human being. The tragedy now is that he is a victim as well.'

To divest Fortune of any redeemable quality is to partake in the blind acceptance in Wexford that made the diocese rich in fractiousness prior to Comiskey's resignation. The soil had not settled on Fortune's grave when *The Irish Times* regaled its readers with how he had all the deadly sins, except sloth. He was a costume in search of a character, who called home the diocese that did not want him. Fortune had acquired a vast array of sobriquets by the time he quit his first curacy in Fethard-on-Sea. Flapper. Father Goldfinger. King Midas. Closer to the truth is an observation by a relative: he was two people, an uncle who never forgot a birthday and a priest who destroyed the lives of others without regret. Some had an uncompromising opinion of whatever complicated and disparate forces made Fortune tick. To Seán Cloney, whose family was at the heart of the Fethard Boycott, and who knew Fortune in Poulfur in his capacity as chairman of the parish hall, 'he was the greatest liar that I ever met'. Fortune had a 'svengali-like influence' over Bishops Herlihy and Comiskey, said Canon Ruddock, who was told that Fortune was evil. The views of the parishioners in Fethard encountered by Fr Thaddeus Doyle in 1984, when he spent a week with Fortune to give a parish mission, are the polar opposite:

I heard much praise for Fr Seán, for the work he was doing, his willingness to go the extra mile in helping people. One person compared him to the then famous racehorse Arkle, saying he was one in a million. There was mention also of the dispute about the community centre and an acknowledgement that he had handled the situation badly, very badly.

When one spends a week in a person's house, one gets to know something of their personality. Fr Seán had good points, very good points. I believe that, despite what we know now concerning his problem and the great hurt that problem has caused, he was at heart genuine. I believed that he got ordained intending to serve God and God's kingdom with all his strength.

He told me that he only slept about two to three hours a night. I know now that isn't good. We need our sleep if we are to handle situations in a calm way. People talk about his collections. He ran a big operation. That costs money. His turnover costs were high. But it must be also said that he was generous, very generous, generous even to the point where he could be taken advantage of. I was invited back to give a couple of further talks in Poulfur and got Fr Seán to give one in Murrintown.

He was always courteous, always enthusiastic, and always ready to give praise and encouragement. Remember, he had absolutely nothing to get from me, yet he was always the same. It was only when he went on administrative leave that I first heard the allegations of abuse. I can honestly say that before that I hadn't heard one word, not one suggestion or allegation.

When the allegations of teenage abuse became known, I realised that they were serious. I accept what his victims say concerning the abuse. I accept that they went through hell. I can only express my deepest sorrow this was so.

(The Curate's Diary)

Doyle, based at St Kevin's, Tinahely, when Fortune died, produced his popular *Curate's Diary* monthly. Fortune had lent him his photocopier in Poulfur to run off 200 copies of the first twelve-page edition for free. Doyle walked with Fortune's family from the Church to the graveyard after his funeral. 'At the graveside I watched one of his nieces, a truly beautiful young girl, sitting on a kerb with her hand on his coffin, crying. I thought of the stuff in the papers. I thought in particular of certain papers and certain reporters. I thought too of those who had been quoted by the papers at this tragic time, for they too had now joined in the hurting cycle. And I wondered what had that beautiful young girl done to deserve all this suffering and who would apologise to her.'

With a forcefulness undiluted by the passing of the years, *The Ferns Report* is unsparing in its depiction of Fortune's reprehensible crimes, a nefarious litany of horrendous and horrific assaults on teenagers, many of whom were involved with the Catholic Church. From the moment Fortune entered seminarian life at St Peter's College, his abuse of boys was assiduous. His arrogance is often referred to by those who crossed swords with him but what else would you expect from a priest who was taught to be the master of his dominion, whether in Fethard or in Ballymurn – rural parishes orbiting the glitzier Wexford – who never disguised his penchant for young men, the more vulnerable the better, who could celebrate Mass after buggering a boy, leaving him a bloody mess on the floor, whose conscience was never troubled by the mental and physical pain he inflicted, or the unabated profligacy of his faith? As the Gardaí discovered, he was a congenital liar.

He drifted in and out of Wexford under the noses of Bishops Herlihy and Comiskey, who believed him to be an abomination, like the cold-hearted tercel in Ted Hughes' *Hawk Roosting*, who resolves, after a life of rupturing the bones of the living, that he is not going to change. There is no sophistry to his behaviour, no attempt to peddle a fallacious explanation for his vices; no effort is made to denude his sadism, not a moment's regret for the horror visited upon boy after boy. The Diocese of Ferns was his own personal playground, luring the innocent to his dungeon. He was never seen in public dressed casually, and therefore he used the distinct garb of priesthood to gain the trust of his victims and to disguise the warped concupiscence of the serial predator. The Catholic Church was his camouflage, an unwitting participant in one of Western Europe's worst examples of clerical sex abuse. His vocation was a calling card which opened doors in Wexford: with 'access all areas' guaranteed, he was unsparing in his selection of victims: scouts, altar boys, boarders, hitchhikers, the sons of friends, complete strangers.

Educated at Gorey Christian Brothers and the Christian Brothers Novitiate in Dublin, Fortune was twenty-six when he was ordained – without any psychological assessment or 'fitness to practise' probe – at St Peter's College. The early signs of the absence of a normal emotional texture was visible in the teetotal seminarian pacing the corridors of St Peter's after dark. In 1976 he raped a thirteen-year-old pupil in a shower cubicle and made him swear on the Bible not to tell a soul. The boy was a boarder and Fortune took advantage of his access to the dormitory to visit the boy's bedroom and to continue the abuse. From the moment Fortune was asked to leave Blackrock College after for one term in 1971 (no explanation was ever given) intending to join the Holy Ghost Order, to his final posting in Ballymurn, which he quit after his arrest in 1995, his career path via Wexford, Belfast, Dundalk, Poulfur and London is littered with the residua of shattered lives. Each time a bishop altered his trajectory, Fortune mastered his new environment and continued to abuse.

He engaged in nocturnal visits to St Peter's dormitory to masturbate boarders; he joined the Catholic Boy Scouts of Ireland and molested patrol leaders in his tent; he subjected the son of an acquaintance of Herlihy's to an eleven-hour ordeal in Poulfur parochial house; he used every form of connivance to seduce students at St Malachy's College in Belfast; he had oral sex with a thirteen-year-old boy who joined Youth Encounter in Dundalk; he abused a friend's son so badly in Dublin that he became violently ill; while director of the National Association of Community Broadcasting, he buggered a teenager attending a Mater Hospital communications course, leaving him to bleed profusely on the recording studio floor; he raped a youth to whom he offered a lift home from hospital; he molested an altar boy in the passenger seat of his car while two elderly parishioners sat in the back; he entrapped a thirteen-year-old boy in a public toilet in Wexford and buggered him; he offered a young man, just off the ferry at Rosslare, overnight accommodation in Ballymurn and raped him in the dead of night; he raped a twelve-year-old boy and then blackmailed him when he was older into having sex with him regularly. When he was in a generous mood and not violent, he offered young boys inducements to sleep with him or give him a blow job. It was the closest his emotionally retarded self ever got to a proposition.

Almost as long as the list of Fortune's perverse iniquities is a record of the occasions when his victims reported their abuse: the standard response was to shift him from location to location. His propensity for targeting young males was known to several dioceses, to the scouts, to youth clubs, to parish committees, but the methodology of dealing with him was as irresponsible as his behaviour. Fortune's predilections were kept under cover, handled in house, attended to on a need-to-know basis but did not include the long arm of the law. Adults had no qualms sending a man they knew to be interfering with young boys to other places where the abuse would continue, but in 1980s' Wexford, vigilance did not extend beyond 'out of sight, out of mind'. Once Fortune was gone, the complaint was shelved. *The Ferns Report* catalogued two dozen instances of terrified victims reporting the abuse to parents, priests, leaders of clubs, bishops, over a time span of twenty years until 1995. Following a string of complaints about his advances to boys while camping, a dossier was submitted to the national headquarters of the Catholic Boy Scouts of Ireland. The leader of the Wexford town CBSI troop, Joe Cuddy, gave a copy to the diocese.

Fortune was summarily dismissed from the Holy Rosary Parish in Belfast after Bishop Philbin of the Diocese of Down and Connor heard from Fr Martin Kelly, Spiritual Director at St Malachy's College, that Fortune had tried to seduce students. The diocese then warned the Administrator of St Patrick's Parish in Dundalk, where Fortune had found refuge, not to let him bring home pupils from the Christian Brothers School (CBS). If it is possible to absolve people from not pursuing complaints, from not walking into the nearest Garda station and giving a statement, and if collective absolution arises from a societal ingenuousness and an undoubted servility to the Church, the Diocese of Ferns has no such excuse. Bishops Herlihy and Comiskey are guilty of the most injudicious management of

Fortune, for common sense should have informed them that, after perusing psychological profiles commissioned by the diocese, Fortune was a habitual offender. Whatever about the source or the cause of his badness, it was not an extractable illness that could be sucked out by prayer or cured by exile.

The years 1979–1981 were among the busiest in the epsicopate of Bishop Herlihy: his work load was immense but he did not shirk from his numerous engagements, including marking the fiftieth anniversary of his ordination, for which he was conferred with the customary freedom of the town by Wexford Corporation (many Church men have received the council's highest accolade, including Archbishop Daniel Mannix, Papal Nuncio Pascal Robinson, Archbishop Richard Downey, Cardinal John D'Alton, Papal Nuncio Alberto Levame, Cardinal Richard Cushing, Cardinal William Conway, Cardinal Tomás Ó Fiaich and Brendan Comiskey). Ordained to the Diocese of Kerry, Herlihy's academic greatness was rewarded with the post of Professor of Sacred Scripture at All Hallows College, Dublin. He was transferred to Rome in 1947 (with future Archbishop of Dublin Dermot Ryan) and became Rector of the Irish College in Rome from 1951 to 1964, when he was – to his surprise – enthroned as Bishop of Ferns. He was, to paraphrase Ó Fiaich, a devoted priest, a kind friend and a courteous gentleman. A hard-working and industrious bishop who coped with the loss of a lung after he was shot by the Black and Tans when he was a boy, Herlihy was on the go to the last, administering confirmation in considerable distress shortly before his death in 1983. The outpouring of complaints about Fortune – from the scouts, from the Diocese of Down and Connor, from a Knight of Columbanus, from parishioners in Poulfur – threatened to turn into a deluge: Herlihy, who did not personally assess Fortune's candidacy for the seminary because of his five years in the Juniorate of the CBS in Dun

Laoghaire and did not apply the recommendations of *Norms for Priestly Training In Ireland,* which insisted on a thorough medical examination of candidates for the seminary, went beyond the parameters of the diocese for a professional insight into his ungovernable priest.

He could not have liked what he read. Monsignor Professor Feichin O'Doherty, Professor of Logic and Psychology at University College Dublin, interviewed Fortune several times while he was doing a postgraduate catechetic course at Mount Oliver, Dundalk, at Herlihy's request. As the encounters increased, O'Doherty's opinion underwent a gradual transformation, arising from Fortune's caprices and vacillations. After asking Fortune about the incidents with the boy scouts, which he famously dismissed as 'just messing', O'Doherty believed that his behaviour was tantamount to indecent assault. Notwithstanding his suggestion that Fortune could succeed in coming to terms with himself and his sexuality, which O'Doherty knew was homosexual ('perhaps the most important thing I can say about him from the psychological point of view is his apparent lack of real feelings about the reality of his situation'), he told Herlihy that Fortune's personality left a lot to be desired. ('I did not get the impression that he takes his most recent episode and present position seriously enough, nor do I think that we have the full story.') Herlihy behaved in a manner unworthy of the responsibilities of his office: dismissing O'Doherty's growing sense of foreboding, he began the arc of destruction for many young lives by posting Fortune to Fethard-on-Sea in the parish of Templetown in southwest Wexford in 1982. 'Extraordinarily ill advised,' said *The Ferns Report.*

In between Fortune's bouts of denial and his examination by half a dozen psychiatrists in Dublin and London in the years ahead, he went on an indiscriminate rampage in south Wexford, abusing teenagers whenever he could, access to whom was often facilitated by the naivety and the innocence of parents. The diocese's handling of Fortune was deeply flawed and irresponsible from the start: Herlihy felt that any misbehaviour by Fortune would not go undetected by the closely knit community of Fethard, and he was right. Fortune's impact was explosive. Herlihy was mistaken, however, in his conviction that Canon William Mernagh – a good man and President of the GAA County Board – and parish priest of Templetown since 1970, would keep the young pup on a tight leash, but that was to completely underestimate the destructive and conniving nature of Fortune and besides, Mernagh was in his sixties.

Shortly after arriving in the coastal parish, Fortune was involved in a dispute over control of the parish hall, compelling the management committee to cancel discos and to post the following notice on the door: 'regrettably we are forced to take this action due to foul intervention and interference by the local curate for the time being, Fr Seán Fortune.' Told that he would have to fork out the admission if he wanted to go into a Macra na Feirme disco in the parish hall, he is alleged to have said in anger that the firstborn of any Macra member would be deformed. So much of what Fortune is reported to have said or done is either unchallenged or exaggerated hearsay, but it is indisputable that he was a hugely divisive figure in Fethard.

Any prospect of a relationship between the new curate and parishioners steadily deteriorated. Seán Cloney has related how he was warned about the priest by a scout leader in advance of Fortune's posting. Unable to have any involvement with scouts, Fortune established the Don Bosco youth club in the basement of his house in Poulfur, a short drive from Fethard, beside a reconciliation room for boys in trouble, and he involved its young members in discussions about sexuality. 'He brought youths from the village on a retreat to Loftus Hall and they were to stay overnight. They were told by Fortune not to inform their parents about what they were doing or what they got up to, but there were nude pillow fights,' said Cloney.

In the 'Fethard and District Notes', which Fortune compiled for a small fee for the *Wexford People*, he had a habit of including the names of the boys involved in the club's activities. Copies of these notes were later submitted to the Gardaí in 1995. Gemma and Declan Hearne, aghast at Fortune's behaviour, communicated their concerns consistently to Herlihy, Comiskey, Cardinal Ó Fiaich and the Papal Nuncio, Dr Gaetano Alibrandi. An anonymous poem, fifteen stanzas in length, 'Thoughts After the Hunt', inspired when Fortune threatened to sue the local hunt after it chased a fox through Church property, and referring to Fortune's recreational activities in Fethard, was posted to Comiskey, with the admonition:

> *Take the lid off the can, crozier-carrying man*
> *Of God, as you value hereafter*
> *It's with you the buck stops, in your court the ball hops*
> *Rip the collar from off this impostor.*
> *Yes I tar with the same brush all who dabble in slush*
> *Give support, or consent with their silence*
> *To an unprincipled cur with a collar, non-fur*
> *Though some suggest others use violence.*

Irrespective of how often you read accounts of sexual abuse, the testament of the victims of Fortune in Fethard and elsewhere still retain the capacity to shock. His behaviour spelled calamity for young men who trusted the Church. Youths such as Paul Molloy ('I would read at first Mass and he would abuse me before second Mass, blessing the Eucharist an hour later.); Pat Jackman ('It was eleven hours of, of a constant torture, which ended up in sexual acts of sorts.'); Colm O'Gorman ('On Sunday mornings, after Fortune had abused me on Saturday night, he'd leave me in his bed in the bedroom in the house and come down and say first Mass.'); Damien MacAleen ('All of a sudden, like after a couple of minutes, he started groping, you know literally rubbing me up and that went on for another couple of minutes.') and Donnacha MacGloinn ('Very, very rapidly he sort of basically pinned me down against the mixing desk and . . . anally raped me.')

Lives were ruined and lives were lost: Peter Fitzpatrick shot himself in the chest in a caravan at the end of the family garden: he was no different from the many young boys who accompanied Fortune on outings. After his death his mother, Monica, told Fortune to his face that he was not welcome at their home or at the funeral. In all, two young men who had come into contact with Fortune, through his weekend retreats or his FÁS schemes, took their own lives.

Alarmed by the cacophony of allegations, new bishop Brendan Comiskey ended Fortune's disastrous spell in Poulfur, telling his long-suffering parishioners that he had signed up for a media course in London, but in reality Fortune's exit was prompted by the necessity for further psychological assessment. In London, leaving behind unpaid bills to the tune of £20,000 in Fethard, he found a new role for himself and started to write columns about religion for *The London Irish News*. In his opinion pieces about renouncing sin and rejecting Satan, Fortune paraphrases a motley collection of obscure sources: Casimir Kucharek, Cyril of Jersusalem and Alexander Schmemann. Exile in London could not last forever but Comiskey, who was acquiring an encyclopaedic knowledge of what his priest was accused of in his former parish, was uncertain how to proceed. His experience as Auxiliary Bishop in Dublin convinced him that he needed hard evidence before he could institute canonical proceedings, an exercise which was as rare in the Irish Church as a breathing dodo. Fortune was assessed by Dr John Cooney in 1987–1988, who recommended a period of in-patient treatment under close supervision as a matter of urgency. It never happened. The blueprint for bishops in the Dublin archdiocese when Comiskey was there was to facilitate the priest, not the child. Consideration for future victims of clerical abuse by the Church was never a prime consideration. Fortune was a law onto himself. Urged by Comiskey to receive two days of counselling at Heronbrook Assessment Centre or the Order of the Paraclete Centre in Stroud, where the sick priests of Dublin were forwarded, he declined. One counsellor, who managed a limited session with Fortune, repeated the assertions of Dr Cooney: Fortune needed residential treatment urgently. He further warned Comiskey that Fortune was a pathological liar. The priest was becoming increasingly rebellious and erratic in his attitude to his bishop. After Comiskey warned him in a letter dated 12 April 1988 not to move from London without his permission, Fortune blanked him.

He was easier to pursue than to trap. A Comiskey procrastination could linger indefinitely and he wrote back to the bishop's secretary eight days later confirming his intention to move to Comiskey's old beat, Bray, and was ensconced in a residential house there by the end of the month, smack in the middle of a large community with several parishes. Both priest and prelate met in July but Fortune declined a suggestion by Comiskey to undergo assessment at the House of Affirmation in Birmingham. It was a long meeting minuted by Comiskey. The bishop admitted that he was unwilling to let him return to parish duties because he knew Fortune could not accept restrictions, but he acknowledged that medical intervention had not helped him to decide whether there was any substance to the allegations of sexual misconduct. Comiskey was 'not in a position to provide a context in which any of our priests have to be kept under a microscope' (*The Ferns Report*). Perhaps, but a plan by the bishop to have three priests (who were 'sworn to secrecy') in the diocese examine the outstanding allegations was scuppered when Fortune retaliated by engaging a solicitor to represent him. Comiskey was in possession of a letter from Paul Molloy, a victim of Fortune's in Poulfur in late 1987 when he was an altar boy, outlining extensive abuse, by which time Fortune was in London. 'There were two different Fr Fortunes,' recalled Molloy. 'The priest who would go up to the altar and give terrific sermons about the evils of drink, sex and sin, and the other one who would talk to young boys about homosexuality, interview them one by one, and abuse them.'

Two years on, Comiskey arranged for Molloy and Fortune to be interviewed separately by canon lawyer Rev. Dr Robert Noonan at All Hallows. Noonan was given no background information about Fortune's recent history and his function was to ascertain if both Fortune and Molloy – based on their oral evidence to him – were believable, and he decided that they were. Noonan asked Molloy several questions and then asked him to write out the allegations on some foolscap. 'I don't know how the bishop looked on this because he never told me,' said Molloy, who initially informed Fortune's replacement in Fethard, Fr Sean Devereux, about the abuse. Devereux, who was kept busy finding out what Fortune had done in Fethard, told Molloy he should contact either Comiskey or the Gardaí.

In between Bray and Fortune's next posting a year later, Comiskey learnt that Fortune's name had come to the attention of Wexford Gardaí and did his utmost to have him clinically assessed. Fortune met with more doctors, each with a separate diagnosis and a different remedy: Dr Ingo Fischer – whom

Fortune voluntarily attended – thought he was heterosexual and was fit for parish work subject to continuing treatment; Dr J. R. W. Christie-Brown, consultant psychiatrist at the Bethlem Royal Hospital and the Maudsley Hospital, London, discovered no evidence of mental or psychiatric evidence but could not say if Fortune was suitable to be a curate. The analysis is not forensic because either Fortune or the diocese declined, for whatever reason, to present an unadulterated version of his recent past. Dr Christie-Brown was not briefed once on the sexual allegations against Fortune and had no medical reports from either Feichin O'Doherty or John Cooney on his patient. Fortune had also lied about his formative years: he painted a picture of a happy childhood, at odds with his later claim that he was abused by a member of the clergy. He exaggerated his academic record, which explains why Christie-Brown felt Fortune had a superior intellectual ability. In his qualified report to Comiskey, Christie-Brown expressed his willingness to look at further documented evidence available on Fortune, but Comiskey was not forthcoming, having decided to give the priest a new parish, despite the advice available to him, including an earlier warning from Dr Cooney that Fortune had an unstable personality, and a recommendation by the Heronbrook Centre that Fortune required urgent residential care.

It is unmistakable that Comiskey wanted somebody in the medical profession to make up his mind for him and Dr Fischer stepped into that role, stressing that Fortune's rehabilitation required accompanying pastoral ministry. Comiskey would always believe that Fortune never abused again after his treatment by Fischer, but allegations listed in *The Ferns Report* suggest otherwise: 'On one occasion when Fortune was chasing him, [the victim] telephoned the bishop's house at two in the morning. He spoke with Fr Tommy Brennan and can remember being very frightened but said that the conversation was very short. He told Fr Brennan he was in Wexford and that Fr Fortune was chasing him. He was speaking to Fr Brennan from his mobile telephone and Seán Fortune was in his car driving up and down the streets. Fr Tommy Brennan told Daniel to call the Bishop the following day. Daniel felt Fr Brennan had taken his complaint seriously enough and that he seemed quite calm. Fr Brennan has confirmed this account of Daniel's telephone call to the Inquiry.' Another victim was blackmailed into working at Fortune's home in Ballymurn on and off for ten months and had to perform oral sex.

After months of psychiatric haggling over the mind of Seán Fortune, the vacillating Comiskey made a decision and stuck to it. Fortune, who had been abusing boys at St Peter's College, Belfast and Poulfur, was appointed to the parish of Ballymurn, the half parish of Crossabeg, much closer to the bishop's residence than Fethard, in September 1989, where he would remain until his arrest in 1995. In a letter, Comiskey advised Fortune to 'win and maintain the esteem, respect and affection of the community' from which he had never received a single complaint against any priest serving there. What Comiskey did not do, in asking parish priest Fr Michael McCarthy to keep an eye on him, was inform him of the sexual allegations against his new curate. Nor did Comiskey enlighten Fr Donald McDonald, who was on the teaching staff of Bridgetown vocational school, where Fortune was to give religion classes.

Much has been made of the close relationship between Comiskey and Fortune in these years, but it has been blown out of proportion. Correspondence would indicate that Comiskey was exasperated by Fortune, that he did not trust him and he kept him at arm's length. The resourceful Fortune was accomplished at inveigling his way into homes and into company. Canon Nigel Waugh has recorded how, on many occasions visiting the bishop's home, he 'wandered in and out of his house to attend meetings without challenge, letting myself in and out, as did his own clergy.' Indisputably, Fortune was often spotted by the public at the bishop's residence at Summerhill and was in attendance at a few of the bishop's social evenings. To suggest that both were social buddies is erroneous: Comiskey never drank on any of his nine visits to Fortune in Ballymurn, but it is more than likely the bishop let his guard down in his own home. Certainly, Fortune did serve wine to guests at a reception for local media hosted by Comiskey, and he would have been sufficiently Machiavellian, as a noted pioneer, to benefit from the bishop's periods of inebriety.

It is beyond all rationale, knowing what he did, for Comiskey to have appointed a loose cannon like Fortune to another parish: faced with other miscreants before and after, James Doyle and Donal Collins, his preference was to stall for time. He never had an instinct for the jugular. Nor, as recommended, did Fortune receive any further treatment from Fischer. All those medical reports commissioned by Comiskey, where Fortune's different personalities are compressed into a few paragraphs, became repositories of dust on a shelf. Fortune is proof that diocesan policy of managing a crisis was crafted on the fly. Fortune was rewarded for refusing to pay obeisance to his bishop.

His tenure in Ballymurn, after a peaceful first year, inevitably has its fractious moments arising from his chairmanship of the Board of Management of the local national school, necessitating an intervention by both Fr Walter Forde and the Department of Education after parents withdrew children. He was forced to resign from teaching religion at Bridgetown vocational school in 1991 on the urging of principal Tony Power, following complaints by parents that he was encouraging pupils to tell lewd jokes and had behaved inappropriately in the classroom.

Despite his less-than-impeccable relationship with parents in Bridgetown and Ballymurn, he held on to the Board of Management Chair until the year of his arrest. *The Ferns Report* has also documented allegations of inappropriate sexual behaviour, almost amounting to extortion, by Fortune at his lodgings in Ballymurn.

His name crops up only once in *The Murphy Report*: a priest, whose redacted name is 'Fr Horatio', used a holiday cottage that Fortune had access to and abused a young girl there. 'Horatio' claimed that the only link he had with Fortune, who gave him the key to the cottage, was that they both happened to be in the same area at the same time.

In February 1995, Colm O'Gorman flew back from London and, at his sister Barbara's house, meticulously delineated his abuse by Fortune in a statement, which eventually took two days to finalise, to Detective Pat Mulcahy. O'Gorman's father, Sean, had been a Wexford County Councillor for sixteen years and contested the General Elections in 1969 and 1973. His son would attempt the feat for the Progressive Democrats in the same constituency in 2006. O'Gorman was fourteen when Fortune first invited him to stay the night at his house in Poulfur, and abused him in his bedroom. 'I wanted to get up and run out of the room but I couldn't. I froze completely. Then he moved his hand down . . .' wrote O'Gorman in his autobiography, *Beyond Belief*. The abuse by Fortune was relentless and continued for two years. O'Gorman fled the country for England when he was nineteen. A month after O'Gorman's statement, the Gardaí interviewed Fortune, who was immediately given administrative leave by Comiskey. A precept was not issued so Fortune was free to say Mass. The redoubtable Mulcahy busied himself meeting and talking to people in Templetown who were able to verify O'Gorman's presence in Fortune's house.

A Garda team, comprising a chief superintendent, a superintendent, two sergeants and Detective Mulcahy, met weekly to discuss the progress of the investigation, which mushroomed as more victims of Fortune came forward. Mulcahy arrested Fortune on the last day of March and quizzed him for seven hours and from there the investigation proceeded gradually:

27 June 1995: Mulcahy's report submitted to Superintendent James Kehoe.

27 June: Kehoe gives the report to the State Solicitor for Wexford, Jack McEvoy.

1 August: the DPP receives the report.

27 October: DPP directs prosecution.

1 November: arrest warrant issued.

15 November: Fortune appears in court on twenty-two charges and is remanded on bail.

18 January 1996: forty-four additional charges added.

January 22: Book of Evidence served.

23 September: case sent forward for trial to Wexford Circuit Court.

11 November: Fortune granted leave to apply for Judicial Review.

17 December 1997: High Court judgement refuses all reliefs claimed by Fortune.

28 January 1998: Notice of Appeal to Supreme Court is filed.

2 March 1999: Fortune appears at special sitting of Wexford Circuit Court.

Despite the unexpected downturn in his circumstances in 1995, Fortune the entrepreneur was letting nothing get in the way of business. He was running twice-yearly media courses at the RTÉ Training Centre, charging £1,000 per student per session and, despite his antagonism to the profession, engaged well-known journalists to give lectures. The grandly titled

Institute of Journalism and Theatre, offering a diploma course in public relations, had appointed RTÉ producer Bill Keating as its president (without consulting him) and among its guest lecturers were Mary Murphy from Carr Communications, RTÉ broadcaster Liam Nolan and Joe Power, religion correspondent for the *Irish Independent*.

By October 1995, Fortune was enrolling twenty-five students per term, but he maintained to the diocese that it was a non-profit organisation. Due to adverse publicity from the tabloids, who regularly doorstepped him at classes, his media career began to founder in 1997: a flurry of letters between Comiskey and Fortune ensued over money, as Fortune claimed – falsely, as he had over £23,000 in an Ulster Bank account – that he was on the breadline. Comiskey acquiesced and the diocese began to lodge £600 a month in a separate account Fortune had with Allied Irish Bank. The diocese also helped him with his legal costs until he sought a judicial review of the charges.

Comiskey was grappling in a war of words with Cardinal Cahal Daly over celibacy in the summer of 1995, calling in public for more transparency in the Church, yet in private with Detective Mulcahy he was anything but. He was asked to give a statement to help Gardaí with their investigation of Fortune on three occasions, and each time he declined. As alcohol took over his life, Comiskey quit his diocese and fled to America. The pressure on the bishop was exacerbated by his knowledge that he was sitting on three other abuse allegations against Fortune that he had not reported to the Gardaí. On his return from America in early 1996, sober and fit, Comiskey had a change of heart. By now serious legal issues had arisen between the bishops of each diocese and their insurer, Church & General, regarding entitlement to indemnity in respect of civil claims under whatever policy they had. While Fortune was being arraigned on sixty-six charges at Wexford District

Court, Comiskey offered the Gardaí full access to all diocesan files. This freed him to tell a press conference at St Peter's that he had never obstructed a Garda investigation. But Fortune's arrest and the subsequent multitude of charges reverberated throughout the diocese, which started to haemorrhage scandal after scandal, with the vulnerable Comiskey floundering in an ever-increasing tide of legal correspondence and prurient media reports. Fortune, meanwhile, was on a hook and the DPP was gradually beginning to reel him in. The DPP delivered twelve affidavits (seven by victims) for the two-day judicial hearing sought by Fortune to prohibit his trial in December 1997.

An order of prohibition was granted by Mr Justice Geoghegan in one complaint (by Paul Molloy), but all the other reliefs claimed by Fortune were refused. A Notice of Appeal to the Supreme Court was served in January by Fortune, countered by a DPP move to cross-appeal the High Court order that restrained the DPP from proceeding with Molloy's case. Fortune's appeal was withdrawn in November 1998 but the Supreme Court allowed the prosecution of the charges involving Molloy.

Finally, four years after Colm O'Gorman gave a statement to Pat Mulcahy, on 2 March 1999 the 45-year-old Fortune, unrecognisably obese and his six-foot frame supported by crutches, shared the same courtroom in Wexford as many of his victims. His ponderous movement was at odds with his early nickname Flapper, so called because he was always in a hurry. He may have been about to lose his anonymity but he had lost none of his conceit, correcting the court record when his name – Seán Fortune – was called out. 'It's Fr Seán Fortune.'

It took quarter of an hour for all the charges to be enumerated (twenty-nine sex abuse charges, including twelve of gross indecency, sixteen of indecent assault and one charge of buggery between 1981 and 1987) and Fortune replied 'not guilty' to each, requesting of Judge Joseph Matthews, midway through, to sit down as he felt weak. O'Gorman, who had resisted last-minute attempts at a plea bargain by Fortune's defence, in which attempted buggery would replace buggery, had been approached by the father of one of the eight victims to have the trial moved from Wexford. 'It's easier for you lads that live away. We have to live here, we have to live with this, you don't.' Fortune's exchanges with the judge bordered on the surreal, from believing that he was being accused of murder to a nonsensical ramble that the proceedings were a dream. He appeared to fall asleep while he was being formally charged in front of a jury of four men and eight women, and was roused by a Garda. If it was play-acting, it would come at a price.

Simon Kennedy, solicitor, who knew Fortune personally, was present in court observing the proceedings, and described the priest's antics as 'the most bizarre case I have ever experienced in twenty-seven years as a lawyer'. In the absence of the jury, Dr Peter Fahy, who had treated Fortune in 1995, told Judge Matthews that Fortune's level of stress would interfere with his ability to meet the case.

Defence counsel, Jeremy Maher, BL, further expressed his concern for Fortune's health and his fitness to undertake a trial. Concerned by Fortune's confusion and the fact that he was on a powerful painkiller (a morphine derivative), Judge Matthews decided that the issue of Fortune's mental and physical fitness should be decided by a new jury and, on being told it could take three weeks to summon a panel, he remanded Fortune to the Central Mental Hospital in Dundrum for treatment until 23 March, much to Fortune's consternation. He argued cogently to oppose it: the transformation from a gibbering wreck to an articulate though pitiful adult fighting for his freedom was seamless. 'I beg you. I'm in pain and the more stress I'm under the more pain I'm under,' said Fortune, but the judge said he was acting in Fortune's best interest because he could receive medical attention for as long as it was required. As Fortune had surrendered bail, he was taken from the court by Gardaí. An industrial strike at the Mental Hospital by SIPTU care workers resulted in Fortune being entrusted to Mountjoy Prison. His first experience of prison was not to his liking and, five days after Mr Justice Cyril Kelly freed him on bail, he took his own life at his barricaded rental accommodation at Bewley Street in New Ross. His housekeeper, Margaret Stamp, had last talked to Fortune on Thursday evening. The Our Lady of Fatima Presbytery at 25 Bewley Street would have to be cleaned, the inevitable post sorted. At night, the exterior of the house resembled a Main Street jeweller's shop with steel shutters covering the windows. The screens and the 24-hour closed-circuit television, which he could view from his bed, were security measures adopted by the 45-year-old Fortune for protection against the increasing hostility of an outside world outraged by the iniquities he was alleged to have perpetrated: a time bomb of paranoia and persecution was ticking inside his head.

He had become noticeably bloated by his intake of medication to relieve stress. Four days after his release from Mountjoy Prison, and following his last call to Stamp and to his caretaker Peter Bennett ('Do not bother coming in tomorrow as I will not be there. I am going away with a priest friend from early. I will not be back until late. Come in on Saturday morning as usual.') Fortune was meticulous in the preparation of his death: a typed note in the form of verse, entitled 'A Message From Heaven to My Family,' was placed on the dressing table adjacent to the bed: on top of the note was an additional handwritten message, an afterthought perhaps, 'from Fr John Fortune, please read this at my Requiem in Ballymurn,' and a third statement in a brown envelope addressed to his brother, Tom. An empty whiskey bottle in a bin, an assortment of scattered tablets,

Xanax and Zydol, and the presence of a white substance in his ordination tankard, indicated the desperate nature of the journey Fortune had planned and executed with grim determination.

In his last conversation with Stamp, his intention was to go away with a priest friend on Friday and to be back by Saturday. He had promised that the shutters on the door would be raised by the time she got there on Saturday. Concerned that Fortune had failed to contact her, Stamp arrived at his house shortly after 11 a.m. on Saturday, having been unable to reach him by phone, and was surprised that the shutters were down. She phoned Bennett, who did an assortment of odd jobs for the priest and who had keys for the house. He arrived within half an hour and opened the quiet house with a latch key. They both entered the tepid darkness in the hall. The ground floor resembled a mini church, with religious figurines, a chalice and a lectern. Bennett noticed that the alarm had not been set, a rare oversight by Fortune, and when they went into the kitchen, he remarked on the 'funny smell' in the house. Stamp hurried up the stairs to Fortune's bedroom, followed by Bennett, who tentatively, after calling Fortune's name, opened the door and switched on the light.

A bespectacled Fortune, his ample six-foot frame fully clothed, was supine on the bed, rosary beads twined around his hands in prayer. He had obviously been dead for some time.

Learning of his suicide from a journalist, O'Gorman did not believe it was cowardice on Fortune's behalf. 'It was ego. No one could be allowed to hold him to account. No one. He would not permit that.' After the airing of *Suing the Pope* in 2002, in which O'Gorman became the public face for his fellow victims' experiences, there was a widespread respect, outside the Catholic Church and pockets of opinion in Wexford, for the enormity of his achievement at the expense of something he had valued the most: privacy.

O'Gorman had launched a civil action against the diocese in 1998, which was settled in 2003 for €300,000, along with an admission of negligence by Bishop Walsh. 'It is now finally possible for me to put down the personal burden in all of this. I can now leave behind me the battle for justice in my own name, the battle for the right to have the harm caused me named and owned in full by those responsible.' The legal process and the road to redress had not been easy for O'Gorman – whose odyssey ended when he returned to live in County Wexford after seventeen years abroad – not by a long shot. 'The approach adopted by the Catholic Church in my own case has been a source of very real hurt and pain, hurt that was entirely avoidable had the Church faced its responsibilities in a more Christian and compassionate way.' He pointed out the hypocrisy of bishops speaking of the need to reach out to victims, while Church lawyers sent out vindictive and intimidating letters. 'That the Church has a right to defend itself in any legal action is beyond dispute, but the manner in which they have defended themselves in mine and other cases is reprehensible.'

Much has been made of a letter written by Fortune and left in his bedroom, an insight into his last hours with empty pill packets here and there, which was handed over to Fr Gerald O'Leary. Fortune said he was innocent of the accusations of abuse and claimed that Comiskey had raped him. He also made several requests which were not acceded to: he wanted to repose overnight at Ballymurn Church and he did not want Comiskey to officiate at his funeral. O'Leary told the Ferns Inquiry that as he believed the letter to be 'a very explosive document', he secreted it to a safe in a presbytery in Ballymitty. It did not enter his mind to hand it over to the Gardaí and after two years he burned it. At the request of Bishop Walsh, he provided an account of the letter for the Ferns Inquiry, which found no evidence to support Fortune's allegations. After

Fortune's death, Fr Colm Kilcoyne warned that 'there are ugly edges to the story that will continue to hurt and destroy long after his death, unless they are faced'.

At Fortune's funeral at St Michael's Church in Gorey on 16 March 1999, Comiskey's homily, which was scrutinised by his legal team, accepted that the prosecution against Fortune had come to an end. 'This development in itself adds further to the pain of all those who had looked to this particular process to alleviate their plight.' Not once did Comiskey mention the words 'victim' or 'abuse' at the funeral of the worst clerical abuser the Diocese of Ferns had ever known. Fortune was interred in St Michael's cemetery. Four hectic days later, in which he was both grieving the death of a sister-in-law and travelling back and forth to America (to deliver an address to the Friends of St Patrick), a contrite bishop once again availed of the voluntary services of his public relations adviser, Barbara Wallace, in response to suggestions that he did not respond appropriately when complaints of child sexual abuse were made to him. 'It is quite true that I received such complaints. It is untrue, however, to say that I did nothing about them.' After Fortune's death, Comiskey's episcopacy was put on life support: 1999 was the penultimate chapter in a saga hurtling towards its end.

It is appropriate that the last words on this harrowing chapter should be left to *The Ferns Report*. 'The Inquiry believes that Bishop Comiskey was correct to seek medical and canon law advice in his dealing with Fr Fortune and it accepts that the Bishop did not feel assisted by such advice which made his task more difficult. Nevertheless, the ultimate decision-making power rests with the Bishop and he must take responsibility for these decisions. In the view of the Inquiry the evidence available to Bishop Comiskey was compelling and dictated the immediate removal of Fr Fortune from ministry.'

3

Fr James Doyle

'Notwithstanding the report's acknowledgement that when dealing with abusers in the past, bishops followed – in good faith – the best psychiatric advice available at the time, clearly in relation to clerical sexual abuse we failed many young people over too long a period.'
Bishop John McAreavey, The Irish Bishops' Conference, 2003

How James Doyle of the cut-glass smile was successfully corralled into the priesthood remains a mystery: a blind motorist passing a driving test could not have achieved more. Prior to his ordination in 1974, Doyle was sending out signal after signal that his behaviour was unbecoming of somebody preparing to act in the person of Christ. As early as the mid-1950s in America, Fr Gerald Fitzgerald, founder of the Congregation of the Servants of the Paraclete, established to deal with problematic priests, was so convinced of the inability of child abusers to change their ways that he recommended immediate laicisation.

The Church would come round to Fitzgerald's way of thinking with the offending priests of the Diocese of Ferns, but with Doyle it took thirty-one years after he attempted to molest a student, while drunk, in the safe haven of St Peter's College, two years before his ordination.

In the vacuum between investigation and prosecution that besmirches the track record of the authorities confronted by allegations of clerical abuse in Wexford, Doyle always behaved as if he did not have a care in the world. His record before his ordination is eczema-ed with controversy. Long before he was charged with assaulting a minor in Wexford, a *cause célèbre* because he was the first priest in Ireland to be brought to book before a court, Doyle had exhibited a history of auto-eroticism. A report prepared for Bishop Herlihy by Professor Feichin O'Doherty in 1982, after he was informed that Doyle might have been interfering with altar boys in Clonard parish, determined that Doyle 'did not face up to celibacy in any realistic sense' and it was desirable that Doyle should not interact with young people.

O'Doherty thought that Doyle's eccentric predilections were manifest during his seminarian years, but passed unnoticed: he was misled, and Herlihy knew he was. During the school term 1972–73, Doyle – then a junior member of the seminary – returned to St Peter's drunk and tried to sexually assault another student. Told about the incident, a priest reported Doyle to the Dean of St Peter's, Dr Thomas Sherwood (who became President of the college in 1976), but he was dismissive. The priest then informed the President of the college, Fr Patrick O'Keeffe, who summoned Doyle to a meeting and gave him the option of joining a religious order rather than the priesthood. Doyle still favoured the latter, so O'Keeffe told Doyle by letter in 1973 that he would not be called to the Deaconate and his suitability for the priesthood would have to be re-examined. O'Keeffe's successor as President of the college, Fr Seamus De Val, approved Doyle for ordination a year later, a move that is believed to have come about because of intervention by Herlihy, although De Val told the Ferns Inquiry that he was not party to the information that prompted his predecessor to postpone Doyle's ordination.

De Val added that while a file would have been maintained by the college on Doyle, as a future priest, he did not refer to it when recommending Doyle for ordination and as such would have been unaware of the year-old abuse allegations. 'These records clearly state that an incident of interfering with boys in the boarding school had occurred but it appears that these records were either ignored or not consulted when James Doyle's ordination was decided upon,' said *The Ferns Report*. Doyle's ordination proceeded without any adherence to the *Norms for Priestly Training in Ireland,* promulgated by the Episcopal Conference a year before: the guidance stressed that an applicant for the seminary should have a thorough psychological assessment 'to ascertain whether he has the necessary qualities of personality for exercising his duties and sustaining the obligations of the life he has chosen' and that each student's position be kept under review; if he is deemed unsuitable, he is to be helped to choose another career. Not a single priest accused of sexual misdemeanours who emerged from the seminary at St Peter's was subject to any meaningful vetting. 'Had they been properly implemented,' said *The Ferns Report*, 'it is difficult to understand how the ordinations of clearly unsuitable men were allowed to proceed.'

Most clerical students were directed to St Peter's by either the Bishop of Ferns or the Bishop of Down and Connor and, if recommended by a bishop, did not have to be vetted.

The inertia displayed by the diocese towards Doyle at crucial moments in his career, not once but on three occasions – by De Val in 1973, by Herlihy in 1982 and by Comiskey in 1984 – demonstrates how the Diocese of Ferns became, unintentionally, an incubator of destructive licentiousness by a handful of priests like Doyle for whom ordination was a ticket of leave from the societal responsibilities that beckoned.

Doyle, like Jim Grennan and Seán Fortune, served his time in Northern Ireland before returning to Ferns. The allegations of abuse against Doyle span twenty years, and at least one is deserving of deeper perusal because of his method of entrapment: in 1980, while returning to Belfast, Doyle, now a curate in Clonard parish, stopped to pick up a seventeen-year-old hitchhiker near Gorey and, after the normal chit-chat, propositioned him. The man was so disturbed by his approach that he immediately contacted the Gardaí, who went in pursuit of Doyle and stopped his car near Wicklow. Doyle was questioned on the spot and the incident was brought to the attention of a local priest the day after by a sergeant in Gorey. The Gardaí had no intention of processing a file: the priest was told, but reassurance was sought that there would not be a repeat of the incident.

The priest informed Herlihy's secretary, and also advised the investigating Garda that he should tell Doyle's parish priest in Clonard. In all, it is believed that three priests were aware of the incident with the hitchhiker, but never brought it to the attention of Comiskey when he was appointed bishop. This was important because under canon law the bishop is responsible for disciplining priests in his diocese. ('The fact that three priests of the diocese, apart from the authorities in St Peter's, were aware of Fr Doyle's activities but did not consider it necessary or appropriate to speak with Bishop Herlihy or his successor, indicates a system of secrecy which did not advance the achievement of child protection in the Diocese'– *The Ferns Report*.)

In or around the time of the solicitation of the hitchhiker, Gardaí in Wexford were also keeping tabs on Doyle, acting on rumours that he might have been interfering with altar boys. As there was insufficient evidence to move against Doyle, the only avenue of approach left to the Gardaí in Wexford was to enlighten Herlihy, and they did. What emerged in the submissions to the Ferns Inquiry is that the Gardaí in Wexford and Gorey had shared their suspicions about Doyle. Although Gardaí in Wexford and Gorey exchanged information about him, and although the Gardaí tipped off Herlihy, no record appears on police files about Doyle at this time, apparently in order to safeguard his constitutional rights.

It was a case of not if but when Doyle offended again; and when he did in 1990, the attitude of the Gardaí had hardened. Toward the end of July, Mr Joe Smyth, senior social worker in the Wexford area of the South Eastern Health Board, contacted Garda Patricia O'Gorman to report an alleged incident of sexual assault involving a priest and a young boy. Garda O'Gorman interviewed Smyth and the boy and his father, who worked for the bishop in an administrative capacity. Comiskey, naturally, got wind of the assault but he was faced with the type of a dilemma only a bishop could have empathy with: he was uncertain whether he should report the incident to the Gardaí or not, so he advised the boy's father – who worked with the finance secretariat in the Diocese of Ferns office – to contact the family doctor and, inter alia, the Health Board.

Comiskey was mindful that Child Abuse Guidelines dating from 1987 made it mandatory for all doctors to report an allegation of abuse. Comiskey's advice was also an unprecedented footnote in his epsicopacy: the first time a complaint of this nature had been directed to the Gardaí. From the court hearing that followed on 21 November 1990, four years before the Fr Brendan Smyth case, we know that Doyle, who was a guest in the boy's home, molested him twice: while the boy was sitting on his knee and again upstairs, when Doyle impulsively pushed him into a corner and fondled the boy's penis. The victim was twelve.

Curiously, when the priest was interviewed by Garda O'Gorman, he said that he could not remember the incident but that he did not deny the allegations. Matters proceeded at a lightning pace. The Garda file was forwarded to the State Solicitor and then passed on to the DPP, who directed that the 41-year-old Doyle should be prosecuted for indecent assault contrary to Section 62 of the Offences against the Person Act 1881 and for common assault, the first priest in Ireland to be made accountable for his misdemeanours with a young child. Superintendent Noel O'Sullivan told the court that it was only when the child became afraid and started to cry, as Doyle used his considerable physical presence to push him into a corner, that the assault was witnessed by the boy's father. No evidence was heard from Doyle: instead his solicitor, Bob Egar, said that the priest was 'aware of the anxiety and disruption he caused to the child's parents' and wanted to indicate how seriously he regarded his conduct.

The only mitigation Egar could offer was that Doyle had himself been the victim of repeated sexual abuse when he was ten at the hands of an eighteen-year-old, a time when he also witnessed the difficulties caused by a chronic drinking problem: Doyle had had a disrupted home life as a child and had grave difficulties adjusting at school, the court was told, which makes it all the more incongruous that he was passed fit for ordination. Two events precipitated Doyle's descent into alcohol abuse: the death of his thirteen-year-old brother when Doyle was seventeen and his work in Andersonstown, Belfast, when he witnessed at first hand the sectarian violence that continued unabated for years.

Doyle's punishment for the offences, for which he pleaded guilty, was soft in the extreme – some might view it now as woefully inappropriate – but it was not untypical of the attitude of due process at the time to the Catholic Church: he received a three-month suspended sentence at Wexford District Court from Justice Sean Magee, on condition that he quit the Diocese of Ferns. *The Ferns Report* noted that the coverage of the trial by the local media, which published a photograph of Doyle with the court report on the front page, provoked a considerable backlash within Wexford, particularly from primary school teachers in his parish, because of the perception that the priest had been badly treated by the positioning of the report. No one, a decade before the new millennium, would have accused the good people of Wexford of an excess of indignation, especially in a town where it is distinctly lacking unless there is revolution in the air. But indignation there was over the media treatment of Fr James Doyle, one of their own, who sang with the Festival Singers and set up the church folk group.

Specifically blackballed was the *Wexford People*, which came out a day after the court case, and published the case on its front page, alongside an unusually big and less-than-flattering photograph of a grimacing Doyle. In light of what was to follow throughout the 1990s, the coverage, with the benefit of hindsight, seems mild. However, no priest had ever been prosecuted in the Diocese of Ferns for meddling with boys and the Doyle publicity came out of the blue for a Church enmeshed in every facet of the community. Six months earlier Wexford Corporation had made Brendan Comiskey the shortest-serving Bishop of Ferns to receive the freedom of the town.

Two months before Doyle's trial, Comiskey issued a press release for the 16 August editions of the local media to announce that Doyle had taken an immediate sabbatical leave of one year 'and is moving to London for further studies'. It was a fabrication, but nobody, except the bishop, Doyle, one or two priests, the little boy Doyle abused and his family, knew different. The sabbatical did not last long. Perhaps to Doyle and the Church's surprise, the Gardaí pursued the investigation of the sexual assault to its logical conclusion, a court appearance. There was a new Superintendent in town, Noel O'Sullivan, from outside Wexford, and he was his own man. The priest had to take a sabbatical from his sabbatical in London, and face the music in Wexford. Such was the esteem with which Doyle was held in his locale that the publicity generated by his case resulted in an onslaught of resentment and loathing toward the newspaper, which received an unprecedented number of letters, prompting its managing director to apologise in the next edition if the editorial slant had offended readers, which it clearly had, but the Fourth Estate had done the right thing, even if it was clearly rattled.

The media had helped expose Doyle for what he was: a clerical abuser of a boy, young enough to be taught by any of the fifty-plus teachers, the majority of them women, spread throughout Wexford, who put their names to correspondence objecting in the strongest terms to either the positioning of the report, or the language of the reporting. Teachers such as the nineteen members of Kennedy Park primary school, the closest to the home of the victim and in the same parish as Doyle, who described the coverage as 'discriminatory', without specifying against whom. Also incandescent with anger were eleven teachers at another primary school in the heart of the town, Our Lady of Fatima, who felt that it was (a) unnecessary to expose Doyle in 'such an undignified manner' and (b) the coverage was a 'gutter press reaction' to a man who had done so much good for the community.

Eight teachers at Rathangan National School described the reporting as 'ill judged and irresponsible', while sixteen teachers – all women – at the St John of God School in the

Faythe, the birthplace of novelist John Banville, deplored the manner in which the case was reported. (Another letter, published a week later, with name withheld, struck a different tone: 'I was surprised and disappointed that of the 54 teachers who signed the four letters in last week's paper, not one of them condemned child abuse – and a lot of them are mothers.') Doyle's supporters within the community came from all walks of life: a former altar boy in Clonard parish who had served Mass with Doyle, lamented the fact that the media did not exercise 'a little discretion'.

Rev. Joseph McGrath, born and reared in Wexford town and who, two years earlier, had succeeded Seán Fortune as C.C. Poulfur, described the report as 'unusual' because of the explicit details of the assault and the use of a photograph of Doyle. Fifty-six residents in Coolcotts, in the shadow of Clonard Church, signed a letter objecting to the publication of the court report. 'While we do not condone his offence, it is obvious that he has a problem, compounded by alcohol, which is being treated.' In others words, it was a minor misdemeanour, carried out under the influence, and it won't happen again.

Only one correspondent had the foresight to see that the unfortunate attachment of one sentence in the report – 'the boy is a son of a senior Catholic Church official' – opened up the possibility of public exposure. Barbara Wallace, then Chairperson of Wexford Festival Opera, whose public relations company was used by Wexford County Council, the South Eastern Health Board and, much later, by Brendan Comiskey, pointed out that 'the reference to the victim's father in Church affairs must, in a small community, make identification relatively easy'. It is instructive that Catholics in Wexford at this time were able to excuse the deviancy of their clergy, or make light of their crime, by their commitment to acts of welfare elsewhere in the community. Priests like James Doyle, Donal

Collins, Martin Clancy and Seán Fortune cultivated a high profile in all walks of life. In spite of their convictions, both Doyle and Collins were happy to pose for photographs for *The Secular Priests of the Diocese of Ferns* in 2000. 'They tended to see the abuse on a scale, which, when weighed against all the good they did in their ministry, could be excused and forgiven,' said *The Ferns Report*. This was the flavour of the feeling within Wexford after the public humiliation of Doyle.

In the wake of the very public cross–community support of the priest, with almost no acknowledgement of the suffering of the victim or his family, one can imagine the sense of isolation and desolation his parents must have felt in Wexford. The tragic repercussion for the family is alluded to in *The Ferns Report*. The boy Doyle abused was the nephew of three priests, one of whom later resigned and left the ministry, and his father had worked with the finance secretariat in the bishop's office. The fate of the boy's father, from the moment he discovered Doyle assaulting his young son in his own home up until his untimely death alone in an apartment on the town's main street five years later, is nothing less than a tragedy. The undeniable trauma for the family was exacerbated by the salacious purloining of his death by the increasingly aggressive tabloid reporting in Dublin of anything to do with the diocese in the mid–1990s, which went so far as to connect the discovery of the body of the bishop's former finance secretary in June 1995 with Comiskey's sudden departure to America four months later. 'Death of Bishop's Money Man May Have Led to Move' screamed the *Sunday World,* which, by identifying the father, identified Doyle's victim, who was still a teenager.

What is undeniable is the role James Doyle and, arguably, the Church had in the emotional distress visited upon the family and the boy's father, hitherto a gifted music producer who had worked with writer Nicky Furlong and director Tomás Mac Anna, a much sought after adjudicator in the South East and a freelance coordinator for RTÉ . His descent into a slow spiral of personal detachment and destitution which culminated in his death at fifty was triggered by the events of 24 April 1990. 'Notwithstanding Bishop Comiskey's expeditious removal of Fr Doyle and his subsequent dealings with him,' said *The Ferns Report*, 'the Diocese did not meet or attempt to meet with this victim or his family in relation to the complaint. The consequences of this case were very serious for the family concerned.' For bringing about the reporting to the Gardaí indirectly by the Health Board, Comiskey found himself under pressure from some priests in the diocese, and met with senior clergy later that year to underline the mandatory requirements of the Child Abuse Guidelines, although there is no direct evidence that the bishop wholeheartedly referred to this policy in dealing with future complaints.

More or less after his derisory sentence, Doyle – who observed the court proceedings with a cold detachment – was now free to molest and proposition young people while attired in clerical garb, as long as it was not within the confines of Wexford. The diocese lost little time in shepherding Doyle to the Stroud Institute in England where, true to form, he was banned from driving for a year after he was convicted of drink driving. It did not seem to occur to the Church that Doyle, who had shown a penchant for hitchhikers, should not have been let near a car, let alone a school. Eighteen months after his discharge from attending the centre in Stroud, which was established by the Servants of the Paracletes in 1959, and where an assessment of his sexual orientation concluded that he was not drawn to children, Doyle undertook unpaid work at a parish in Southwark, where he worked on and off as chaplain to a co-education secondary school with 600 pupils, with the tacit agreement of Comiskey and the school management, who knew about his recent history but presumably not the recommendation in Professor O'Doherty's report to the diocese in 1982: 'it would also seem desirable that he should have a change of role, away from working with young people.' The first that parents in England knew of Doyle's past was when a report about him appeared in *The Observer* in 1994.

Doyle then returned to Ireland. Archbishop of Dublin Desmond Connell, asked Comiskey to have Doyle removed from working in a halfway residential out-patient support house for adults, but Comiskey had no idea how his priest had come to be there in the first place. Doyle was operating as he pleased without supervision and was not accountable to anybody, but Comiskey was satisfied that the centre was an appropriate place for him. Encouraged by Connell, the Bishop of Ferns informed the Gardaí of Doyle's latest location. Connell went one step further. He issued a decree forbidding Doyle from exercising any ministry, including public celebration of Mass, in the Dublin diocese, and from wearing clerical attire. After Comiskey's resignation, his temporary replacement in Ferns, Bishop Eamonn Walsh, established an ad hoc advisory panel to clean up the diocese, and he issued a precept to Doyle to have no unsupervised access with teenagers, that anyone involved with him should be made aware of his history, that his work must be solely a bookkeeping one, that he refrain from saying Mass in private or in public, that he cease having any chaplaincy role and that the Gardaí be informed of his whereabouts.

Shortly after his arrival in Wexford, Walsh learned of another allegation against Doyle dating back to 1981, when the victim was eleven, a time when priests in the diocese and Gardaí had entertained misgivings about the priest. The boy found a watch at a local GAA pitch (Clonard parish house is next to Wexford Park – hallowed home of the GAA) and brought it to Doyle who said that if the owner was not found, the boy could keep the watch. Doyle then undid his own and the boy's clothing and exposed himself, encouraging the boy to touch him. When the boy returned a number of days later to see if the watch had been reclaimed, Doyle tried to expose himself again, though no actual assault took place. The boy kept the incidents to himself, but reported it to the Apostolic Administrator in 2002, and the Gardaí in early 2003. By then, the diocese had clearly had enough: Doyle was invited by his bishop to consider laicisation but declined, so the Pope, on the application of Walsh, dismissed him from the priesthood in 2004.

4

Canon Martin Clancy

'The verbal or pictorial portrayal of the perpetrator as a man of unmitigated evil is frequently inaccurate and often misleading, resulting in parents failing to appreciate that the child abuser may be someone with a kind and pleasant appearance, capable of warmth, affection and generosity and of intellectual and professional worth.'
The Ferns Report

'*How many?*' The question reverberated through the newsroom of *The Wexford Echo* on that Tuesday in October 2005 as two of its editorial staff dispatched to Dublin began sifting through *The Ferns Report*, hot off the government press, diligently filtering the shocking contents by phone to their colleagues on standby in Wexford. '*Twenty-five priests!*' Like many weekly provincial newspapers, the century-old *Echo* was printed on Tuesday evenings and was on the shelves in newsagents from New Ross to Gorey and from Rosslare to Bunclody early on Wednesday mornings. As the publication of *The Ferns Report* was well flagged for 25 October, *The Echo* had a time frame of about three hours to (a) collect a copy of the voluminous report in Dublin, (b) return to Wexford, (c) make facsimiles of the relevant chapters to distribute to reporters, (d) distil the contents, and (e) write and prepare reports for ten news pages. It was not that time was of the essence, because newspaper deadlines wait for no one, but that analysis and writing would have to be conducted on the wing and at a furiously fast pace. To facilitate the process, a reporter was given a priest to shadow in advance of the publication of the report: the priority names were James Doyle, Seán Fortune, James Grennan, Donal Collins and Micheal Ledwith.

They had been subjected to either a Health Board or a Church inquiry or had been before the courts, with the conviction of two for sexually related assaults. It was not anticipated, in spite of press speculation, which could be inaccurate, that the report would investigate as many as twenty-five priests. It quickly emerged in several of the urgent phone calls from Dublin that another priest in the report was culpable of the most heinous allegations of child abuse, but somehow his name had slipped under the media radar when he was alive: Martin Clancy. He had been identified, without being named, by Bishop Eamonn Walsh as a child abuser in 2003 in the parish of Ballindaggin. But little was known about him because he had died suddenly ten years earlier. Here was the original invisible man of *The Ferns Report*. Reporters took to *The Echo*'s diocesan archives and sifted through the copious cut-outs for any scintilla of information about Clancy. People in his parish said that rumour surrounded him like a fog, and that it escalated in 1991 when he became the first priest in living memory to resign his parish in favour of a curacy.

Finally, armed with a copy of *The Ferns Report* still warm from the oven, the crimes of Clancy, whose funeral in 1993 was presided over by Comiskey and attended by fifty priests, were laid bare: he had been abusing schoolgirls for thirty years, had fathered a child by a victim he had raped and had left money in his will for his daughter's education. Unlike Fortune, Doyle, Grennan or Collins, he had never been the subject of a whispering campaign in the media but families had good reason not to leave their daughters alone with him. Like James Grennan, he was a priest who wrought divided loyalties in a small parish. Comiskey had said at his funeral that he was 'in love with his vocation'. He was in fact an unworthy priest: of no one of whom so much was written in *The Ferns Report* was so little known. The report demolished his reputation. The earliest recorded abuse by Clancy dates as far back as 1965 and it continued until the late 1980s. For three years in the 1960s – three or four times weekly – Clancy molested Maeve, the first time after her mother consented to him going to the girl's bedroom to speak with her. Clancy would ask after her physical development and whether she had boyfriends, and his molestation in her home became full intercourse when he brought her to the parochial house in Ballindaggin. Clancy never stopped trying to have sex with her. To get away from Clancy, she fled to England for about a year when she was fifteen. Two years before he died, by which time she had already informed two priests about the abuse, one of whom took ten years to inform the diocesan authorities, Clancy arrived at her house and made a botched attempt to kiss her.

Clancy's lust was rapacious. Among the other victims that he pitchforked into their own private hell was a girl, just twelve, who alleged that a teacher of the national school had directed her to the parochial house for a private talk with Clancy who assumed charge of sex education classes. He molested her in his study, the latest in a steady stream of victims ushered to his den. 'I was a child when I went into that room in that house, but when I left I was not a child,' a victim named as Judy told the Ferns Inquiry. Clancy was recognised throughout the county for his interest in and passion for traditional music. Comhaltas Ceoltóirí Éireann, which Clancy helped co-found and of which he was the inaugural chairman in Wexford, issued a lengthy statement after his death, remarking that 'Irish traditional music's loss is heaven's gain'. His extra-curricular devotion to music and the many events organised by Comhaltas Ceoltóirí Éireann gave him unrestricted access to young musicians, one of whom was first molested when she was eleven by Clancy when he was stationed in Wexford town, in the dressing room of a concert hall. Three years later, after repeatedly abusing her, sometimes in his car, Clancy got the girl pregnant.

Like others, she felt she had no option but to flee Wexford: her family brought her back from England six weeks later and her daughter was born in 1975. Only when the baby's mother turned sixteen did Clancy acknowledge his daughter: he wrote out two pitiful cheques, £500 each, for her upkeep, although years earlier the rebarbative priest had threatened to have his daughter taken away from her if she breathed a word about his identity as the father. Three months after Clancy's death in Dublin, she received an extraordinary letter from Fr John Sinnott, who was executor of Clancy's will and had worked alongside him for fourteen years. Attached was a cheque for £3,000 and a note from Sinnott, acknowledging the money as 'invested by Canon Clancy and which I send to you on maturity. It was his wish that this money is to be used for your further musical education. I hope it will help you in your pursuits and I wish you success.' Sinnott had no knowledge of Clancy's daughter.

A decade on, Bishop Walsh visited Ballindaggin parish, which includes the churches of Kiltealy and Caim, and apologised for Clancy's crimes, just as he had done a year earlier in Monageer. He urged anybody who had ever been abused by Clancy to come forward and to meet with him. Complaints of child sexual abuse by priests were received in an administrative capacity by the diocesan delegate. As a result of Walsh's appeal, made before a hushed congregation at St Colman's Church, three victims the Church did not know about would come forward, including the mother of Clancy's child. That Clancy was highly thought of in the diocese is an understatement: born the eldest of a family of six in Clare, but raised in Campile, Clancy was ordained into the priesthood in 1942 after studying at St Peter's College, ministered in Carrigaholt in the Diocese of Killaloe, Hexham near Newcastle-Upon-Tyne, until D-Day in 1944 and returned to Ferns upon his appointment as curate in Tomacork in 1945, serving in Templeduigan in 1948 and Wexford, where he remained for two decades, in 1954.

Clancy sought easy access to young people and became chaplain to the 2nd Wexford (St Columbanus) Scout troop for many years. He was appointed parish priest of Ballindaggin – which he quickly dubbed 'Lanestown' because of the warren of narrow roads – in 1972, where he remained in contented bliss until 1991, when his bishop decided to move him after receiving correspondence that alleged Clancy was an abuser. He swapped places with his curate in Kiltealy, Fr John Sinnott, who had been privy to innuendo about Clancy. 'In the 1980s and 1990s, you'd hear outside that there were rumours, you'd hear that girls were saying "I wouldn't trust him" – but you'd hear all that indirectly. No one came to me and said: "This is what's happening." So there was no way you could go and follow it up.' It must have been a difficult situation for Comiskey to comprehend: Clancy as a man of action was not dissimilar to Monsignor Horan in Mayo. He was the driving force behind the community centre in Ballindaggin, he brought an entrepreneurial zest to improving the national school, the cemetery, the presbytery and the eighteenth-century church, and directed a project that culminated in the publication of *Memorials to the Dead – Ballindaggin*.

Music was his first love. One of his first duties upon his arrival in the parish was to revive traditional music, and the organisational skill he had brought to the early years of Comhaltas Ceoltóirí Éireann was much in evidence in Ballindaggin, as was another practice he enjoyed in Wexford, teaching music to young children. Those who had dealings with Clancy will say that persistence and persuasiveness were the hallmarks of his character: he had traditional views on the evils of alcohol, immorality and contraception. Outwardly, he busied himself upgrading the infrastructure and facilities of the village: he water-blasted and sealed the front wall and bell tower of St Colman's Church; he helped the parish raise £28,000 toward the £236,000 cost of adding a five-classroom extension to Ballindaggin Primary School, which was blessed by Comiskey in 1984, and he was instrumental in the building of St Colman's Community Hall at a cost of £43,000. Money was in short supply in Ireland of the 1970s and early 1980s, but Clancy had the gift of securing it.

Clancy as father of his parish was the man Comiskey thought he knew when a bombshell landed on his desk in April 1991. It was a letter from a former pupil of Ballindaggin national school who had been repeatedly molested and abused by Clancy in the parochial house after he promised to teach her how to play music. The recalcitrant Clancy, in reply to Comiskey, denied that he had molested her but accepted that he 'momentarily touched her on the upper thigh and immediately realised I was very wrong'. The old priest's halo had slipped. He admitted that he found the girl 'a good looking, red headed youngster, provocative etc.' She was twelve. 'To suggest that I fondled her breasts, rubbed her vagina or interfered with her clothing is absolutely without foundation.' Such was the nature of the correspondence that passed between the bishop and one of his most senior clerics. Clancy's obscurantism must have damaged any certitudes Comiskey may have held. 'The bad example I did give on this occasion troubled me greatly and I have referred the matter on many occasions to many confessors and retreat masters, who have told me to forget about the incident,' said Clancy. And he did.

Comiskey took Clancy out of Ballindaggin, moved him down the road to Kiltealy, so that Clancy could avoid the penance of retirement to which he was psychologically unsuited. The bishop decided that he could not have him monitored until he had met the alleged victim face to face, to determine her credibility, an astonishing decision in light of the fact that Clancy had admitted touching the girl, and still had uninhibited access to schoolchildren. His demotion was presented in a totally different light in a tribute in the *Wexford People*: 'Such was his love of the area that he took great pains to persude Bishop Comiskey to appoint him to Kiltealy curacy in a swop with Fr Sinnott.'

Comiskey 'had a credible complaint and an admission of inappropriate behaviour from Canon Clancy, which should have allowed him to require the priest to stand aside immediately', stressed *The Ferns Report*. The girl's story has an unusual twist: her father had become aware of the abuse of his daughter and sent a threatening letter to Clancy, saying he would go to the *Sunday World* unless he paid him £20,000. The father's letter was brought to the attention of the diocese, which forwarded it to the Gardaí via a solicitor, although the letter from the girl, detailing the abuse against Clancy, was not given to the Gardaí. A meeting between the father and two local Gardaí took place in a patrol car outside the family home, and he was advised, according to testimony by Gardaí to the Ferns Inquiry, to make a formal complaint rather than seek money from the priest. The Gardaí, though acquainted with the rumours surrounding

Clancy, did not launch an investigation of the priest, who was still in ministry, even after they had the discussed the allegations of abuse with the father. No official Garda record exists of the conversation between the father and the two Gardaí. In 1996 the man's wife in correspondence with the diocese, claimed that her husband, who had since died, had been warned by the Gardaí not to go public with the allegation. Disturbingly, one of the Gardaí present in the car had received a complaint about Clancy from a young woman in 1981. The dogs in the streets in Ballindaggin knew about Clancy's reputation for years, but he was never interviewed by the Gardaí. Life in the village went on as if nothing untoward had ever occurred. 'The Inquiry is satisfied that rumour, suspicion and innuendo had come to the attention of members of the Gardaí as well as members of the teaching profession, the medical profession, the Church and the general public, and were never acted upon,' commented *The Ferns Report*.

The term paedophile is, more often than not, wrongly used against priests like Seán Fortune and Donal Collins: as far as we can establish, their interest lay in youths about the age of puberty – hebephilia – or post-pubertal adolescents – pederasty. Clancy was a paedophile, the accepted definition of which is someone who, over at least a six-month period, has recurrent, intense sexually arousing fantasies of a prepubsecent child (thirteen or younger). Individuals with paedophilia generally have an attraction to children of a particular age range. The majority of Clancy's victims as recorded in *The Ferns Report* range from twelve to fifteen, though one girl was just eight.

Months earlier, in response to consternation over the James Doyle affair, Comiskey met with senior clergy to discuss child abuse guidelines. The policy Comiskey intended to adopt included relieving the accused priest temporarily of his duties in order to protect other children at risk. What he did with Clancy was the direct opposite: he moved him from Ballindaggin to Kiltealy with no restrictions placed on him whatsoever. The paramountcy principle did not apply, where protection of children takes priority over the rights of the priest. At the time of the correspondence with his bishop, Clancy had been raping one girl weekly for four years.

He had started when she had gone to him for music lessons. She was eight, and the abuse continued from her time in primary school to secondary school and only stopped when the bishop moved Clancy out of Ballindaggin. Clancy pestered her – she was now twelve – to keep on the classes in Kiltealy. She refused. After Clancy's death, the sixteen-year-old told her principal, Sister Madeleine Ryan, that Clancy had been abusing her. The principal contacted both her parents and Bishop Comiskey, asking him to pay for counselling expenses in Dublin for the girl and her parents. Comiskey agreed. It must have been an awakening for the bishop to know that if he had pursued his old policy of leaving the priest *in situ*, like he did with James Grennan, the abuse of the girl by Clancy would have continued.

When Clancy slumped and died on the third floor of St Stephen's Green car park in the company of Sinnott (they were in Dublin for the funeral of architect Eamonn Hederman), Comiskey compounded the suffering of victims by presiding at the obsequies, paying a glowing tribute in his homily, and standing by as children from Ballindaggin and Kiltealy national schools undertook important roles in the liturgical celebrations. Clancy's funeral took place in the same week as the Kilkenny Incest Case report was presented to the newly appointed Minister for Health, Brendan Howlin, who promised the full implementation of the Child Care Act.

The laity, naturally, was less deferential to the Church when *The Ferns Report* spilled the beans on Clancy. After reading a pastoral letter from Bishop Walsh at a weekend Mass, days after the contents of the report had been digested the length and breadth of the country, Sinnott faced a barrage of questions from angry parishioners about Clancy. The parish priest, visibly upset, said he was equally as shocked by the revelations. The public obloquy was not confined to Ballindaggin, but sent a shockwave throughout the diocese.

5

Fr John Kinsella

'Moral contradiction underscores the Irish public's disillusion with a religious institution once regarded as all powerful and untouchable.'
Robert Savage and James Smith, *Sexual Abuse and the Irish Church: Crisis and Responses*

If the past had overtaken Brendan Comiskey in early April 2002, it was catching up with Fr John Kinsella in the rural parish of The Ballagh. Kinsella and Comiskey had history, but with Comiskey gone, Kinsella's new adversary in Wexford was Eamonn Walsh, and he did not stand on ceremony. As Apostolic Administrator, he had access to every diocesan file that Comiskey had maintained but prioritised those containing allegations of a sexual nature against clergy. His new policy, which would blow through the shattered diocese like an Arctic wind, was to remove any priest against whom a credible allegation was made. Walsh locked horns with Kinsella almost immediately, and the ensuing confrontation was to leave a priest who vehemently denied any allegations against him to feel deceived by his diocese and unfairly stripped of his ministry.

Little was known publicly about John Kinsella the priest: he was educated at Monamolin National School, St Peter's College and St Peter's Seminary, where he was ordained in June 1974, the same year as Fr James Doyle. While Doyle, about whom Bishop Herlihy already had reservations, was sent on a temporary mission to Belfast, Kinsella was placed closer to home in Enniscorthy, where he remained until his transfer to The Ballagh, famous for its hurling and camogie prowess.

In November 1995, Patrick Doyle gave a statement to Garda Tom Murphy in Enniscorthy, alleging that he had been abused by Kinsella shortly after he was posted to the town. He was a fifteen-year-old altar boy, and Kinsella would ask him to attend to the parochial house to help him with parish work, whenever he was on duty. Doyle claimed to the Garda that the abuse was initiated when Kinsella brought him to his bedroom and asked him to remove his clothes and try on a pair of swimming trunks. Kinsella took off his clothes, lay on top of the boy for quarter of an hour, and masturbation took place. As Garda Murphy took notes, he heard that Kinsella was alleged to have abused the boy three times a week for four to five years. Paul McGannon was fifteen when he went to the home of Kinsella, now based in The Ballagh, on a summer's day in 1993, to discuss problems he was having at home. He would allege to the South Eastern Health Board that, while he was upset, Kinsella knelt before him and started to rub his crotch for about half an hour. Kinsella was accused by McGannon of abusing him on a regular basis for about a year. Anthony Doyle, a brother of Patrick's, gave a statement to Gardaí in 2002, alleging that he had been raped by Kinsella when he was an altar server in Enniscorthy, beside a pond in a field near his home. After his Leaving Certificate, he entered the seminary at St Peter's College and discussed the incident with his Spiritual Director. As it came under the seal of confession and was confidential, the Spiritual Director was unable to discuss specifics of the allegations with a third party.

Symptomatic of the problems infesting the Diocese of Ferns during Bishop Comiskey's term is the length of time it took to get priests to inform on other priests and for priests to remove themselves from ministry once an allegation of abuse was brought to their attention. Comiskey first learned of the accusations against Kinsella in 1995, but despite his best efforts to have him removed, involving consultation after consultation with canon lawyers, Kinsella was still at his post when Comiskey absented himself from his, seven years later. It took Bishop Walsh less than a month to oust Kinsella from the picture.

The case of Kinsella was a watershed moment for Comiskey: it was the first allegation of clerical child abuse to be managed under the Catholic Church's Framework Document of 1996 but by adhering to the letter of the law, the process dragged on interminably. Between 1995 and 1996, allegations by all three men against Kinsella had come to the attention of both the Gardaí and the South Eastern Health Board, but Comiskey had received no direct complaint until the Board informed him of McGannon's allegations in March 1996, just weeks after the bishop's return to Wexford following a recuperative break in America. The Board was careful not to identify McGannon to the bishop, who was still none the wiser after three months, so the diocese contacted both the Gardaí and the Health Board in July seeking assistance so that its Advisory Panel could process its own investigation. The diocese learned of another allegation against Kinsella in September (by Anthony Doyle) and was in a position to meet his older brother, Edward, a month later. Edward's allegations were thereafter put to Kinsella, who strenuously denied them.

In advance of an Advisory Panel meeting in December, the

diocese was busy investigating Kinsella's past: priests who had worked alongside him in Enniscorthy were questioned about his behaviour and, though nobody had a specific complaint, there was disapproval at the large number of boys who used to hang around the parochial house. The diocese's concern was exacerbated when it was discovered that Kinsella was known to have taken one of the victims on holidays with him. Comiskey finally came face to face with one of Kinsella's accusers early in the new year. Accompanied by a social worker, McGannon detailed abuse allegedly committed by Kinsella. Comiskey acted. Shortly after his meeting, he wrote to Kinsella recommending that he step aside from active ministry, but the priest, who always maintained his innocence, refused.

Whether Comiskey expected this opposition is unknown, but Kinsella's solicitor informed the bishop that he could not defend his reputation without a full and thorough investigation of the allegations which, in their current state, were a matter of hearsay. If Comiskey was hoping for a helping hand from the Gardaí, who were investigating Kinsella on the strength of the statements from the Doyle brothers, it was not forthcoming. When Patrick Doyle sat before Garda Murphy on 27 November 1995, and asserted a litany of abuse by Kinsella stretching over five years, he was asked to consider whether he wanted to make a formal complaint, because he had made an informal one in the past. He was also advised by Murphy to receive counselling, which he did. In February 1996, in tandem with Comiskey ending his sabbatical abroad and returning to Enniscorthy, an anxious McGannon walked into the local Garda station and gave a statement claiming that he had been abused by Kinsella. He withdrew it two months later.

By then, the Gardaí had put the allegations to a startled Kinsella who, in two tense meetings, in which he would maintain he was put under pressure to give a statement – which the Gardaí denied – the priest is reported to have conceded to having had a consensual sexual relationship with Patrick for four years from the late 1970s, which began when Patrick was nineteen. Kinsella would deny any relationship to the Ferns Inquiry. Gardaí spent the summer preparing a file on Kinsella for the DPP, recommending charges of gross indecency perpetrated on Patrick (McGannon had by now withdrawn his statement) when he was a minor, during a four-year spell, 1974 to 1979. While the State Solicitor examined Patrick's testimony, Anthony Doyle in September furnished the Gardaí with the first of two statements, alleging that not only had Kinsella abused him but the priest had secreted photographs of Doyle semi-naked in his parochial house. This was a year before the enactment of the Criminal Justice (Miscellaneous Provisions) Act, so the Gardaí were powerless to search the house. Anthony had also submitted a collection of poems, detailing abuse of sorts at the hands of an unnamed priest, for publication to *The Wexford Echo*, but their potentially defamatory nature meant they were unpublishable.

Matters became even more convoluted when Kinsella sent a letter to the Gardaí alleging a sexual assault by Anthony, who had been having sex with the priest after he reached the age of consent. In March, McGannon, who had apparently withdrawn his statement because of pressure from his family, resubmitted his statement to Gardaí with two changes. The imbroglio facing the Gardaí in Enniscorthy in the spring of 1997 constituted the following: Patrick Doyle, whose claim that he had a sexual relationship with Fr John Kinsella for three years after he was nineteen would be refuted by the priest, claimed Kinsella abused him when he was fifteen; Anthony Doyle, after years of therapy, remembered that Kinsella had apparently raped him in a field, but he had consensual sex with Kinsella when he was an adult; Kinsella alleged that he, in turn, had been sexually assaulted by Anthony Doyle, while Paul McGannon, after alleging that he had been abused by Kinsella in February 1996, withdrew this statement, but in March 1997, changed his mind and re-entered his original complaint. (In September 2002, Anthony made a fresh claim to Gardaí that Kinsella had buggered him when he was eight: in April 2002, McGannon gave a statement to Gardaí claiming, for the first time, that he had been buggered by the priest. The DPP, within months, directed no prosecution in any of the cases.)

McGannon met with the South Eastern Health Board and was suspicious that Kinsella might have abused the children of a third party. The Board, though McGannon's hunch was exactly that, was obligated to interview one of the parents of the children, who clarified that they were more than happy with the safety of their children in the company of Kinsella: the parents were annoyed by McGannon's claim, which they believed to be false, but it did have the effect of Comiskey asking his priest to remove himself from ministry. While the Gardaí did their best to untangle the tapestry of allegations made against Kinsella and on his behalf, the diocese engaged in what became a fruitless effort by Comiskey and his Advisory Panel to do something constructive about its priest in The Ballagh. It was suggested that Kinsella should undergo assessment at Stroud, where the troubled priests of the Dublin and Wexford dioceses had been sent in the past, but he declined.

Comiskey, on advice, invoked Canon 552 ('an assistant priest may for a just reason be removed') toward the end of 1997 to force Kinsella to take administrative leave, but the priest said he would appeal the ruling to Rome, thus temporarily blocking Comiskey's decree. The bishop had done almost everything in his power to alter the landscape at The Ballagh but after correspondence with Kinsella lasting months, and despite the best canon law advice made available to him, nothing had changed. Relief for Kinsella came from the Gardaí. The DPP in May resolved that there should be no prosecution of Kinsella in relation to Patrick Doyle (difficulty in proving lack of consent) and Paul McGannon (due to inconsistencies in his statements). After a month, the DPP's verdict on Anthony Doyle was the same – no prosecution. McGannon made another statement to Gardaí in September, which prompted the DPP to ask Gardaí to obtain reports evaluating his psychiatric and psychological condition, but exactly a year later McGannon asked the Gardaí to close the file. In March 1999, the DPP said a prosecution in respect of McGannon's complaint would be unsafe, though nobody in the Gardaí thought it prudent to inform the man at the core of the allegations, Fr John Kinsella, an oversight *The Ferns Report* called 'unusual'. Immediately after Comiskey resigned, McGannon made fresh complaints again to the Gardaí, followed by Anthony Doyle, which necessitated Kinsella being arrested and questioned twice.

In between the latest bout of allegations by Doyle and McGannon, there was another twist in the tale of the life and career of Kinsella: Apostolic Administrator Eamonn Walsh had adopted a 'no smoke without fire' policy to any priest with a question mark over his head, and Kinsella withdrew from his parish in a blaze of publicity. Just a month before that Gardaí learned from the DPP that Kinsella did not have a case to answer, although he was the last to find out. Kinsella, declining to dissimulate like other priests, typed out a detailed statement on 15 April 2002, which was then forwarded to *The Wexford Echo* by his solicitor, in which he categorically denied that he was ever involved in any act of child sexual abuse. 'It is very difficult to explain and articulate one's feelings when one has been wrongly and falsely accused, particularly when the allegations are of a sexual nature involving children, as it is my view that once these allegations are in the public domain and no matter what is said or what conclusion is made on the issues in hand by any party, body or forum, it is inevitable that my reputation as an individual and a priest will be manifestly damaged.' Kinsella viewed the DPP's decision not to prosecute him as a declaration of innocence. In June 2003, Kinsella's canon lawyer wrote to Bishop Walsh and said it would be an injustice not to restore Kinsella 'to being in a position of good standing'. Unmoved, Walsh's response within weeks was to issue a precept against Kinsella prohibiting him from ministry pending the completion of all inquiries, which would have included any civil cases.

In May 2007, both Doyle brothers and McGannon initiated a High Court action for damages against Kinsella and Bishop Walsh, in his capacity as Bishop of Ferns and thus vicariously liable for the acts of his priest. The diocese had contended that the action was statute barred because of the delay in bringing the proceedings. Patrick Doyle repeated the substance of his statements to Gardaí at the hearing before Mr Justice John Quirke, namely that Kinsella had first abused him when they lay naked on a bed after trying on swimming trunks and he continued to be abused twice a week from the age of fourteen to nineteen. With the permission of his parents, Doyle, despite the allegations of abuse, went on holidays with Kinsella to Florida in 1978, west Cork in 1979 and France in 1981.

McGannon alleged that Kinsella had committed acts of gross indecency upon him at the parochial house in The Ballagh, including an alleged rape by Kinsella and another unnamed man. However, the action by the three plaintiffs, which was the first civil action taken against a diocese in Ireland that proceeded to a full trial, and a counterclaim by Kinsella, was struck out by Justice Quirke mid-hearing, with no order. In a subsequent interview on radio, Kinsella's accusers said they were happy with a financial settlement reached with the diocese, but it is also clear that Kinsella paid not a cent to McGannon or either of the Doyle brothers. 'If another party made such a payment, then it was done on foot of no finding of impropriety against me in the civil courts and no admission of impropriety on my part,' added an adamant Kinsella.

The priest, however, was not out of the woods. A year after the High Court action, Kinsella was defrocked by Pope Benedict, a decision which Kinsella called a serious miscarriage of justice perpetrated by the diocese. 'Despite overwhelming evidence against the accusers, the diocesan authority callously pursued the path of a kangaroo court to judge me in the harshest way possible. Due process, an indispensable requirement to any civilised society, was ruthlessly disregarded.'

Not for the first time, Kinsella was the last to know. He was stunned when the 'dictatorial style ruling' was conveyed to him by a family member who read it first in a newspaper. *The Ferns Report* found that where a credible allegation of sexual abuse was made and was capable of being believed (it was not necessary to establish that it was true or even probably true), it was correct for the diocese to ask a priest to step aside from his ministry and, if necessary, to require him to do so. Nevertheless, the report stated that it was 'fully conscious of the pain caused to any priest who is required to step aside as a result of an unproven allegation of a repugnant offence, but the paramountcy of protection of children requires that some priests and other persons in employment may be required to endure this apparent injustice in the interests of the common good'. The report was concerned by the delays in the canon law legal process that Kinsella had to endure, 'caused to an extent by the piecemeal nature of the reporting of allegations'.

6

Fr Donal Collins

'It is a scandal and an obstacle to the faith of the people that those who have abused children sexually should act in Persona Christi.*'*
Bishop Eamonn Walsh in a letter to defrocked priest Donal Collins

Was Donal Collins assuaging remorse on an April morning in 1998 when, after years of stalling and denial in which judicial review proceedings came before the High Court on fourteen occasions, he finally entered a plea of guilty at Wexford Circuit Court to charges of indecency and indecent assault on pupils at St Peter's College? If his contrition was sincere, why seek a judicial review in the High Court to have the charges quashed? Why decline to help investigating Gardaí with their inquiries? His plea, when it came, was unexpected but it did not discourage his victims from successfully imploring the trial judge to hear their testimony, much to the chagrin of their former teacher whose deviant pederasty, over three decades, was about to be exposed. 'Sorry', for Collins, was always the hardest word until it was too little, too late. He had assumed that a guilty plea would obviate the need for evidence from his victims, now all adults, who had waited years for this day of reckoning, and result in a shorter hearing. It was not to be.

The public image of Collins – principal of St Peter's College, man of science, man of God, living on £300 a month – was taken apart by the unsettling and astounding evidence of four former pupils who had the rare courage to step into the breach forsaken by the majority of Collins' victims, whom we are unlikely ever to know about. In the witness box, facing their tormentor, some reverted to their teenage selves, occasionally sobbing as a catalogue of abuse by their teacher was revisited. Unable to shirk this confrontation, Collins stared at his feet. His unmasking was a day of infamy for the Diocese of Ferns: one of its leading intellectual lights had abused his position as principal of Wexford's most celebrated boys' school to bully and to coerce pupils into depraved acts. The scrupulously nurtured persona, which had charmed bishop after bishop, and school committee after school committee, and which could switch from pedagogy to criminality with pernicious alacrity, was torn asunder in the alien environment of the courtroom. Until his fall from grace, the public perception of Collins had been unaffected by his regular appearances in court, often alongside Seán Fortune, for he was never identified. Both priests were together at Wexford Circuit Court in November 1997 – Collins in civilian garb – seeking judicial reviews of their cases and both were remanded on continuing bail.

They had much in common, but were poles apart. Collins was the private academic and Fortune the public sycophant. Fortune was cocky and almost indifferent in court, but Collins was attentive and, on the surface, even respectful. He did not care to draw unnecessary attention to himself.

Both became increasingly incapacitated for the ordeal of court. Collins used a cane to get about on the day of his hearing (he had suffered a fall) while Fortune, for his last appearance in court, was buttressed by a pair of crutches. The indignant and cumbersome gait of Collins and Fortune – was their physical incapacity a ruse to garner sympathy? – served only to highlight their separateness from the events going on around them, from the normal behaviour of ordinary people. The atrophied Collins, undoubtedly, bore the scars of ill health: the legacy of a heart bypass operation was evident in the pallid hue of his face, the skin under his eyes as saggy as sackcloth. At the Circuit Court, Collins pleaded guilty to a multitude of offences, all but one at St Peter's, where he had contributed the entirety of his existence to the advancement of the school – though the judge ruled that it could not be identified by reporters – between 1972 and 1984.

The long list of charges was read out first: a charge of gross indecency on a date unknown between 1 September 1976 and 31 December 1976; a charge of gross indecency on 8 January 1978 at Ballsbridge, Dublin, which coincided with the annual Young Scientist competition in the RDS; a charge of indecent assault on a date unknown between 1 September 1975 and 31 December 1976; gross indecency on a date unknown between 1 January 1979 and 30 June 1979; indecent assault on a date unknown in September 1972; indecent assault on a date unknown in December 1972; indecent assault on a date unknown in October 1982 and gross indecency on a date unknown between 1 January 1984 and June 1984. Michael Counihan, SC for the DPP, pointed to a pattern to the abuse of the four teenagers. The pupils were summoned to the priest's private rooms in an older building of the school 'for a chat'. Collins told them he wanted to see if everything was progressing with their physical development ('measuring up') and he asked them to remove part of their clothing so that he could examine them. Collins would touch their private parts, a transgression which led to masturbation. In two instances, requests were made by Collins to the boys to do the same to him. One of the charges arose during an overnight stay at a guest house in Ballsbridge, Dublin, while attending the Young Scientist competition.

There was no violence involved, added Counihan, but there was psychological persuasion and manipulation by Collins in all cases and, with one boy, the threat of expulsion from St Peter's. Collins used his position as a priest and teacher to take advantage of the students in his care. Through years of judicial hearings of his case, Collins, acting on legal advice, declined to help Gardaí with their inquiries and had decided to enter a plea of guilty only on the morning of the hearing. There had been a considerable amount of psychological trauma for the victims as a result, Counihan added. Pat Geoghegan, a Detective Garda stationed at Wexford, told the court that one of the victims had first contacted him about Collins in November 1994, and gave a written statement, conspicuous for its recollection of various sexual abuses perpetrated by the academic.

Geoghegan outlined in detail the nature of the abuse that took place in the school, including fondling, masturbation and oral sex. Asked how the first victim had progressed since the abuse, Geoghegan said there was little doubt that he had been deeply affected, and as such had sought medical and psychiatric help in the USA and Ireland. Collins' second victim had been severely traumatised: despite the anguish of what he had endured as a teenager, he had decided to come forward to make a statement in order to protect others. The third victim had felt the same, Geoghegan explained. In the case of the fourth victim, it was implied by Collins that he would be expelled from the college if he did not comply with his sexual demands. The latter was urged to sleep with Collins, was given alcohol and shown a pornographic film. Collins' victims, one by one, were called to the stand and told in poignant detail the disastrous effect the abuse had on their lives: feelings of guilt, of shame, of inadequacy, broken relationships and other personal difficulties were recalled. Two of the victims had married and two had remained single; some had sought therapy and counselling to cope with the abuse in school. One of the men, visibly upset during the evidence of another, withdrew from the courtroom. All of the victims were critical of Collins' attempt to delay legal proceedings.

The earliest abuse investigated by Gardaí was in September 1972, when Collins invited one of the boys, just fifteen, back to his private room, ostensibly to discuss a school project. After making the pupil comfortable, Collins raised the subject of the boy's physical maturity and proceeded to molest him. The boy abruptly left the room. When the boy returned to Collins' room in December to inform him that he wanted to be removed from the project, Collins sat him down, put an arm around him, opened the top button of the boy's trousers and tried, unsuccessfully, to masturbate him. The legacy of these incidents was twofold: he went from being a promising student at Inter Certificate level (he got seven honours) to just about passing his Leaving Certificate exams and, because he had lost faith in the educational system after his encounters with Collins, he missed out on university. His evidence against Collins was the first time a victim of clerical abuse in Ireland had his voice heard in court: observers and commentators of events in Ferns had hitherto been in the unsatisfactory position of relying on speculation.

How abuse by a priest affected a boy throughout his adult life had never been publicly disclosed prior to the trial of Donal Collins. Even factoring in the blinkers of ignorance, nobody could know how victims felt. The Collins trial changed that. Victim Impact Statements – first introduced in California in 1974 and in Ireland by the Criminal Justice Act 1993 – were intended to empower victims at the sentencing stage of the criminal process, and Collins' victims illustrated the effect of his assaults on them.

'I rebelled against education. The thought of trusting a teacher ever again was alien to me. I changed my friends, my habits, everything,' he said. He had told his wife just three years before. 'There is still not a waking day I don't think about this.'

A second victim – then in his mid-thirties – said that he would not consider himself an emotionally demonstrative person, 'but I can give some indication of the damage that man has caused'. He was a fourteen-year-old second year student when, on a date unknown between September and December in 1975, Collins summoned him to his office and asked him if he was 'developing properly'. He ordered him to strip, massaged the boy's penis and masturbated him. The abuse continued at different times and occasionally Collins, as officious and pedantic as a mid-ranking doctor at a concentration camp, measured the boy's penis and recorded the results in a notebook, a precursor to showing the terrified boy pornographic films and performing oral sex.

Long after he left St Peter's, the victim became suicidal, and it was only through therapy that he was able to establish a secure footing in his life. 'This man stole my youth and tainted my whole life. What should have been some of the best years of my life were instead a wretched experience. The sad, perverted, grotesque introduction to sexuality that he gave me when I was a teenage boy filled me with feelings of shame, self-hatred and the sense that there was something wrong with me.' He could not date a woman until he was past thirty. 'There was a great fear that people would discover my secret and this led me to being guarded, withdrawn and defensive with other people. By trusting him, I had been trapped in a nightmare and I lost my capacity to trust other people. I became cynical and suspicious.

He deprived me of the chance to mature in a normal way and left me with the feeling that sex was something sneaky, shoddy, shameful and unloving.' The abuse had a domino effect on the man's family. 'All of this has been a cause of immense pain and deep distress to my parents. They are devout and highly committed Catholics who would never have imagined they would be betrayed by a Catholic priest.' Collins' indifference to the welfare of the pupils in his care was amply demonstrated by his abuse of the third victim: once again he asked the young boy, some time between September and December 1976, to come to his room. The priest dilly-dallied in conversation before he asked him about sex, specifically wondering if he had onanistic habits. Collins encouraged the boy to masturbate while he watched, and then they both did it at the same time. Having groomed the pupil, he ensured that he was part of a school entourage that travelled to Dublin for the annual Young Scientist Exhibition at the RDS. The group stayed over at a guest house near Ballsbridge: Collins went to the boy's room later in the night and molested him.

Pupils were enrolled at St Peter's by parents for an education to prepare them for life but, thanks to encounters in the school with priests like Donal Collins, Seán Fortune and the priest named in *The Ferns Report* as 'Fr Delta', who abused boys at St Peter's in the mid-1960s, their future was shattered. Nobody at the school intervened. It took ten years for the third witness to 'get back to being a normal person'. He had been a brilliant student at St Peter's, gaining a place at University College Dublin to study medicine, but he could not concentrate on his studies, dropped out of college and became involved in petty crime. He was no stranger to the courts, having twice appeared before a judge. 'It is only in the past year that I sought help. For nineteen years I was in complete denial and did not talk to anybody, even my wife. It was like a black hole in my head. I now have a child myself and I think it is very important that man should never be let near children again.' Facing the imminent tidal wave of publicity that they voluntarily evoked demanded from Collins' victims a rare and uncommon courage.

The acuteness of the loss felt by these men well into their adult lives was also voiced by the fourth victim. He was shy at St Peter's even before the abuse began. In October 1982, a month of great excitement at the college (see Chapter 1), he was asked by Collins to collect other boys' copy books from the study hall and to bring them to his office. He did as he was told, leaving them outside the door, but as he started to walk away Collins saw him and invited him into his room. His physical growth was raised by Collins, whose sincerity, as usual, contained nothing less than a shoal of red herrings. He told the boy to remove his clothes: after he did so, Collins produced a ruler and measured his penis, a prelude to masturbation. The abuse continued for several years. Two years on Collins plied him with booze, showed him a film from his pornographic collection, molested him and performed oral sex. When the boy had a disagreement with him, Collins threatened him with expulsion from the school. The emotional tones of the man's testimony, fighting back tears as he recalled his miserable experience at St Peter's, reverberated in the sober atmosphere in the court. 'I have thought about this every day for seventeen years and it just won't go away. Words cannot describe what that man took away from me. I've been trying to shut it out for years. I never sought help and never told anybody.'

Ian Murphy, a member of St Peter's College advisory body, was called upon to enlighten the court with a professional profile of the defendant: Collins, the teacher, had shown commitment and dedication to his craft, was an innovator and an energetic worker who had contributed much in the field of education.

'He worked above and beyond the call of duty,' Murphy said. Remarkably, according to Murphy, Collins played a key role in helping St Peter's become one of the first diocesan schools to put in place a Board of Management, and Collins initiated a number of measures to improve its performance.

Dr Patrick Walsh – a specialist medical consultant and director of the Granada Institute and director of psychological services at St John of God's, which offered counselling and help to both perpetrators and victims of sexual abuse – gave evidence of the psychological treatment Collins had undergone since the offences were first investigated by Gardaí. Walsh said Collins was first referred to him in 1994 after complaints of sexual abuse had been made against him. He initially saw Collins on an individual basis, but later the defendant attended group therapy sessions. Collins' behaviour was explored over a considerable period of time and at great depth, and showed most of the features of similar abuse cases. While there had been an initial difficulty in fully acknowledging what he had done, Collins 'had cleared the barrier of denial' by the time of his trial and had accepted his actions. Collins – who never gave a statement to Gardaí and refused to sign any notes by the investigating detective – was a man who thought things through analytically and this made him 'emotionally unavailable' at times. There was, Walsh suggested, an intellectual appreciation by the priest of the impact of his abuse on the boys who suffered, but he needed the same appreciation at an emotional level, and was receiving counselling for same. If Collins was at liberty, there was little, if any, real risk of him reoffending: an aftercare programme would guard against a relapse of his behaviour. Walsh added that Collins' extended family too had been extremely shocked by news of the abuse and it had caused them enormous pain and great shame. Their feelings ranged from wanting to murder him to ambivalence as to how to deal with or support him.

Erwin Mill-Arden SC, read out an apology to the court from Collins, admitting he had behaved 'very badly' and had betrayed the trust placed in him. Collins, apparently, had no idea of the effect of his abuse on his victims while it was occurring. Mill-Arden contended that, by pleading guilty, Collins had saved his victims the 'discomfiting experience and embarrassment' of a trial: there was no need for the victims to be in attendance, he said: they had addressed the court only in so far as they chose to under legislation. It was unusual, added Mill-Arden, for a well-known teacher and a priest like Collins to find himself on trial for abuse. 'There was one corner of Collins that was evil and bad,' added Mill-Arden, but he asked that Collins' work as an educator be weighed in the scale of damage done to the victims. He detailed Collins' illnesses: two heart bypass operations and a fracture to his right hand. If the matters had come to light earlier, argued Mill-Arden, it may have resulted in a different situation and a different man would have been before the court. 'I ask you to look upon this as a very unusual case and ask that you measure the penalty so that justice is done and seen to be done, but take into consideration these matters,' said Mill-Arden. 'I would be hounded from this court with cries of "shame" if I asked for leniency, but is it not that any one of us can be evil – any one of us can fall?'

The evil before the court was from a different man, from another era almost, he added. Judge Olive Buttimer, summing up, took into account the lapse of time since the offences took place, the fact that there was no violence involved, the medical problems and age of Collins, combined with his guilty plea and the disclosure that he had sought psychiatric help. Against that, she had to balance the fact that Collins had been in a position of trust and the victims entrusted to his care. She imposed a four-year term of imprisonment for indecent assault and a two-year term for gross indecency on each count to run concurrently, with the sentence to be reviewed after twelve months.

After a year behind bars, Collins was released. His debt to society was risible. A year on, at Wexford Circuit Court, a familiar roll call of players attended. Mill–Arden stood before Judge Buttimer to praise Collins' unique contribution as a teacher of science and physics to Irish education. Nor had his skills been wasted during his term behind bars, as he used his time to teach his fellow inmates. Collins, added Mill–Arden, was unlikely to reoffend and, if released, he would attend the Granada Institute and reside in Wexford. The judge, who had 'an excellent report' from the governor of the prison, suspended the final three years of the sentence on condition that Collins ('in terrible ill health for a man of sixty-two', said Mill-Arden, though Collins lived for another twelve years) continued his treatment. Meanwhile, earlier in the same courtroom from which Collins walked a free man, charges brought against his former St Peter's colleague, Seán Fortune, were struck out, owing to his suicide a fortnight earlier. No despair ever wrung from Collins an explanation for his behaviour, and no statement expressing sympathy to the victims ever wrung from Brendan Comiskey an explanation for the diocese's failure to detect, when all the warning signs were there, this serial abuser in their midst. Comiskey, 'deeply saddened' by the events which culminated in Collins' conviction, said it was a cause of 'great pain, regret and sadness' that a priest in his diocese would betray the trust placed in him.

He added that the principle that the welfare of the child is of paramount importance was at the heart of *Child Sexual Abuse: Framework for a Church Response. Report of the Irish Catholic Bishops' Advisory Committee* though he did not add that it had not been granted a recognito by the Holy See, so the recommendations to protect children had no legal status in canon law. Nor could it be espoused voluntarily by any Irish bishop: not for the first or last time, Comiskey went on a solo run. (The feeling, admittedly, among the hierarchy was that Rome was less than helpful in developing a strategy to cope with the onslaught of abuse complaints in Ireland, a disenchantment which lasted until 2001, when the Vatican issued new instructions for the handling of allegations, *Sacramentorum Sanctitatis Tutela*. All allegations were to be fast-tracked to Rome.) 'The recommended policies and structures of this report have been operational in this diocese since that report was issued in 1996,' Comiskey added. This assertion, however, turned out to be less than true.

Collins was one of St Peter's worst-kept secrets. Although no documentation was produced to shed light on why he was removed and sent to the Diocese of Westminster in 1966 for two years, the then Dean of the seminary, Fr Patrick Curtis, informed Collins that there were suspicions that he had been acting improperly with the boarders in the Attic dormitory, a new dormitory. Curtis and Fr Tom Sherwood reported to Herlihy's secretary that Collins had been measuring about twenty pupils' penises in the dormitory. Herlihy would have been all at sea faced with Collins' priapic obsession. After his sojourn as a curate with the Emigrant Mission in Kentish Town, he was brought back to Wexford by a forgiving Herlihy, who insisted that he avail of accommodation in the priests' house rather than in rooms adjacent to the students' quarter. Collins' exile was considered sufficient penance by Herlihy who viewed sexual abuse as a moral failure rather than a criminal act: he gave Collins a teaching post in 1968, thus ensuring that he was back at St Peter's for the 150th anniversary celebrations of the college, and placed him in charge of swimming lessons in 1974. He augmented his standing in Wexford and throughout Ireland by his active role in the annual Young Scientist Exhibition

(1969–1981), serving as Chairman of the Irish Science Teachers' Association for two spells in the 1970s.

The abuse of pupils continued after his reinstatement. This is clear from testimony given to the Ferns Inquiry and from the statements given to Gardaí. One priest, who lived downstairs from Fr Collins for two periods, in the early 1970s and mid-1980s, was cognisant of the steady stream of pupils ('traffic on the stairs') going back and forth to Collins' rooms, even after lights out. 'There was not the slightest suspicion of anything untoward,' he recalled. This is hardly credible but it is symptomatic of the miasma of delusion that shrouded the college. Many boarders went to Collins' room who were not abused, to watch television, to use his phone, to listen to music. 'It was easy to go up and down to his room without being noticed, as the other two priests in his part of the building were often away,' Colm Tóibín recalled in *The London Review of Books*. 'His stereo system was amazing. I listened to *Tommy* there and *Jesus Christ Superstar*. He always had a box of sweets. I could ring home on his telephone. On Saturday nights after lights out, with his full connivance, we could break all the rules and sneak up to his room and watch *The Late Late Show*. We were often there until midnight.' According to *The Ferns Report*, the sweets, the music, the television, were more than likely tools used by Collins in a well thought out grooming process to increase the frequency of contact with pupils outside the classroom. Tóibín would become the first Wexford writer to fictionalise the impact on a family of a son who is charged with clerical sexual abuse, in *A Priest in the Family* from his collection of short stories *Mothers And Sons* in 2006; he revisited the subject of clerical abuse in 2010 in his book, *The Empty Family*, in the short story 'The Pearl Fishers' (a priest, Fr O'Neill, a science teacher in a Wexford secondary school, has been prosecuted for abuse):

According to the evidence given, it was only after our time at St Aidan's that he brought boys to his room and fucked them. But maybe there was other evidence that would have implicated him much earlier, and maybe it all happened in front of our noses. The idea of a priest wanting to get naked with one of the boys of St Aidan's and stuff his penis up the boy's bottom was so unimaginable that it might have happened while I was in the next room and I might have mistaken the grunts and yelps they made for a sound coming from the television.

On the day Donal Collins was jailed, a statement was released by a support group for abuse victims, Survivors: 'It is inconceivable that over the long period that this abuse occurred, that no doctor, no nurse, no social worker, no teacher, no Garda, no clergyman, no public representative or no other responsible member of society ever became aware of what was happening to young boys at this school.' When Comiskey went searching for a new principal of the college in 1988, he did not receive a single complaint against Collins, despite corresponding with every member of the teaching staff. Comiskey had met Collins before he became Bishop of Ferns: the bishop-elect met with a fifteen-strong planning committee in the diocese prior to his installation, and Collins was an esteemed member.

Unfortunately, the two priests who had first brought Collins' tendencies to the attention of Herlihy, Curtis and Sherwood, died within two years of each other in 1975 and 1977, the latter suddenly at the age of forty-seven, and with their deaths were interred the only verifiable accounts of what might have happened in 1966. (Until 1985, when the roles were separated, the president of St Peter's was also the principal: daily running of the school ceased to be part of the president's remit after 1989 when a Board of Management was set up.

The college's first lay principal was appointed in 1995.) The warning signs were as glaring as neon, not alone the 'traffic on the stairs' of young boarders to Collins' rooms, particularly after school hours, but the suspicion that something was askew with Collins. Two priests warned Comiskey about the wisdom of appointing Collins as principal, while a lay teacher told the Ferns Inquiry that his behaviour was 'well known in the school', but he never informed the bishop of this.

A year after Collins was appointed principal in 1988, and seven years before he appeared in court, Comiskey received the first recorded allegation of sexual abuse against Collins from a staff member in the seminary. This was backed up by a second allegation within a month by the parent of a former pupil, which coincided with lurid graffiti about Collins on the walls of the college.

Comiskey needed to act but he was blinded by the pig-headed fidelity to canon law that blighted the response mechanism of most Irish bishops at the time: he discussed the allegations with Collins who denied them aggressively, and Comiskey's response was to do nothing for the next two years. Collins, against whom not one but two allegations of abuse had been made, continued as principal. In June 1990, Comiskey was given the Freedom of the Borough by Wexford Corporation and among the forty or so priests invited to the conferring was Collins. A third complaint, in 1991, resulted in a bizarre sequence. In response to an anonymous letter from a new victim of Collins, Comiskey agreed to place a coded advertisement in a national newspaper indicating a willingness to communicate with him. This time Collins was prepared to concede to his bishop that he had engaged in indiscreet contact with young boys – while rejecting the specific nature of the charge against him – and was prepared to consider his position as principal.

In the hermetic world of his bishopric in 1991, Comiskey was floundering: he had already mismanaged allegations against James Grennan in 1988 and James Doyle in 1989 and now the principal of one of the elite secondary schools in his diocese had admitted in private to improper contact with pupils. Comiskey wisely subscribed to insurance cover after it emerged that dioceses could be held liable for clerical abuse. By 1990, most dioceses in Ireland had insurance policies with Church & General: Comiskey took out a policy a year earlier, which was on a claims-made basis. The limit of indemnity was £100,000 for any one claim and a maximum of £200,000 in a given year.

Comiskey was obligated by Church & General to remove a priest from his duties if there was a reasonable suspicion of unacceptable behaviour and to have the priest receive proper medical care before he could return to his duties. This may chiefly explain why Collins and other priests – Seán Fortune and James Doyle – were sent by the bishop for assessment. (The Stewardship Trust, established by the Irish bishops in 1996, was a £4.3 million settlement agreement with Church & General placed in trust to provide assistance to any bishop faced with an abuse-related claim: within a decade of its inception, the trust paid out €8.77 million in compensation to 143 victims of 36 priests. Though the Church had insured itself against abuse claims as far back as 1987, which made a mockery of its claim that it did not appreciate the full gravity of abuse until the Fr Brendan Smyth case in 1994, the laity were in the dark about the Church & General policy and the Stewardship Trust until 2003.)

Again the diocese shipped Collins abroad, to the University of South Florida, Tampa (he took an MA Degree), in the expectation that he would avail of counselling. Collins did not receive any because he was not interested. There are echoes of the poor inter-diocese communication between Ferns and Westminster and Ferns and Florida: neither was informed why Collins had been deposited there and so he revelled in parish duties in both. Comiskey insisted that Collins receive treatment for his aberrancy in the belief that he could be rehabilitated and receive a Certificate of Fitness to Minister on his return, though giving Collins a position of responsibility within the diocese was the last thing the bishop intended.

Comiskey, through his extensive network of contacts in America, had Collins admitted to The Institute of Living Treatment Center in Hartford, Connecticut – one of the first mental health centres in the country – run by Fr James Gill, at the time counselling three to six priests a year: the centre would decide if Collins could serve in a diocese again. Dr Peter M. Zeman contacted Comiskey and recommended that Collins could be appointed to a parish if he received continuous counselling. This prognosis was not what Comiskey had expected (he was prepared to give Collins a role in the diocese, but certainly not on his own in a parish). Later, the bishop discovered that his priest had withheld specific information from his assessors in Hartford, an allegation that Collins did not deny when they spoke in March 1994. Collins' reasoning was symptomatic of the obfuscation he could summon at will when backed into a corner. As befitting a liar and an abuser, Collins disclosed the truth when it was approached obliquely. Back in Ireland, Collins told Comiskey that he had expected any inaccuracies of his to be unearthed by the diligent assessment procedures at Hartford, but that he had been prudent to ensure that no revelation would be used against him in any future litigation. For Comiskey, this translated as denial on Collins' behalf. Comiskey asked Collins to attend the Granada Institute centre run by the St John of God Brothers in Shankill, outside Bray, when he had more or less accepted that many of the allegations made against him were true, although Collins denied ever abusing a pupil after he became principal. A year to the month after Comiskey learned that Collins had been economical with the truth at Hartford, Collins wrote to his bishop agreeing to his suggestion to retire on the grounds of ill health.

The exact number of St Peter's College boys abused by Collins will never be known: though four men initially gave statements to the Gardaí, evidence from these and more were given to the Ferns Inquiry, such as Sam, abused by Collins on six occasions in his office or in the dormitory in the late 1960s; such as Rory, abused four to six times a year for four years (he was paid compensation by the diocese in 2000); such as Edmund, a bright science pupil, whom Collins attempted to bugger and who received compensation after 2002; such as Richard, warned by a nurse of the college not to be alone with Collins who serially abused him; such as George, who said he was molested by Collins when he was principal of St Peter's. All the names of victims in the inquiry, whether published elsewhere or not, were redacted and all evidence proffered was unsworn. The Inquiry protected the anonymity of priests against whom unproven allegations were made by ascribing pseudonyms taken from letters of the Greek alphabet, such as 'Fr Delta', a contemporary of Collins at the college, against whom many instances of abuse were alleged: compensation was paid by 'Delta' to one victim which, when it came to the attention of the diocese in 2002, caused his retirement. His modus operandi was similar to Collins: he fondled a boy's penis to ensure that 'everything down there was in working order'.

Even when Comiskey finally believed that Collins had been abusing pupils for a long time, he took no corrective course of action, such as informing the South Eastern Health Board or tipping off the Gardaí. The bishop was culpable of a paralysis of management that made no sense then and makes no sense now. His conviction that his responsibility for Collins, or for that matter any Ferns priest, extended only to their presence in the diocese – Comiskey approved of convicted child molester James Doyle's tenure as a chaplain to a secondary school in England – wavered once he fully realised the potential for litigation against the diocese. 'It was unacceptable that Bishop Comiskey should have made erroneous statements to the Gardaí and the media in view of the information available to him in relation to Fr Collins,' concluded *The Ferns Report*.

When Collins was jailed on 25 March 1998, Comiskey released a prepared statement to the media. 'The principle that the welfare of the child is of paramount importance lies at the heart of *Child Sexual Abuse: Framework for a Church Response. Report of the Irish Catholic Bishops' Advisory Committee*. The recommended policies and structures of this report have been operational in this diocese since that report was issued in 1996,' he said. If only. A year earlier Comiskey met with Gardaí and in his statement he maintained that Collins had denied any wrongdoing, but this was untrue. Wasn't Collins' concession in 1993 that he had 'interfered with pupils' the wake-up call that made Comiskey realise that he could never again appoint him to a parish? After 1996, Ferns was still exporting its troubled priests to parishes outside the diocese. After a year in jail, Collins was again at liberty with, while Comiskey remained Bishop of Ferns, certain privileges: Comiskey encouraged him to work on the diocesan directory, to be available for temporary duty at St Senan's Parish, Enniscorthy and, though it was tempting fate to allow a convicted abuser of boys access to the Internet, whether on Collins' solicitation or not, allowed him to help establish the diocese's first website (Collins' email address was then advertised in the Ferns Diocesan Bulletin, *The Forum*.)

The Secular Priests of the Diocese of Ferns, an impressive

400-plus-page tome by the late Canon John V. Gahan, was published in 2000 to coincide with 1,400 years of Catholicism in Wexford: among the hundreds of priests and bishops profiled is an entry for Collins, without a single mention of his crimes. It is preceded by a recent monochromatic portrait, taken by a studio photographer, and a sharp and spruce Collins looks a million miles away from the man led in handcuffs to a prison van just two years earlier. A new portrait of James Doyle also appears on another page with, among others, Micheal Ledwith. Comiskey's resignation marked the beginning of the end of the last chapter in Collins' life and career, which had begun so promisingly in September 1963, when he joined the staff of St Peter's College as a teacher of science. The diocese was without a bishop (Bishop James Staunton had died on 27 June 1963, and Bishop Donal Herlihy was not enthroned until 13 December 1964). Because of the leniency shown by both Herlihy and Comiskey and the ever-widening gulf between their intentions and the common good, Collins had leverage to split his personality into that of an excellent teacher and a depraved abuser: a man of science who had no qualms about invoking God by reason of the sacerdotal consecration he received on his ordination, he was anything but Christian to the pupils he assaulted. This made him a self-deluded criminal, an achievement not listed among his many qualifications in *The Secular Priests of the Diocese of Ferns*. The Gardaí received more complaints about Collins in 2002 and 2003, but the DPP directed that no further action should be taken because of potential difficulties with judicial review proceedings.

With the arrival of the Apostolic Administrator, Bishop Eamonn Walsh, the Church made it a priority to impose order in Ferns. By the summer of 2002, Walsh was inclined, acting on the assistance of an advisory panel, not to entrust Collins with the *cura animarum* (the care of souls). Despite entreaties from

Collins, a canonical precept was imposed on him withdrawing permission to celebrate Mass. He was denied access to the Ferns' website and, though he said he would not, was told to consider voluntary laicisation. Without skipping a beat the Vatican, on the application of Bishop Walsh, dismissed Collins as a priest in December 2004.

'It is a scandal and an obstacle to the faith of the people that those who have abused children sexually should act in *Persona Christi*,' Walsh wrote to Collins. On an April morning in 2010, Collins was found dead at his home in Curracloe. Five days later, about thirty people – including some former pupils – turned up to mourn his passing at a low-key funeral Mass at Rowe Street Church in Wexford town. Secrecy, which the diocese excelled at, surrounded this final farewell to Collins: although half a dozen priests were in attendance, there was no homily. The coffin, with a single wreath of white lilies, was brought to Crosstown cemetery across the harbour and Collins was laid to rest with his parents.

7

Fr James Grennan

'Fr Grennan continued in his role as Chairman of the Board of Management of the national school in Monageer after this controversy occurred without any investigation by the Department of Education or the Diocese as to his suitability for such a role.'
The Ferns Report

*T*he Ferns Report concluded that Bishop Comiskey's handling of the allegations against Fr James Grennan by a group of young school girls resulted in unnecessary suffering for them, their families and the people of Monageer, today a byword for a haunting chronicle of shattered lives. Bishop Eamonn Walsh visited Monageer in 2002, fourteen years after the allegations first surfaced, and his acknowledgement of the pain of the pupils, an admission by the Church that Grennan was culpable, was received angrily by the dead priest's extended family, who believed him to be innocent, for no charges were ever brought by Gardaí. His family was not alone in their belief that Grennan was above suspicion. He is still highly regarded in the parish of Poulpeasty, where he ministered for a decade: when a history of the churches of the curacy was published ten years after the events in Monageer, it included a portrait of Grennan – resembling a young John Wayne – in a clerical roll of honour.

The events of Monageer are a tangled web of intrigue, facts, speculation and mystery but, despite inquiries and investigations, it is unlikely that the truth of what occurred, not just the alleged abuse, but the apparent connivance of the Gardaí and the diocese, will emerge. Monageer, like Banquo's ghost, haunted the old Health Board in the wake of Grennan's death, an unfortunate aspect in this story's trajectory because the Health Board did more than the Church or the Gardaí to have any impropriety thoroughly investigated. Accusations have been levelled at the Board that it did not do enough. The facts, however, indicate that the Board acted in a professional manner, motivated by the welfare of the children, but was not helped by an intransigent diocese and by senior ranking Gardaí in Wexford.

The Board, on 27 April 1988, sent a social worker, Kathleen Kinsella, to Monageer to talk to ten local National School girls a day after they had informed their principal, Pat Higgins, that Grennan, the parish priest, had behaved inappropriately with them in the church. Higgins had first contacted Childline (an ISPCC freephone) and was advised to refer what he had been told to the Health Board; he spoke with the Director of Community Care, Dr Patrick Judge, who discussed it with Senior Social Worker Joe Smith. (Ironically, had it not been for a complaint about the fifth and sixth class childrens' behaviour by Grennan to Higgins, what was to unfold might never have materialised: Higgins identified the pupils who had been apparently rude to the priest, and gave them homework. As he prepared to close the school, the principal was surprised that seven of the girls were still in the classroom. They asked if they could talk to him, and thus the allegations surfaced. Higgins, who had been principal for fourteen years, advised the girls to tell their parents and he promised that he would seek advice on how best to help them. He was as good as his word.) Higgins was in an invidious position: Grennan was also Chairman of the school's Board of Management and by informing the Health Board, Higgins was reporting his employer's apparent misconduct to an outside authority.

The girls were interviewed collectively by Kathleen Kinsella on different days in a room in the school set aside by Higgins. Disturbed by what she was hearing, Kinsella met with and then recommended to the parents of each child that they be brought to the Community Child Centre at Waterford Regional Hospital for further assessment. The parents of three of the children would decline. Kinsella reported her findings to Dr Nora Liddy, Senior Area Medical Officer in Community Care in County Wexford, and suggested that the children should be interviewed by Dr Geraldine Nolan. A qualified paediatrician, Nolan had studied methods of assessing child abuse claims in the UK and Canada, and her responsibility as Validation Unit Medical Officer with the Board was to determine if the allegations were credible. This was uncharted territory for the Board: Monageer was its first recorded allegation of clerical sexual abuse and it happened while the Board was in the process of establishing its validation unit. After talking to the girls individually, Nolan then discussed the allegations, which were consistent in the detail, with Dr Judge, on 4 May. In her report, she said:

> Confession was a major time that the girls felt unhappy about. This was held on the altar with Fr Grennan sitting on a chair and the children kneeling on red cushions at his feet … The rest of the class remained in their seats and were told to keep their eyes closed because they were in a house of God and to show respect. They were told that if their eyes

were closed their prayers would go straight to God. If they opened their eyes while the confession was occurring, Fr Grennan would chastise them.

The girls told Nolan that Grennan during confession would grasp their hands and pull them towards the zip in his trousers, described as half-down. 'He would pull the child close and rub his face and mouth around their jaw while asking them questions about their families. He was also described as putting his hands under their skirts and fondling their legs to mid-thigh level only,' said the report. When the priest was alone with the girls in the vestry as they were preparing for lessons or readings, Grennan touched them under their upper garments while ostensibly examining a pattern.

Nolan's report continued: 'Some of the children also described either in his own house or in his sitting room or at their house or a relative's house, sitting on his knee and being fondled, but in the presence of other people it was made to look like tickling.' The report concluded: 'Fr Grennan's actions in many cases have been going on for two or three years and in some cases over the past school year. They are not allegations that would be made up for any malicious intent, and the girls described much the same activity in different ways.' Some of the girls, a decade and a half later, came forward to relive their experiences to the Ferns Inquiry: one said she had been abused by Grennan as a little girl, but long before the episode in Monageer. This must have been after Grennan was appointed to Poulpeasty in 1971. What she is alleged to have endured as a child is by no means representative of the character in village life in County Wexford in the 1970s, but her experience is indicative of the unhealthy proximity between priest and parents in an isolated rural setting. In *The Ferns Report* the girl is known as Deborah: she maintained that

Grennan attempted to have intercourse with her when she was seven and he was allowed by her parents to share her bed. Her mother confirmed to the Inquiry that Grennan had indeed slept in her daughter's bed when he stayed overnight in the family home: she was 'quite certain' that if anything untoward had happened, her daughter would have told her. But her daughter did not. Deborah took her own life in 2002.

Grennan, a seminarian at St Peter's College where he was ordained in 1958, had served in four parishes before Monageer, including Larne in Antrim and Oulart in Wexford. He was a sociable priest, later fond of a drink, and he established friendly ties with families and members of other denominations wherever he was based. In all, ten children complained. Of these, three, including two sisters, were not allowed by their parents to be further assessed by the Health Board in Waterford. Grennan was a weekly visitor to one of the families for dinner and there were several photographs of him and Brendan Comiskey on the sitting-room wall. The third girl was told by her mother to apologise to Grennan. Dr Nolan's brief was not to establish the veracity or otherwise of the claims but to decide if they were credible. The last line of her report concluded: 'I feel that Fr Grennan has been abusing these children especially over the last year, both sexually, emotionally and physically, and I feel it is important that these children be protected from further abuse.'

Judge familiarised himself with the contents of his colleague's report and became alarmed by the possibility that the priest might have been abusing the girls throughout the school term, not alone in the church but in the parochial house. He endeavoured to bring what he knew to the attention of the Bishop of Ferns, and within a hectic 24-hour period, Judge met with the diocesan Vicar General, Grennan, Higgins and the Gardaí. Nobody can accuse the Health Board doctor of having proceeded laboriously. He went to Wexford Garda station but was directed back to Enniscorthy by Inspector Michael Gilhooley, as Monageer was in its Garda District. Judge met Superintendent Vincent Smith and handed him the validation report, the first time the Health Board actively involved the Gardaí.

Because Bishop Comiskey was away, Judge attended an arranged meeting with the Vicar General, Monsignor Richard Breen, at the bishop's house at Summerhill, Wexford. The outcome of the meeting was disappointing for Judge because his recommendation that Grennan be removed to protect the girls from potential harm – though he had no authority to do so – could not be expedited by Breen. Back in Monageer, Judge had a meeting with Higgins and he warned him that in future the pupils should not be left alone with Grennan. This was a new development, which the principal would have to handle delicately because of Grennan's role in the school: Higgins felt that it was not up to him to deny a child the opportunity to serve at a mid-morning Mass like a wedding or a funeral with Grennan, so he drew up a permission slip for parents to sign which exonerated the school from any liability while the child was out of school.

A day after his encounter with the doctor, Monsignor Breen met Grennan in the village and informed him of Judge's allegations. Grennan, shocked by Breen's disclosure, sought out Judge who, while listening to Grennan's denials during the acrimonious encounter ('a concoction of lies'), remained adamant that he believed what the pupils had said to be true. Judge had acted unflinchingly and with urgency, motivated by the approaching confirmation a month away. At this juncture, what was brewing in Monageer was known to the Church, the Health Board, the Gardaí, parents and the school's principal. Meetings took place but, in the absence of the bishop, nothing could be determined. A Garda, who was a Knight of Columbanus, urged another Knight, Wexford businessman John Jackman, to help persuade Comiskey on his return to have Grennan removed temporarily from the parish in a calculated effort to defuse the tension in Monageer. Jackman – who had already reported an allegation of abuse against Fr Seán Fortune to Comiskey's predecessor Donal Herlihy – communicated this message by phone to Breen, who was powerless to act while the bishop was out of the diocese.

Comiskey returned to Wexford from his holiday in the last week of May and busied himself with the allegations against Grennan as chronicled by Breen. By then, several weeks had passed since ten young girls claimed that their parish priest had used their hands to rub his privates. Comiskey was in a quandary: he was misled (not by Breen's memorandum, which did not mention it) into thinking that Grennan was alleged to have exposed himself at the altar. Comiskey believed this too incredible to be true. Why did Comiskey think Grennan was accused of exposure? Could it have arisen in his conversation with Grennan, after he had been briefed by Breen, or was he misinformed by a Garda? How Comiskey responded was partially influenced by his mistaken belief that the young girls had accused his priest of exposing himself in the church. They had done nothing of the sort: they had said he had put his hands under their skirts and had fondled their legs.

It is debatable if Comiskey, in the weeks approaching the confirmation, was ever fully cognisant of the true extent of the allegations. He dismissed any accusation of exposure as incredible and mischievous, and adopted Grennan's position that for him not to appear at the forthcoming confirmation would be tantamount to an admission of guilt. For a man of his education and intelligence, it is baffling that the bishop chose not to speak to Higgins, or the Health Board officials (Comiskey felt Judge was anticlerical) and though Comiskey had been tipped off that the Board's validation report had been given to the Gardaí, he chose not to examine its contents, only doing so two months later. With tensions running high, Chief Superintendent James Doyle in Wexford town spoke first with the Administrator in Wexford, Fr Jack McCabe, and eventually with Comiskey in person at the Bishop's house. We do not know what transpired between the Chief Superintendent and the Bishop of Ferns because no official record was kept, but a note by Comiskey says the Gardaí were keeping a watch on Grennan's house for fear of him committing suicide. Doyle would claim to the Ferns Inquiry that he had no doubt that he made Comiskey aware of the nature of the allegations. What we can assume is that Comiskey, during the countdown to the confirmation, felt confident that no criminal charges would ever be brought against his priest, and he had every intention of allowing Grennan to participate in the confirmation.

Comiskey's short-sightedness in believing Grennan's denials and his neglect of contrary opinion prepared the ground for the next chapter in this saga, which would prove as divisive in the village as the events that led to the Fethard Boycott in the 1950s. On the day of the confirmation, 20 June 1988, Comiskey appeared in Monageer Church in the company of the very man the Health Board thought was a threat to children, James Grennan. As both made their way up the centre aisle, at least two families stood up and abruptly left the church. Comiskey remembers the day as 'very joyful and happy' but, on the other side of the fence, it was viewed rather differently. Higgins recalls that some families were visibly upset by the appearance of Grennan alongside Comiskey, an image perceptively interpreted by Colm Tóibín: 'So Bishop Comiskey and Fr Grennan stood proudly on the altar waiting for ten little liars to come up and be confirmed.' Surprised by reports in the local media about the walkout,

Comiskey arranged a meeting of the Council of Priests, and arising out of this collegiality of spirit, a letter of support was sent to Grennan who remained on at Monageer as Chairman of the school's Board of Management until his death. Unbelievably, the Council of Priests was kept in the dark about the details of the Health Board's report.

A year after the allegations, Grennan attended Dr Peter Fahy, a psychiatrist in the Blackrock Clinic, for treatment for strain. Dr Fahy wrote to Comiskey: 'I cannot see how he could have done what he is accused of doing in full view of the congregation.' Comiskey, by now familiar with the validation report, still did not attach any credence to what the girls claimed had occurred. Why? Comiskey was not an innocent abroad when it came to confronting abusive priests: as auxiliary bishop of Dublin, he was fully aware of complaints and rumours of sexual abuse by clergy, and he would have been, like Bishop Dermot O'Mahony and Bishop James Kavanagh, party to reassigning priests to different parishes, subject to Archbishop Dermot Ryan's approval. Comiskey came to Ferns well versed on how problem priests were managed in Dublin: abusive clergy – like Thomas Naughton, who served in four parishes in a ten-year spell – were verbally reprimanded, but left in ministry.

Comiskey's bungling of the Grennan allegations from the moment the issue landed on his lap might be understood if seen as the diocese exercising a responsibility to one of its priests, but it is next to impossible to understand or explain why the subsequent investigation by the Gardaí came to nothing. There was, between the apparatchiki of the diocese and the Gardaí in Wexford, a frustrating incompetence in their attitude to protecting vulnerable children from the very real threat of future interference or abuse. Peripheral to the shadow boxing of the Catholic Church and the Health Board in the early rounds of the Monageer story were the Gardaí, but not for long.

After being directed to the old Enniscorthy Garda station from Wexford, Dr Judge presented a copy of Nolan's validation report to Superintendent Smith, whose office would have been a fifteen-minute drive from Monageer. Because Monageer National School falls into the Ferns Garda subdivision, three Gardaí from the station in Ferns – Donal Behan, Sergeant James Reynolds and James Sheridan – were asked by Smith to investigate the complaints in the Health Board report. While the Gardaí were busy interviewing the ten girls in the village, though only seven gave statements, James Doyle, who was the divisional officer at the Wexford station, made it his business to contact Comiskey to mark his card that some parents were threatening to boycott the confirmation if Grennan attended. Chief Superintendent Doyle, who had been based in Wexford from 1974 and was in the force for almost forty years, was considered an old-school Garda, something he elaborated on when he received a Mayoral Reception from Wexford Corporation to mark his retirement in 1991. For Doyle, day-to-day policing was guided by the least possible disturbance to the majority of law-abiding people.

Doyle had been sticking his nose into the Garda investigation in Monageer. He asked Detective Tony Fagan, operating from Enniscorthy, to pay a visit to Grennan to persuade him to leave the parish until after the confirmation (though Doyle would later deny this). Would he not have been more proactive instructing the investigating Gardaí already on the ground to interview Grennan, rather than asking a detective to encourage him to abscond? Before the investigation by the rank-and-file Gardaí had concluded, Superintendent Smith asked Sergeant Reynolds to forward the girls' statements to his office in Enniscorthy. The statements had not been typed and did not have a cover report but Smith wanted them because, he said, the Chief Superintendent was anxious to see the notes (though Doyle would also deny this). And there the official Garda investigation into the first reported allegations of clerical abuse in the diocese entered a cul-de-sac. The statements vanished into thin air after Reynolds gave the notes to Donal Behan and directed him to hand them over to Smith. Behan would tell the Ferns Inquiry a decade on that, after the notes were sent to the law officers for a direction, he later raised the issue with Smith, who confirmed that he had discussed the matter with Doyle. 'I concluded at the time that it was just quashed and that was it,' Behan told the Ferns Inquiry. The State did not get an opportunity to explore the culpability of Grennan, and Grennan did not get an opportunity to clear his name. To this day, the Monageer file is lost. So what happened?

The report of the Garda investigation into Monageer, carried out by two detectives from Cork in 1996 at the request of Deputy Commissioner Pat Byrne, concluded that Smith was contradictory in his response. 'On one hand he says he read the statements and was satisfied that the kids had been molested by Fr. Grennan. On the other hand he says he was not satisfied there was sufficient corroboration to justify further action. The latter is a statement of convenience.' The 1996 inquiry was critical of the failure of the Gardaí to interview Grennan: 'Whether Fr. Grennan would have admitted committing the acts alleged by the girls or not, a complete investigation file should have been sent to the law officers for their consideration as to a prosecution or not.' The 1996 inquiry's verdict on Doyle was damning. 'It is indeed difficult to understand or justify the inaction or the lack of interest of ex-Chief Superintendent Doyle in not following up or enquiring into the final outcome of this serious matter of which he was well aware occurred in his area of command.' The 1996 inquiry accepted that the girls and their parents had been let down, that the system had failed them badly. The report says: 'The blame must lay fairly and squarely on the Garda Siochana . . . It is also very convenient for Bishop Comiskey to say that in the absence of a positive result from the Gardaí, that he assumed there was no case against Fr. Grennan. The warning signs were there for him at the same time.' The 1996 inquiry found that the Garda investigation was poorly directed and 'showed a marked reluctance to confront this highly esteemed senior clergyman. This is no doubt attributable to a culture prevailing at that time which unfortunately failed to accept any wrong doings by the clergy, especially in sexually related matters.'

We are asked to believe that Doyle, who intervened when it was unwarranted, chose, after the statements compiled by the Ferns Gardaí were lodged with Smith, to ignore the case and was forevermore incurious about the minutiae of the statements from the girls. Doyle was a family man with children of his own. The gulf between the intentions and actions of all the Gardaí involved in Monageer, one sergeant, one Chief Superintendent, one Superintendent, two Gardaí and one detective, made the 1996 Garda inquiry consider bringing criminal proceedings. 'The matter of criminal proceedings was considered for perverting the course of justice,' said the 1996 inquiry. 'In view of the age now of the officers concerned and in view of ex-Superintendent Smith's explanation, no charges are recommended.'

There appeared to be, even though only eight years had elapsed, a violent opposition of values within the Gardaí between 1988 and 1996. It is probable, based on the decisions he would make later, that Smith's undertstanding of what he read in the validation report was ambiguous. He visited some of the girls' parents, though not the majority of them, and convinced himself that they were anxious not to have an investigation carried out. Garda Behan began the investigation initially on his own and was then joined by Sergeant Reynolds and Garda Sheridan.

Seven of the girls gave statements. The perception of the Gardaí was that if the nature of the abuse was questionable, at least the girls' statements tallied with the validation report. Behan agreed with the tone of the Health Board report, conceding that some of the allegations in the statements to the Gardaí were of a more serious nature. Reynolds believed that the incident in the church needed to be investigated fully as the substance of the statements was of a criminal nature. Smith chose the path of least resistance. His understanding of the situation in Monageer would have been clearer if he had requested his Gardaí to interview Grennan. This did not happen.

The file he had on his desk had no chance of being considered for prosecution without an interview with the alleged assailant. That the file ended up on his desk in the manner it did – no covering form and not typed by the investigating Gardaí – was an anomaly (original documentation is maintained by the investigation team) that only Smith could explain. He told Reynolds that the Chief Superintendent in Wexford wished to see the file. Doyle would deny this, saying that his only input was to call on Comiskey to advise him on the prevailing mood in the village. The state of affairs among the Gardaí entered the realm of the absurd with Doyle's failure to remember asking Detective Tony Fagan to meet Grennan in an advisory capacity to discuss the possibility of him taking a sabbatical from parish work. Fagan arrived in Monageer unaware that his colleagues in Ferns were investigating allegations of abuse against the man he himself was seeking to remove from the village. The 1996 Garda inquiry, after quizzing Doyle, noted: 'what is clear is that the Chief Superintendent had a far greater input into the whole affair than he is prepared to admit.'

Doyle's failure to recall seeing the Garda file or ordering Fagan to talk to Grennan 'is puzzling'. (Pat Higgins became seriously disillusioned that the probe, launched with such urgency by the Health Board, dragged on and slowly fizzled out: both principal and school chaplain, who remained respected by many parents, continued to work together in a professional manner, though in a difficult and strained way.) Somebody succeeded with the alchemical dis-appearance of the Monageer file. Rather than ring-fence the children in Monageer, the Gardaí ring-fenced the Church. Though completed in 1996, the inquiry into the activities of Gardaí in Monageer remained an internal document, until excerpts were published by a newspaper in 2003. The 1996 inquiry, which the author has seen in full, blamed the inadequacy of the Garda investigation. 'There was a reluctance to pursue the investigation in the manner demanded.'

The Ferns Report would endorse the findings of the 1996 Garda inquiry, regretting 'that the report was not forwarded to the DPP as recommended by the investigating officers'. Smith told the Ferns Inquiry that he had contacted the Garda station in Ferns and requested the statements from the girls to be brought to his office. After reading the statements, he was personally satisfied that they had been molested by Grennan. Smith then went to Wexford and had a meeting with Doyle, who read the investigation file. Without commenting, Doyle handed the file back to Smith, who retained the statements. Smith told the Ferns Inquiry that he was not satisfied that there was sufficient corroboration to justify further action. 'He stated that he has no idea what became of the statements but is adamant that he did not dispose of them,' said *The Ferns Report*. 'Superintendent Smith conceded that he was reluctant to prosecute Fr Grennan and thought it would only damage the complainants further. He accepted that he should have sent the file to the DPP with a recommendation not to prosecute rather than take the decision himself. He had no doubt that the complainant girls were interfered with and he knew the matter was serious but thought a prosecution was not the answer.'

Chief Superintendent Doyle also cooperated with the Ferns Inquiry though his version of events clash significantly with his Superintendent's. He claimed that he never saw any file, that he never read any statements by the girls and that he never saw the Health Board report. His meeting with Comiskey, claimed Doyle, was his sole involvement in the case.

Gary O'Halloran was a barrister in his mid-thirties and a Fine Gael member of the South Eastern Health Board when he read an article by Veronica Guerin early in October 1995 in the *Sunday Independent*, one of a series of reports concerning the travails of Comiskey, who was in America at the time receiving treatment for alcoholism. Guerin, who had written extensively about Comiskey, alleged that the Health Board was aware of an earlier allegation of abuse somewhere in the diocese against a priest but had not informed the Gardaí. The Health Board vehemently denied this. Roused, O'Halloran raised the allegation at that month's meeting of the Health Board in Kilkenny eleven days later: a memorandum by the Board records that CEO John Cooney had no knowledge of the case to which O'Halloran, bereft of specifics, had referred. With Comiskey away, the media, local and national, was engaged in a daily feeding frenzy, with the diocese as dinner. At the November meeting of the Board, O'Halloran tabled a motion calling for an independent enquiry into its handling of the case referred to by him a month earlier.

There was confusion with the actuality of the motion: O'Halloran's case, derived from Guerin's story, is said to have taken place in 1987. Could he have meant 1988? Probably, because a day prior to the meeting, O'Halloran contacted Martin Hynes, Programme Manager Community Care, to clarify the exact case he was referring to. 'In fact on the first occasion on which he rang me he, himself, was not aware of Monageer or the name of the alleged abuser. It was on his third telephone call that he was able to clarify these for me. Up to that point the executive did not know what case Councillor O'Halloran was seeking information on,' said Hynes. Minutes before the Board meeting, which was held in public, Fine Gael TD Phil Hogan approached Cooney over unease about O'Halloran's motion: O'Halloran would consider withdrawing it if he could have a private questions-and-answers session with the CEO on a confidential basis. Cooney agreed, and O'Halloran asked the following questions:

- Did the Director of Community Care report the matter to the Gardaí under the 1987 guidelines?
- What information have we about Garda involvement in the investigation?
- What information have we about Garda conclusions about the investigation?
- What information have we about the reasons for the Garda conclusions?
- Was a report on the matter sent to the Bishop?
- Was any response received from the Bishop?
- Was a copy of the response in our possession?
- Was a copy of it on file?
- Was it ever on file?
- Did the Bishop accept responsibility for the incident?
- Did the initial complaint come from a reputable member of the community?
- Was the Department of Health involved?
- Was there any contact between the Director of Community Care or anybody else in the Health Board with the Chief Medical Officer of the Department of Health?

- Did anyone from the Department of Health meet with the Director of Community Care or was there any other contact between the Director of Community Care and the Department of Health?
- Were there any assurances given by the Health Board to the victims?
- Did the Health Board promise counselling services to the victims and did they deliver on these promises?
- Was any assurance given that the abuser would be removed?
- Was any assurance given by the Health Board that the alleged abuser would not be present at the confirmation ceremonies that were shortly afterwards?

Satisfied with the replies he received, O'Halloran indicated a willingness to withdraw the motion if Cooney issued a statement to the meeting repeating much of the information he had just given him. In anticipation of the motion going ahead, the Board had already prepared a draft statement. It felt that its staff had 'responded well' to the allegations in 1988. Cooney read his statement ('The Medical Officers' conclusion from the professional assessment was that the allegations were not malicious, that abuse had taken place and that the children needed protection from further abuse') and O'Halloran backed off his motion. Speaking briefly on behalf of a guardian of one of Grennan's victims, O'Halloran said children were hurt by how Monageer was dealt with by both the Church and the Health Board. The last comment flew in the face of Cooney's conclusion that in 1988 'the Board's local staff dealt quickly and competently with the case and not only did they comply with the then recently introduced Department of Health guidelines on child abuse, but they went beyond these'.

The ceasefire between O'Halloran and the Board did

not rest easily. O'Halloran submitted a handwritten letter to Cooney seeking information 'which was received from any other person, agency, or Health Board, concerning allegations of abuse'. He was, in turn, asked by Martin Hynes for precise details of what case he had in mind, but O'Halloran did not reply. O'Halloran next sent correspondence to both the Department of Health and the Department of Justice raising his concern about the investigation in Monageer. He made a number of allegations, but the one with the loudest reverberation was the following paragraph: 'Sadly, persons in superior positions in the Church of the Diocese of Ferns, in the Health Board and in the Garda Síochana either breached the trust placed upon them, or turned a blind eye when such a breach occurred.'

Arising from O'Halloran's correspondence with the departments, the aforementioned 1996 investigation into the conduct of Gardaí in Monageer in 1988 was initiated at the request of Deputy Garda Commissioner Pat Byrne: in February Gardaí met with Cooney, who gave them access to all the Board's files. The Gardaí, after extensive interviews of the main players, would conclude in the 39-page report that the Health Board had fully complied with its obligations. The Board was next contacted by the Department of Health on 2 April, and Hynes, in less than a fortnight, submitted a full report to Frances Spillane, Principal Officer of the Department's Child Care Policy Unit. In reply to O'Halloran's allegation that 'persons in superior positions' in the Board had turned a blind eye to allegations, Hynes framed the following response:

> It is not clear if we have the full text of Councillor O'Halloran's letter or if what we have is an extract from some wider document. A number of questions arise in regard to his statement as follows: What 'old boys network' does he refer to? What 'conspiracy of

silence' does he refer to? What 'constitutional rights of violated children' does he refer to? When he says 'It is difficult to accept that the correspondent duties in this case were discharged in a proper fashion,' to whom and to what does he refer? i.e.: Parents and families; teachers/school authorities; Health Board staff/management; Gardaí; individual clergy/the Church. If Health Board 'Staff in front line discharged their duty in an exemplary fashion' what is the problem in this case? What people 'in superior position – in the Health Board – breached the trust placed upon them and turned a blind eye when such a breach occurred?' Councillor O'Halloran's aspersions are widely cast. Clarification of the allegations he is making would be helpful in view of the fact that staff of the Board

- validated that abuse had occurred
- informed families and gave advice
- informed Gardaí
- advised the teacher
- advised ecclesiastical authorities and made the validation report available
- confronted the abuser

The question arises as to what breach of trust was involved? In what way could we be said to have 'turned a blind eye'? The executive of the Board has answered queries and briefed Board members in committee. Councillor O'Halloran stated: 'All that was ever sought in this case was an honest explanation of what happened and a simple apology.' Does he imply that explanation/answers given by us were not honest? From whom and for what is an apology sought? The alleged abuser always denied the allegations. While he might have been able to explain or elaborate on some aspects of the case, he is not now alive and able to do so. Even if he were alive it is unlikely that he would now admit the abuse and offer an explanation. By whom, from whom and for whom is 'a simple apology' sought? Neither the Board or its staff perpetrated the abuse. Indeed Councillor O'Halloran has commended front line staff for their action. When Councillor O'Halloran says 'now that the abuse of the victims has been maintained and continued' what does he mean? As outlined earlier, experienced staff of the Board have had recent contact with all of those whose abuse is validated. It is the predominant wish of the victims that the constant publicity now being given to the case would cease and that they could get on with their lives. There is the possibility that the extensive publicity recently given to the case could in itself become more abusive of the victims than the abuse which was perpetrated in the Church in Monageer in 1988. Parents who are disbelieved, or felt isolated by their community in 1988 might well feel somewhat pleased that their story is now being believed. This does not mean that their daughters can feel pleased with the attention the case has recently being receiving.

(South Eastern Health Board)

(Pat Higgins, as a Department of Education employee in 1988, reported the allegations against Grennan to his regional representative of the INTO but received no reply: he reported it to his local school inspector but received no communication from the Department of Education.) O'Halloran never relaxed from pursuing what was fast becoming the most lauded conspiracy theory in the national media. He repeated his assertions at the June meeting of the Board in 1996 that it had not done enough to help the victims of Monageer: at the July meeting, Cooney asked O'Halloran to put his allegations in writing and, according to a report in *The Wexford Echo*, Chairman Tom Ambrose and O'Halloran became engaged 'in a verbal exchange of considerable intensity'. O'Halloran's charge that the victims had been left isolated by the Board 'could not be further strengthened by a written submission'. The Board was satisfied that the Monageer case was handled skilfully and confidentially, which did not imply secrecy and, as regards O'Halloran, if he experienced difficulties in getting information from the Board, it was due to his 'imprecise questions based on erroneous press reports'. Added Hynes: 'One may well ask if this and other child abuse cases in County Wexford are central or peripheral to many of the stories which have been written and which have had the Bishop as their focus.'

After the release of *The Ferns Report* a decade later, O'Halloran was interviewed on RTÉ Radio 1 and (1) claimed that Pat Higgins and Patrick Judge were not supported by the 'upper echelons' in the Health Board and (2) he accused the 'hierarchy in the Health Board and the Garda authority and the Church authority and indeed the political establishment, of working together to deny justice to the victims of abuse'. His allegation is at variance with the 1996 Garda inquiry: 'There is no evidence of any collusion between Church and State organisations to stifle, obstruct or abandon this investigation.' *The Ferns Report* believed that a 'proper formal communication in the form of a liaison' between the Health Board and the Gardaí in 1988, followed by monitoring of the situation, would have concluded in a more effective investigation.

8

Monsignor Micheal Ledwith

Ich bin der Geist der stets verneint (I am the spirit who always denies)
Mephistopheles in Goethe's *Faust*

'The new dean, Dr Ledwith, was young and friendly and open and very good looking. He was also reputed to be very smart. One of my friends knew him from home so he often stopped to talk to us. He was a new breed of priest; he had studied in Europe and America. Many of the new teaching priests spent their summer in parishes in America so they were full of new ideas. Everything was open for discussion, or almost everything. I went to a brilliant lecture by Dr Ledwith on ideas of paradox within Church doctrine. It was whispered that he would one day be a great prince of the Church,' recalled alumnus Colm Tóibín about Ledwith's time at St Peter's College in *The London Review of Books*.

Monsignor Micheal Ledwith, handsome and erudite, was certainly a new breed of priest who would have a distinguished career at Maynooth but, alone among those investigated by the Ferns Inquiry, he abandoned the Catholic Church in his prime, settled in America, joined a New Age religion and penned books with the colourful if esoteric titles of *The Great Questions in the Hamburger Universe* and *The Orb Project*. He was multidisciplinary (editor, lecturer, actor, writer) and multifaceted (from President of Maynooth College to senior lecturer with the Ramtha School of Ancient Wisdom), reinventing himself with ease by changing his Christian name to Miceal, a metamorphosis that helped put considerable distance between himself and the Catholic Church, which laicised him.

L'affaire Ledwith began in 1983 with a nod and a wink, but a layman ploughing through the industrious report of Denis McCullough SC might conclude that it was much ado about nothing, a cat-fight among the righteous. The 'Inquiry into Certain Matters Relating to Maynooth College' is also a fascinating insight into the machinations of Church personnel at the highest level. The inquiry, which commenced in 2002, was prompted by the sudden revisiting in newspaper columns of events twenty years earlier when seminarians at Maynooth apparently accused Ledwith, who was then a college Vice-President, of sexually harassing students.

Five seminarians, who had come to Maynooth together and were late vocations, took exception to Ledwith's worldly lifestyle – he liked flying and good living – but when their disapproval was repeated and reached the ears of some bishops, Ledwith stood accused of sexual impropriety with students.

The seminarians, three of whom would later leave the priesthood, were in the senior division at Maynooth, and first sought advice about their concerns from Brendan Comiskey, then auxiliary bishop of Dublin, who gave them a shortlist of bishops to contact. They confided in the Dean, Fr Gerry

McGinnity, with whom they were close and to whom they reiterated their unease about Ledwith's behaviour. The implication was that Ledwith was guilty of favouritism. McGinnity, appointed Senior Dean at Maynooth in 1978, transmitted their grievances to Cardinal Tomás Ó Fiaich, his Ordinary, whom Comiskey had earlier recommended to the seminarians, and Bishop Kevin McNamara.

The seminarians, who met as a group and formulated a strategy, believed that Ledwith was treating McGinnity, their mentor, unfairly. The timing of the decision to meet with several bishops coincided with speculation that Ledwith was tipped to succeed Donal Herlihy, who had died, as Bishop of Ferns, an unpalatable choice for them. Individually, or in pairs, they met with Bishop Cahal Daly in the infirmary at Maynooth; with Bishop Edward Daly while he was giving a retreat at Maynooth; with Bishop Colm O'Reilly in the sacristy at Maynooth; with Bishop Eamon Casey outside the grounds of Maynooth; and with Archbishop Joseph Cassidy in the Long Corridor at Maynooth. A more concerted effort to besmirch the reputation of a teacher could not have been orchestrated. They were motivated by disapproval at the nature of the training they were receiving, by concern at the alleged animosity shown by Ledwith to McGinnity, by opposition to Ledwith's materialism (he owned a boat and, gosh, flew an aeroplane!) and by hostility to Ledwith associating exclusively with good-looking students whom he took from Maynooth for weekend breaks. When they came back, apparently, they said they would not go again. It was rumoured that Ledwith owned a horse, that he took his favourite students shopping and, unforgivably, that he wore a hairpiece.

Ledwith was being pilloried behind his back by a bunch of ultra-conservative seminarians who found time outside of their studies to lobby as many bishops as possible for one outcome, to sully a college Vice-President, and to prevent him from acceding to the top job in Ferns. They could have succeeded. The Papal Nuncio had requested the views of bishops regarding various candidates, Ledwith being one, for a shortlist for the Ferns vacancy, and Bishop Edward Daly had submitted a document that made reference to the complaints by students.

McCullough's inquiry, established by the Trustees of Maynooth to discover if allegations of sexual harassment were made in the 1980s, brilliantly teased out the subterranean tensions in the college at a time when the two leading protagonists in this drama, Ledwith and McGinnity, had it all to play for and all to lose. However, the decision by the students to solicit the bishops to their point of view, and which had the endorsement of McGinnity, backfired. McGinnity was highly thought of but so was Ledwith. Did McGinnity shoot himself in the foot? He had involved himself in a process to weaken Ledwith's standing with the bishops but would only undermine his own. Writing to Archbishop Thomas Morris in August 1983, Bishop McNamara said he was completely satisfied that there was no truth in the rumours about Ledwith. 'Having lived in Maynooth in the early 1970s, I am not surprised at what somebody like the man in question may have had to put up with – given the stand he took in regard to the dismissal of two staff members some years ago, his general support for the Trustees, his theological orthodoxy, not to mention his many distinguished talents and successes he has achieved. It is really a great shame that the story circulated about him should have gained such currency among the students.'

There were other issues that needled McGinnity and with which the cohort of plotters was fully acquainted: one Sunday at Mass in the main chapel at Maynooth, Ledwith, sitting beside McGinnity, spotted a handsome student. He asked McGinnity if he knew the student's name, and he later went on to become friendly with him. McGinnity told the seminarians about the incident from which they arrived at the conclusion that Ledwith was a stalking homosexual.

The key to understanding the background to the contretemps between two senior churchmen at Maynooth is one paragraph on p. 33 in the McCullough report: 'There were two theological camps in Maynooth at that time. Some of the students and some of the staff members identified more with the pre-Vatican Council group. Monsignor Ledwith would have been seen as a totally outrageous liberal ... Bishop Daly felt that McGinnity would have been in the more conservative group.' The dispute pitted Ledwith's liberalism against McGinnity's conservatism. After the seminarians had expended their energy orchestrating a campaign against Ledwith, a meeting of the administrative council of the college (Ledwith and McGinnity were members) was held early in May 1984: President of Maynooth Michael Olden had received complaints from bishops about the seminarians' allegations. On the advice of McGinnity, the council decided not to make good a consideration to revoke the students called to the diaconate, although in practice a serious reason was required to justify postponement of ordination. It just wasn't cricket for students to lambaste a senior and respected member of college staff to bishops, especially when the accusers were short on specifics.

Bishop Cassidy, for one, was taken aback by their approach. And Professor of Sacred Scripture Fr Sean Quinlan had already told Cahal Daly that there had been a breakdown of discipline in Maynooth, with a pervasive sense of demoralisation and drift. Sensing that the tide had abruptly turned and fearing a denial of ordination, the rebellious seminarians turned to McGinnity for advice.

'An atmosphere of tension obtained. They did not

know where to turn. They voiced their worries to me,' said McGinnity, who passed on their concerns to Bishop Kevin McNamara, Archbishop Dermot Ryan and Cardinal Tomás Ó Fiaich. Toward the end of the month, Bishop Eamon Casey, while attending a meeting of the College Visitors (eight bishops acting on behalf of the Trustees of St Patrick's College) took time out to square up to McGinnity near St Mary's Library, and broached the subject of the Ledwith rumours, which had assumed a grotesque caricature of their own. Casey, believing that the Dean had accused the Vice-President of sexual impropriety to Ó Fiaich, demanded of McGinnity that he produce a student who had been molested by Ledwith. McGinnity could not, because he had never made an allegation of that nature. He told Casey that the students had reservations about 'apparent propensities rather than specific offences'. Casey accused McGinnity, who denied it, of having spoken to the Nuncio, Dr Gaetano Alibrandi. McGinnity had been contacted by the Nuncio in a confidential document. 'I was taken aback that such a confidential and private consultation was known of by anyone other than the Nuncio who sent it. But doubtless he must have had his own reasons for revealing it,' he said.

What began as 'apparent propensities' by a senior staff member at Maynooth was developing into a crime without a crime scene, discussed by the Dean of the college, the Nuncio, eight bishops and five seminarians, but nobody was quite certain what Ledwith was alleged to have done wrong. Pedagogy giving rise to preferential treatment exists at every level in education, from primary school to university. After the confrontation with McGinnity, Casey attended the College Visitors meeting and gave an account of the exchange. A discussion of sorts followed and the Visitors agreed that a senior dean who had made a serious allegation against the Vice-President of the college but could not substantiate it could no longer continue in office. That McGinnity was a conduit between students and bishops was an irrelevancy.

The bishops decided McGinnity had to go, and the extent of their investigation into the allegations by the students began with Casey's robust chat with McGinnity and ended with McGinnity's removal. McGinnity had no chance of survival against the politics of collegiality. As Ó Fiaich was McGinnity's bishop, he took it upon himself to ask McGinnity to take a sabbatical year, after a decade in office, from Maynooth. Toward the end of the sabbatical, McGinnity was visited in Rome by Ó Fiaich who asked him about his future plans. When McGinnity repeated his desire to go back to Maynooth, Ó Fiaich ruled it out because of the Ledwith affair and proceeded to exact his dean's resignation. Ó Fiaich added that if the resignation was voluntary, there would be no blot on McGinnity's record. A letter was read out at a future meeting of the Trustees from McGinnity seeking leave for one year. McGinnity, not unnaturally, felt he was being scapegoated and victimised by the bishops because he had placed the welfare of seminarians first. The cloak-and-dagger nature of his disappearance from Maynooth conveyed an impression, for McGinnity, that he was guilty of a serious transgression. The minutes of a meeting of the Trustees in June 1984 recorded that sabbatical leave was granted to McGinnity, and the minutes of a meeting of the Trustees in June 1985 recorded his resignation.

'From the point of view of where I had come from, it was both humiliating and degrading,' McGinnity wrote in *The Irish Times* in 2002. 'Any direct efforts by myself to obtain some rationalistion of my position were met with polite indifference. Eventually, it was the sympathetic and generous intervention of academic colleagues which led to a slightly more equitable arrangement of duties.' McGinnity accused

Maynooth of a dirty-tricks campaign to sacrifice his reputation in an attempt to conceal the truth. McGinnity was livid that confidential information ('*sub pontificio secreto*' – beneath the pontifical secret) that he had sent to the Nuncio – expressing his concerns about Ledwith – had been passed on to other bishops. He declined to engage with McCullough's inquiry because he had no confidence in its terms of reference.

Was McGinnity aware that Cahal Daly had already deemed as 'far fetched' a story he had told him in June 1983? That while travelling in a car driven by a colleague, the driver placed his hand upon McGinnity's leg? Daly had referred the incident to the McCullough inquiry as 'a bizarre story' in which McGinnity implied that his colleague was a homosexual. The net effect of the meeting in Rome with Ó Fiaich in 1985 is that McGinnity was exiled, and the man at the centre of the 'apparent propensities' storm, Micheal Ledwith, the precocious Wexford boy who was educated at St Peter's College, became President of Maynooth at the age of forty-three, and was on the road to becoming the great prince of the Church as posited by an adolescent Colm Tóibín.

The Ferns Report found that the bishops' punitive decision to make McGinnity take a break after his meeting with Casey could only deter bona fide complaints to Church authorities. 'By any standard, the concerns as communicated by the seminarians and expressed by Fr McGinnity were inadequately investigated,' said *The Ferns Report*. 'They also appear to have been wholly misunderstood.' The riddle of who said what, and what exactly was Ledwith accused of, could not be fully resolved by the Ferns Inquiry: the original group of seminarians maintained that they raised the issue of Ledwith and homosexuality, but the bishops are insistent that they did not.

A year before the Ferns Inquiry was established, both

the bishops and the former seminarians were engaged in an unsavoury war of words in the press that would have had Archbishop John McQuaid turning in his grave. It was claimed, in a report in *The Irish Times* on 25 May 2002, that the seminarians contacted nine bishops about sexual harassment of students by Ledwith between 1983 and 1984. Six days later, in a letter to the newspaper signed by Cardinal Daly and three bishops, it was denied that any such allegation was ever made to them. Denis McCullough, in his 2005 inquiry, found discrepancies in the accounts of both sides, though what they had in common was an acceptance, contrary to the report in *The Irish Times*, that no complaints were ever made of sexual harassment by Ledwith.

The confrontation between Casey and McGinnity, which was robust and potentially combustible, arose from a belief by Casey that McGinnity had reported a sexual impropriety by Ledwith to Ó Fiaich and McNamara. If this is true, it would explain why the bishops sought the removal of McGinnity, but it would not explain why no further attempt was made by the Church to find out the truth. 'Despite the allegation having been made and notwithstanding Bishop Comiskey's very strongly held view when he first met me that he could not have proposed Monsignor Ledwith as President of the College if he had been aware of any allegation of homosexuality against him, Monsignor Ledwith was made President of Maynooth College in 1985 without, so far as I am aware, there having been any intervening investigation,' remarked McCullough.

The correspondence between McCullough and Comiskey reveals a bishop whose memory is a sieve: it began with a letter in November 2002 to Comiskey in what was a traumatic year for him – he had resigned from Ferns just months earlier. Comiskey remembered meeting four seminarians on behalf of Archbishop of Dublin Dermot Ryan, at the residence of the

Pro Cathedral, to hear their grievances about Ledwith, which were (a) extravagant lifestyle, (b) his luxury house on Lough Neagh, (c) ownership of a seaplane, (d) ownership of a horse and (e) favouritism. 'Nothing of a sexual nature was either stated or hinted at in this regard,' added Comiskey. 'There was no mention of sexual harassment of seminarians at Maynooth College in the early 1980s or at any other time. The first I heard of such was in the newspapers in recent times when Fr McGinnity or some seminarians commented on this. This was literally news to me. It would appear that revisionism is operating in a big way.' Comiskey added that he was willing to sign sworn testimony to counter Eamon Casey's suggestion that Comiskey knew about the allegations before they became public.

In his reply, McCullough explained his difficulty with Comiskey's efforts to reposition his memory: Casey told McCullough that he had talked with Comiskey about McGinnity's allegations to Ó Fiaich and McNamara. Comiskey then did a U-turn about when he first learned of the sexual allegations against Ledwith, saying: 'Some time after I had met the seminarians, possibly in or about April 1984, I found out that Fr McGinnity had made allegations to Tomás Ó Fiaich and Kevin McNamara of inappropriate sexual behaviour towards a student by Monsignor Ledwith. I was at that time Bishop Elect of Ferns. I contacted Bishop Eamon Casey and asked him to meet me for breakfast. I don't know where I heard the information from ... I may have heard about it from Monsignor Ledwith himself. I do remember him speaking to me about Fr McGinnity who was annoying him at the time.' After the breakfast, Casey literally drove the length and the breadth of the country, from Armagh to Kerry, where he discussed the McGinnity allegations with Ó Fiaich and McNamara.

Comiskey maintained at a meeting with McCullough that he could not have endorsed Ledwith for the presidency of Maynooth College a year later if he had known of the allegations against him. But, by his own admission and on mature reflection, he accepted that he knew Ledwith's lifestyle had antagonised the reputable McGinnity and a small coterie of seminarians, but he still made a glowing speech nominating the Wexford man for President. His explanation was: 'I did not think of the allegations which Fr McGinnity had made. It may be that I believed and accepted that Fr McGinnity's allegations were unfounded and he could not be relied upon.' As Comiskey was not on the Board of Visitors, it was not his duty to investigate any allegations against Ledwith. McCullough accepted that Comiskey 'either forgot about the allegation entirely when proposing Monsignor Ledwith for President in March 1985 or, alternatively, felt that the allegation was wholly unfounded and that Fr McGinnity was not a reliable source. Bishop Comiskey does not seem very clear which of these explanations is most likely.'

The verbal fisticuffs with McGinnity were not the beginning of the end of Ledwith's fruitful relationship with Maynooth and his bishops nor the end of the beginning of his new life as President of Maynooth, and he set about fulfilling the potential others had long ago seen in him: from 1980, he served three terms on the thirty-member International Theological Commission, of which he was chairman, charged with advising the Holy See on theological matters. He helped clear a huge debt on Maynooth College and set about with his trademark energy and zest in renovating many buildings. But nine years into his presidency of Maynooth his world started to crumble. This time his adversary was not an academic heavyweight but a teenager, and the hierarchy could not afford to treat their favourite son with kid gloves.

The events which brought about Ledwith's defrocking shortly before *The Ferns Report* was published are what concern us here. In December 1994, Comiskey found himself embroiled in another investigation of Ledwith, and this time he demonstrated a straightforward response to the situation he was presented with. He contacted both the Health Board and the Gardaí. Raymond, as he is named in *The Ferns Report*, alleged that he was first abused by Ledwith in the early 1980s when he was thirteen. This continued for two years, although the age of the boy was subsequently disputed by Ledwith, who maintained that he only met the youth's family after he turned fifteen.

The young man first informed the Bishop of Limerick, Jeremiah Newman, a former President of Maynooth College, about the allegations but he was dismissed abruptly: Newman's secretary, Fr Liam O'Sullivan, pointed Raymond in the direction of Cardinal Daly, who was more forthcoming. He arranged a face-to-face meeting with Raymond to discuss the allegations. Daly was obligated to pass on what had been alleged to Comiskey because Ledwith came under the aegis of the Diocese of Ferns and he took the precaution of informing the Congregation for Catholic Education in Rome. Comiskey met Raymond who claimed that he had been abused by Ledwith at the family home and at Ledwith's house.

Comiskey asked Fr Walter Forde, an experienced diocesan spokesperson, to examine the allegations to see if they were credible. Even though Ledwith was not interviewed, Forde acquainted himself with Raymond's claims and concluded that there was enough substance in the allegations to support their veracity. Comiskey was not in a position to identify Raymond to either the Gardaí or the Health Board because he had been given his name in confidence, but he disclosed the name of the Raymond's solicitor to the Gardaí, who conducted limited surveillance on a holiday home used by Ledwith, and he informed Dr Antoinette Rogers, Acting Director of

St Peter's College Seminary in Wexford. Within a random five-year period selected by the Ferns Inquiry, ten priests who were in St Peter's came to the inquiry's attention as being the subject of child sexual abuse allegations.

Three of the priests who feature in this St Peter's College class reunion of the pupils of 1968 in the late 1980s were defrocked by the Vatican. They are (in second row from front): Fr Donal Collins (first left), Fr James Doyle (third left) and Fr John Kinsella (far right).

Fr Seán Fortune, ordained at St Peter's College in 1979, was never media shy until his arrest in 1995 following a ten-month investigation by Gardaí into allegations that he was a serial abuser of teenagers.

Seán Fortune arrives at Wexford Circuit Court in March 1999 to face twenty-nine sex abuse charges.

Fr James Doyle, ordained at St Peter's College in 1974, had the ignominy of becoming the first priest in Ireland to appear before a court on a charge of indecent assault against a boy in 1990.

Doyle, seen here in 2006, declined to apply for laicisation. Pope John Paul II dismissed Doyle from the priesthood in 2004.

Canon Martin Clancy, ordained at St Peter's College in 1942, was a serial abuser of young girls who came to his house in Ballindaggin for music lessons. When the diocese received a credible complaint against him from one of his victims, he was moved to a neighbouring parish without any supervision or monitoring.

Fr John Kinsella, ordained at St Peter's College in 1974, was the first priest in the diocese to publicly refute allegations that he had abused three teenagers. Despite his protestations of innocence, in which no charges were ever brought against him by the DPP, he was defrocked in 2008.

Fr Donal Collins, seen here two years before his death in 2010, was appointed Principal of St Peter's College in 1988. Ten years later at Wexford Circuit Court, he pleaded guilty to charges of indecent assault and gross indecency on former pupils.

Fr James Grennan, ordained at St Peter's in 1958, was alleged to have molested girls preparing for their confirmation. A Garda investigation of the affair in the village of Monageer went nowhere because a file of statements and interviews went missing from a Garda station and has never been found.

Monsignor Micheal Ledwith was appointed to the seminary staff at St Peter's College in 1969. He became President of Maynooth College in 1985, a position he held for nine years, until his departure following an allegation that he sexually abused a teenager, which he denied. He was laicised shortly before the publication of *The Ferns Report* in 2005.

Bishop Donal Herlihy was enthroned as Bishop of Ferns in 1964. He was severely criticised by *The Ferns Report*, which said it was 'inexcusable' for him to have ordained Seán Fortune.

Brendan Comiskey (left) succeeded Donal Herlihy as Bishop of Ferns in 1984. He resigned his post over his mismanagement of priests like Fr Seán Fortune in 2002. He is pictured with his successor, Fr Denis Brennan, ordained at St Peter's College in 1970 and installed as Bishop of Ferns in 2006.

Bishop Eamonn Walsh was appointed Apostolic Administrator to the Diocese of Ferns in the wake of Brendan Comiskey's resignation in 2002. *The Ferns Report* found that his apology to the parishioners of Monageer and Ballindaggin was unequivocal and may have gone some way towards healing the hurt in the parishes.

Community Care with the Health Board, of Ledwith's identity. Lawyers contacted Ledwith on Raymond's behalf and said it was their intention to issue legal proceedings, although a civil trial did not happen as Ledwith agreed to pay Raymond compensation with no admission of liability. There was a confidentiality clause (referred to in *The Ferns Report*) inserted into whatever agreement was reached by the two parties: the Ferns Inquiry never got to discuss the allegation of abuse, which Ledwith has always denied, with Raymond.

Comiskey and Ledwith, erstwhile friends and allies in the earlier fracas with McGinnity, were quickly at loggerheads. Comiskey, acting on recommendations by Forde, asked Ledwith to book himself into a treatment centre run by Fr Stephen Rossetti in Maryland in the United States, though why Ledwith would contemplate this, considering his plea of innocence, is baffling. Rossetti had conducted scores of workshops for priests using psychospiritual health and was an advocate for blending modern psychology and orthodox Catholic theology. The healing programme at the St Luke Institute in Maryland – a mental health treatment centre for priests – which Ledwith was encouraged to attend, has become a paradigm for the co-existence between psychology/ psychiatry and Catholic theology.

Rossetti's career brought him to the forefront in the prevention of clerical child sexual abuse and with raising awareness among priests of the devastating effects of abuse on victims. He was a member of the 1993 Think Tank for the United States Conference of Catholic Bishops (USCCB) on child abuse, which warned that the hierarchy's authority and credibility was being eroded because of a perceived inability to deal effectively with the growing crisis. Rossetti published a study documenting the spiritual damage to victims of sexual abuse by priests, and he instituted the policy of recommending that abusive priests never be returned to any unsupervised work with minors. Rossetti favoured putting offenders through psychological treatment and only then returning them to limited, supervised work (either inside or outside the Church) that did not include involvement with young people. Ledwith did not follow through on a pledge to attend Rossetti's institute, even after certain safeguards were put in place for his welfare, as he was concerned by the use of chemical and electrical tests. Comiskey, unimpressed by Ledwith's stalling, asked Monsignor Richard Breen to conduct an inquiry into Raymond's allegations under Canon 1717, which sets out guidelines for a bishop to investigate a delict (or violation of the law) and to decide on any penalty. It was a lame-duck exercise from the beginning: seven weeks passed before Ledwith was informed of the exact nature of the allegations against him.

In the interim, Comiskey was receiving further canonical advice as Ledwith, on sabbatical from Maynooth, was based in Seattle. He informed the bishop there of Ledwith's whereabouts but he was uncertain how to proceed against a priest in another jurisdiction. The conundrum was easily solved when he was informed that the alleged abuse was over ten years old and had exceeded the Vatican's statute of limitations. Yet again an inquiry into Ledwith by the Church fizzled into thin air. (In 2010, in response to global disquiet at the Vatican's response to clerical abuse, the Pope doubled the statute of limitations to twenty years.) Ledwith's brush with canon law was far from over: the Trustees of Maynooth were waiting in the long grass.

At a meeting of three health boards, the South Eastern, the Mid Western (the region where Raymond was living) and the Eastern Health Board (in whose region Maynooth College is based), in November 1995, it was agreed to inform the Department of Education of the allegations against Ledwith, while the Eastern Health Board would recommend to Monsignor Matthew O'Donnell and Dr William J. Smyth at Maynooth that Ledwith should not have contact with young people. Ledwith knew of the unease within Maynooth about his tenure there, and Trustees went as far as to inform Ledwith's solicitors that a resolution for his dismissal from Maynooth was on the cards at a forthcoming meeting.

The confidentiality agreement in the settlement between Ledwith and Raymond was a huge obstacle to Maynooth, and Ledwith saw no reason to waive the clause because he felt the process instigated by Maynooth was deeply flawed, and he may have had a point. The chairman to the body of Trustees that had looked into Raymond's allegations was Cardinal Daly, who had first reported the allegations to the Diocese of Ferns, so it is understandable why Ledwith would have made an issue of Daly's conflict of interest and his impartiality. Arising out of a hearing by a subcommittee of the Trustees (which Ledwith, accompanied by a legal team of four, attended at the Archbishop of Dublin's residence in Drumcondra), Ledwith followed through on a decision he had considered months before the allegations became known, to retire from the college as a professor and President in 1996.

His career had come full circle, or almost. Comiskey's successor, Eamonn Walsh, attempted to contact Ledwith to inform him that he had been subject to a precept (recommended by the Ferns Advisory Panel) with various conditions attached: he could not celebrate Mass and he could have no unsupervised contact with minors. But Ledwith, who had changed his name to Miceal and was making a living lecturing for the Ramtha School of Ancient Wisdom in America, was not easily available to the clutches of the diocese, and he did not respond to Walsh's request to seek voluntary laicisation. While the draft report of the Ferns Inquiry, with which Ledwith cooperated, was in circulation, the Congregation for the Doctrine of the Faith in

Rome dismissed its golden boy from the clerical state.

Assessing his career with the Ramtha School is another day's work, but suffice it to conclude from the cursory preamble of his lectures or his appearance in the film *What The Bleep Do We Know?,* the insights and the intelligent quotient that you might expect from a once leading Catholic theologian are much in evidence, but perhaps insufficient to counterbalance the vapidity that oozes from the so-called quantum mysticism.

In August 2010, ten men undertook the first tentative steps toward a life in the priesthood at Maynooth, teeming with 350 lay students and 66 seminarians. As they embarked on a life of devotion to God, they were the beneficiaries of a welcome greeting from Monsignor Hugh Connolly, President of Maynooth, who, paraphrasing the late Pope John Paul II, said that the Church needs them 'to mould their personality in such a way that it becomes a bridge and not an obstacle for others in their meeting with Jesus Christ'.

9

Canon Law

'The religious response, the criteria, the manner of viewing things which a bishop uses are different from that of a politician. Different in the sense of belonging to a different realm of things.'
Bishop Comiskey, 1986

The love affair between Bishop Comiskey and his people in the Diocese of Ferns, which began with mutual admiration, slowly became a parody and inevitably concluded with a separation. A sober reappraisal of his career cannot ignore his contradictions, touched upon time after time by *The Ferns Report*. Comiskey made himself available to the Ferns Inquiry on two occasions in 2004, the first time for eight days of oral hearing, which must have been exhausting but to which he responded with 'efficiency and courtesy', and the inquiry publicly acknowledged his high level of cooperation.

Once you delve into the minutiae of *The Ferns Report*, a different Comiskey emerges: cautious, hesitant, officious, dismissive, indecisive and negligent. After Donal Collins was sent to Florida for treatment, Comiskey did not try to limit his ministry as a priest; though fully aware of the threat James Doyle posed to young men, Comiskey had no reservations about him working in a secondary school; his public and private support of James Grennan made liars out of the young girls who claimed they had been molested; though concerned about his relationships with young men as early as 1985, Comiskey allowed Seán Fortune the freedom of the diocese until his arrest; he did not ask Martin Clancy to cease pastoral work after the priest admitted to inappropriate behaviour with a young girl. Comiskey was never going to yield an inch to the increasingly inquisitive media. He was a big monarch in a small diocese, encysted in a system that preferred to keep its dirty linen private.

If you could erase his mishandling of clerical abuse cases in Ferns from his epsicopacy, a very different man emerges: articulate, highly intelligent, sociable, witty, aesthetic, ambitious, alert and curious. He set his stall by personal achievement: in 1969, he was elected Provincial of the Anglo-Irish Province of the Congregation of the Sacred Hearts; in 1974, appointed Secretary General of the Conference of Major Religious Superiors; in 1979, appointed Auxiliary Bishop of Dublin, becoming the first Catholic Bishop to graduate from Trinity College, Dublin with a MSc (Org. Behaviour); in 1984, appointed Bishop of Ferns; in 1990, made a Freeman of Wexford and in 1999, made Chaplain to the International Council of the Alliance of Catholic Knights. His earlier academic achievements – he studied philosophy in New Hampshire, USA, pursued studies in theology and the classics at the Lateran University in Rome, taught Latin in California and moral theology in Washington, D.C. – are evidence of an extremely bright and highly capable individual. He could quote the life of President John F. Kennedy and the poems of his fellow Monaghan native, Patrick Kavanagh, chapter and verse.

As Bishop of Ferns during its most traumatic and divisive episode, he was able to detach himself from the reality of the cruelty taking place on his doorstep. For an explanation as to how he was able, morally and psychologically, to insulate himself within the confines of his diocese, we need an insight into the matrix of episcopalian rule.

When Bishop Eamonn Walsh was sent to restore order to Ferns in 2002, he did the exact opposite to his predecessor: he invested paramount importance to one of the guidelines of the 1996 framework document – a report commissioned by the Irish Catholic Bishops Conference to frame a response within canon law to allegations of clerical abuse – namely that 'the safety and welfare of children should be the first and paramount consideration following an allegation of child sexual abuse'. Walsh interpreted this as a licence to remove any priest suspected of sexual abuse. Two days after arriving in Ferns, he met with the four Vicars Forane (also known as deans: they keep a watchful eye on priests in their district) to discuss the ongoing crisis in Wexford and followed this up with a meeting with all of the priests (there were 133 in 2002) in the diocese four days later.

The message which he would bring to most of the forty-nine parishes over the next two years is that no priest would remain in ministry who had abused children, suspect priests would no longer be moved from parish to parish and all complaints would be made known to the civil authorities. Walsh did not procrastinate: he sought Donal Collins' voluntary laicisation five months later and had James Doyle dismissed by the Pope in 2004. He further turned over to the Ferns Inquiry every report and legal document he could put his hands on, way beyond what was required or what could have been compelled. Walsh was referring to Comiskey and the Ferns diocesan authorities when he told the laity: 'The Church acted like a family within a family. Instead of reaching out to the wounded she gave her first and sometimes exclusive support to the offending priests. In that way the Church created a family within a family. In doing so the Church allowed other innocent children to suffer sexual abuse later on.'

As Comiskey had the 1996 framework document guidelines at his disposal, it is perplexing why he proved so ineffective and inefficient in applying them. He circumnavigated the guidelines with the greatest of care but perhaps he had reasons: he relied on the absence of guidelines prior to 1996 to justify not doing nearly enough. Comiskey's career has two distinct speeds: the upward path of the young auxiliary bishop in Dublin and the downward spiral that became Wexford, whose priests were a law onto themselves, protected by a culture of secrecy and obstinacy. When Walsh summoned a meeting of priests within days of his arrival, he was listened to and obeyed: when Comiskey circulated forms to all priests to provide information about themselves in 1984, fewer than twenty were returned.

Against this backdrop of many independent republics within the diocese, and Wexford is exceptional in Ireland because curacies are considered half-parishes, Comiskey's administrative responsibilities were not helped by (a) seminary admission to St Peter's College until 1988 and (b) canon law. Current selection procedures for candidates for the priesthood are extraordinarily diligent compared to Comiskey's time. The *Norms for Priestly Training In Ireland* (1973) recommended that a thorough psychological and medical assessment be made during the assessment of candidates for admission to a seminary. The Ferns Inquiry could not find a single reference to these norms at St Peter's. 'Had they been properly implemented, it is difficult to understand how the ordinations of clearly unsuitable men were allowed to proceed.' It is known that Fortune was engaged in sexual abuse while he was a seminarian, that colleagues had misgivings about his temperament, but he was adopted by the diocese and his ordination proceeded without a hitch because his background was not checked. A cursory probe between 1971 and 1979, when he was ordained, would have set alarm bells ringing. He went to Blackrock College for a year intending to become a member of the Holy Ghost order, but was discouraged because he was 'unsuited' to missionary work. He was admitted to St Peter's without being assessed in 1973, where the earliest known allegation of abuse against him surfaced in 1976. Fortune's victim was thirteen and the abuse started with oral sex, followed by violent rape in a shower cubicle. It did not end there: the boy was raped several times in a college bedroom.

The pupil reported the abuse to a senior staff member, who responded coldly to the allegations, but he must have said something to Fortune because he stopped interfering with the pupil. Did the teacher report the matter to Herlihy? It seems not, and there was no obstacle to Fortune's ordination. It is improbable that Comiskey had any written record of Fortune's violent abuse of the pupil. No allegation was documented. It is also unlikely that Comiskey saw a Catholic Boy Scouts of Ireland report furnished to Herlihy shortly after Fortune's ordination in 1979, outlining other unsavoury incidents. Is this why Herlihy dispatched Fortune to the Diocese of Down and Connor, and why that diocese dispatched him back to Ferns? In the period between 1965 and 2005, child abuse allegations were made against 47 of the 2,000 priests who served in Northern Ireland.

The prequel to the ordination of James Doyle also makes for depressing reading. A heavy drinker, he found his suitability for a life as a priest being questioned and his ordination postponed in 1973. Despite the availability of memoranda outlining Doyle's excesses, a new college president recommended Doyle for orders without examining a single sentence in his file.

Herlihy lost no time in dispatching Doyle to the Diocese of Down and Connor. When Comiskey arrived in Wexford in 1984, Doyle and Fortune were well ensconced in his diocese, both having been subjected by a worried Herlihy to psychiatric evaluation, with less than promising prospects.

A horrifying reflection is that in the school term 1973–74, three of the worst miscreants in the clerical abuse scandal in Ferns – Donal Collins, James Doyle and Seán Fortune along with other priests whose names were redacted in *The Ferns Report* – were roaming the corridors of St Peter's College, selecting pupils at random. Three years before, Dr Conrad Baars and Dr Anna Terruwe presented a paper, *The Role of the Church in the Causation, Treatment and Prevention of the Crisis in the Priesthood*, at the World Synod of Bishops meeting in Rome. Its conclusions were startling. Having observed 15,000 patients (10 per cent of whom were priests) over 40 years, Baars and Terruwe deduced that 20–25 per cent of all priests in Western Europe and North America had serious psychiatric problems – neuroses and chronic alcoholism – and a figure as high as between 60 and 70 per cent of priests were handicapped by emotional immaturity, which precluded them from being effective in their work. Baars and Terruwe happened upon priests with identity problems: 'Priests who were uncertain in their attitude toward life, felt unloved, lonely and depressed, and whether they realised it or not, awkward in their interpersonal relationships. Psychosexual immaturity expressed in heterosexual or homosexual activity was encountered often. Many experienced difficulties in matters of faith, or suffered from severe scrupulosity, while a growing number of them seriously considered leaving the priesthood. Virtually all of them were non-affirmed men, suffering from a severe to moderate frustration with or without an associated obsessive-compulsive neurosis and alcoholism.' Or, as the evangelist

Matthew surmised concisely: 'by their fruit, you shall know them.'

Monsignor Professor Feichin O'Doherty, Professor of Logic and Psychology at University College Dublin, interviewed Fortune in 1981 and Doyle a year later. Fortune's 'personal history leaves a great deal to be desired. He gives an account of behaviour problems both before and during his seminary days which nobody seems to have noticed. I did not get the impression he takes his most recent episode and present position seriously enough, nor do I think that we have heard the full story yet,' wrote O'Doherty. The parallel with Doyle is striking. He had 'a history of auto-eroticism and homo and heterosexual behaviour. These problems were manifest during his seminary years but passed unnoticed. As far as one can see, he did not face up to celibacy in any realistic sense.' And at Donal Collins' trial, a psychiatrist described him as 'emotionally unavailable' at times, but perhaps his solicitor was closer to the mark: 'There was one corner of Collins that was evil and bad.' The Baars–Terruwe paper warned that 'a priest without identity, without a firm sense of self worth, cannot reveal to others their personal worth. Because he cannot affirm, he cannot love others in a way which strengthens both them and the Church.' Both Doyle and Fortune would claim that they had been victims of abuse in their childhood.

Further, the Baars–Terruwe research advised bishops that a priest, once frustrated in his search for affirmation, 'will attempt to affirm himself through acquisition of material goods, sexual exploits, power, fame or notoriety'. In the experience of both Baars and Terruwe, priests who find celibacy burdensome 'are either emotionally underdeveloped, or they chose the priesthood for less spiritual and altruistic motives than for self-seeking ones, such as the desire to get a college education or make a career, the fear of alienating parents who want a priest in the family at all cost, or the need to make amends for past sexual sins, or the promise of affirmation not found at home'. It was a tragedy in the making in Wexford that in priests like Fortune, Doyle, Collins and Martin Clancy and others identified in *The Ferns Report* the demarcation between celibacy and chastity was blurred. They betrayed their vow of chastity and hid behind their vow of celibacy, and once committed to a mortal turpitude, their abuses could not be contained. Thirty-two years after the Baars–Terruwe paper was circulated to bishops, the Irish Bishops Conference commissioned research into clerical abuse in Ireland. *Time to Listen, Confronting Child Sexual Abuse by Catholic Clergy in Ireland*, a report undertaken by the Department of Psychology of the Royal College of Surgeons, found that clergy on the ground described the strategy adopted by the Church in relation to child sexual abuse as an attempt to prevent scandal first, and protect the Church as an institution second. The other key findings were as follows:

- A majority of priests reported that their initial awareness of clerical sexual abuse was raised through the media and that their own knowledge of the effects of abuse on victims was limited.
- The public learned about child sexual abuse by priests from the media (95 per cent) but tended to overestimate the proportion of abuse.
- Both the abused and family members felt a great sense of guilt because they had chosen to report the abuse to the Church, rather than the Gardaí.
- Many felt that other children might have been protected from abuse if they had chosen to report it to the civil authorities instead.
- Family members of convicted clergy also described major

negative consequences on discovering that an uncle, a brother, a son or a cousin had sexually abused children.

– Convicted clergy who were polled reported mixed feelings about the support received from Church personnel during legal proceedings and time spent in prison. Nobody representing the Bishop of Ferns attended the trial of Fr James Doyle.

– In the postal survey of bishops and delegates, fewer bishops than delegates (45 per cent vs. 80 per cent) reported being satisfied with their handling of past allegations of child sexual abuse.

– Other Church personnel described the Church's overall management strategy in relation to child sexual abuse as an attempt to prevent scandal first and protect the Church as an institution.

– Public perception (77 per cent) felt that the Church did not deal with the problem of abuse adequately. Only 42 per cent believed that the Catholic Church would safeguard children entrusted to its care, while only 40 per cent trusted the Church to handle problems with its own clergy.

– Most (70 per cent) of the Irish public surveyed believed that the individual abuser was responsible for the occurrence of child sexual abuse, while 39 per cent saw the Church hierarchy as having responsibility for its management, with 41 per cent considering civil authorities as the ones responsible for management.

The many recommendations of Time to Listen were far reaching, though the majority of them had already been put into practice in Ferns for over a year by Eamonn Walsh:

– The Church must study the systems being put in place

in other organisations to identify and manage various types of risk and to respond in a prompt and effective manner to crises.

- The Church should actively seek to work in cooperation with other agencies in the best possible protection of children.

- Prevention strategies should be communicated to all Church personnel, to the wider Church community and to the general public.

- Church procedures for prevention should be audited at appropriate intervals. This could be done by the Church or by an external agency using a quality assurance approach.

- A clearly defined protocol for managing complaints, based on a standardised approach, should be put in place and be facilitated by a national Child Protection Office. Such a protocol would facilitate those who do not wish to approach clergy, would broaden the categories of Church personnel against whom complaints could be made and would improve accountability for the management of complaints.

'Notwithstanding the report's acknowledgement that when dealing with abusers in the past, bishops followed – in good faith – the best psychiatric advice available at the time, clearly in relation to clerical sexual abuse we failed many young people over too long a period,' commented Bishop John McAreavey. Bishops had an à la carte approach to 'the best psychiatric advice available at the time', and chose either to ignore or misinterpret the warnings explicit in the Baars–Terruwe report. Selection procedures for the diocesan priesthood since the free-for-all admission exercised during the 1970s and early 1980s at St Peter's – which was closed as a seminary by Comiskey in 1998, a year after the boarding school – has changed utterly. The canonical power of the bishop to examine the suitability of a candidate is assisted by professional advice and even a psychological assessment, which helps trace their sexual history (active heterosexuals must spend a period of celibate living); homosexuals are considered unsuitable for admission to the seminary; less than chaste seminarians are considered incompatible with the vocation; students must have a mature understanding of sexual integration; and the Church's child protection policy must be fully complied with.

The Ferns Report gives the lie to a conviction of the Church that homosexuality is or was a factor in clerical abuse, and draws attention to the irrelevancy of sexual orientation in either the treatment or recidivism of the perpetrator. But the Church thought differently and, days after *The Ferns Report*, the Vatican Congregation for Catholic Education placed a blanket ban on gay candidates for seminaries. This, according to Eoin Collins of the Gay & Lesbian Equality Network, was essentially 'an incitement to discrimination and hatred'. David Norris, in a Senate debate on the report, accused the Church of organising a witch hunt against homosexuals.

If the Catholic Church in Ireland wanted to get to the origin of why so many of its priests were ungovernable and undisciplined, it had to look closer to home. In 2009 *The Murphy Report*, probing the procedures adopted by Clonliffe College in the 1970s and the 1980s, was unable to obtain a single record of an evaluation carried out on a student. Bishop Eamonn Walsh, Dean of the college from 1977 to 1985, explained: 'I always recall Brendan Houlihan, as President, saying to me when a priest is ordained he should leave the college with a clean record. If we have approved him for ordination, he should start from scratch and maybe that accounts for the attitude towards records, that once you promoted the person for ordination, then he is a graduate and let the file begin from that day forward.' St Peter's introduced a screening process of sorts in 1988, though it was far too late for Fr Patrick McCafferty, a seminarian at St Peter's who was abused while on vacation by a priest of Down and Connor. 'Within the diocesan and seminary systems, at that time, there was no one to turn to for help and it would have been unthinkable, on account of shame and fear, to tell anyone in authority. I believed if I had reported the incidents, I would be the one in serious trouble and not Fr X.' A methodical and officious attention to the minutiae of the interview process was incorporated in *The Irish Bishops Document of Child Sexual Abuse: Framework for a Church Response* in 1996.

Better late than never, perhaps, but the writing was on the wall as far back as 1971 in the Baars–Terruwe report, commissioned by the Church but not assimilated by bishops. It had warned: 'A sound home and seminary life can be founded only on an intelligent grasp of a proper philosophy of life and a correct psychology of man.' Dr Derek Smyth, a priest in Foxrock parish, Dublin, has questioned the ethos of priests distrusting themselves and remaining silent. 'This behaviour was reinforced in our seminary training. We were conditioned to surrender to the institution, to the teachings, structures and disciplines of the church. Upon ordination we made a promise of obedience to the local bishop, and even our own letter of acceptance of a diocesan post was scripted for us.'

Canon law, or *jus canonicum*, is an ancient body of laws for the government of the Catholic Church, subject to tinkering and misinterpretation, ever since the schism that separated the Eastern and Western Churches in 1054. For the latter, there was no significant interruption until the Reformation in the sixteenth century. As the Catholic Church cannot function in a legislative or executive sense without authority, bishops are invested with the binding rules of canon law, and as the bishop acts as a vicar of Christ in his own diocese (and not as a vicar of the Pope), he can exercise his power personally. 'The way the Church works,' explained Bishop Walsh, 'is that each parish is responsible to the diocese, but each diocese in Ireland and in every country is independent of every other diocese, and there is this perception that they are like a bank, with twenty-six branches and a head office that says, do this and do that. It doesn't work like that.' Concepts of canon law have influenced civil law and jurisprudence throughout most of Europe from medieval times, such as marriage – from which the law of nullity developed – and the law of criminal procedure. The development of the State derives from ideas conceived by medieval canonists whilst formulating the constitution of the Church. The necessity to codify the tattered matrices of canon law was addressed by the Church, particularly Pope Pius X, at the turn of the twentieth century, in the shadow of seismic changes in science and medicine, a huge undertaking because the classification of the rules of canon law had not kept up with the evolution of secular law throughout Europe after the French Revolution. As the substance and precise details of canon law were strewn throughout the collections of the *Corpus juris canonici*, it was difficult to manage. What was the solution? The Pope established a commission of sixteen cardinals, with himself in the chair.

The schemata of the five books (over 2,000 canons) prepared in Rome – universal norms, personal law, law of things, penal law and procedural law – were reworked in the commission between 1912–1914. To ensure the unity of the codification, another commission was established in 1917 for the authentic interpretation of the new code: the *Codex juris canonici* (Code of canon law) was completed, promulgated and became effective by 1918, the first exclusive codification of all universal Church law, and it was soon to be put to the test in

Ireland. A decree of removal was issued in 1919 against a parish priest in west Cork who, by all accounts, was as divisive in the village of Eyeries as Seán Fortune would become in Fethard: the view of the diocesan authorities was that the regrettable state of affairs in Eyeries (the priest was paranoid), made it 'incumbent on us to take remedial action in discharge of our obligation to provide for the good of souls'. A move by the priest to have the decree of removal declared illegal and *ultra vires* (without authority) by the High Court failed and was appealed to the Supreme Court. As canon law regulated inter-Church relations, the Supreme Court held that the bishop had acted correctly: it was a term of the contract made in Ireland, that 'both parties were bound by a foreign law regulating their respective offices'.

The removal was appealed to Rome, where it too failed. Archbishop of Dublin for over thirty years, John Charles McQuaid reasoned that a diocese had only one teaching authority who, under the Pope, is competent to bind the laity and the religious to moral law, and that is the bishop. His view was shared by the fledgling Irish State with the absolute connivance of the body politic. Subservience by Catholics to the rule of the Church was absolute during McQuaid's reign, 1940–1970, particularly in the 1950s, a decade that opened with a legal landmark for McQuaid's Church. The Tilson case gave canon law's edict on mixed marriages in Ireland legal force: the President of the High Court, Justice Gavan Duffy, made the *Ne Temere* promises signed by a Catholic wife and a Protestant father (that their children must be raised as Catholics) enforceable in Irish law, owing to the special position of the Catholic Church enshrined in Article 44 of the Constitution. Gavan Duffy, whose ruling was also upheld by the Supreme Court, said that the father, by removing some of the children to a Protestant institution after the couple split up, had acted in defiance of a holy pledge, rubber-stamped by Irish law and enforced by Church muscle. Obeisant governments from 1937 to 1959, so terrified of a belt of McQuaid's crozier, deferred – for his private consideration – proposed legislation likely to stray into Church territory. It was McQuaid, while president of Blackrock College, who helped copper-fasten the Church's special position by working alongside a college alumnus and leader of the country, Éamon de Valera, as he prepared the 1937 Constitution. His bid to reform the country as a Catholic fiefdom was made easier by a gift from McQuaid of the 1918 *Codex juris canonici*. Their Constitution, observed Tim Pat Coogan, visualised a country that, while democratic in practice, would be theocratic in precept.

McQuaid's consecration as Archbishop of Dublin in 1940, a position his political sponsor de Valera lobbied for, and McQuaid's subsequent role as both a feared and fearless consigliere and tough underboss for the Church hierarchy established an Irish Catholic State. The word of the Catholic Church became law. This was the poisoned chalice that McQuaid had worked tirelessly for and handed down to a future generation of bishops, like Brendan Comiskey and Eamon Casey. 'The Dáil proposes, Maynooth disposes,' wrote Seán Ó Faoláin, though Seán Lemass might have begged to differ: his refusal – as a new Taoiseach – to bend to McQuaid's entreaties in the Liquor Bill in 1959 showed that, as John Cooney reflected, 'the citation of canon law no longer automatically held sway in the Dáil'. Dermot Keogh, ordained by McQuaid, has maintained that the friendship between the Fianna Fáil leader and the archbishop never clouded their concept of duty. 'It is all too facile to hold, a priori, that de Valera and McQuaid sang consistently from the same hymnal.' One of McQuaid's closest colleagues was the Bishop of Ferns, James Staunton. Throughout his career, he was a personal ally of McQuaid and collaborated as the Catholic noose was tightened around the young democracy. In his suffragan bishop in Ferns, McQuaid found a confidant, a loyal mouthpiece and disciple. As early as 1934, Staunton – then a mere canon – and McQuaid – then a mere mortal – conspired to oppose an advisory council pressing to allow lay teachers a greater say in school policy. Staunton was among the Church triumvirate that greeted Minister Noel Browne in 1950 to make clear, in a missive aimed at the coalition government's midriff, that the Church would fight the Mother and Child Scheme with whatever arsenal it could muster. As Bishop of Ferns, he refused a Church of Ireland appeal (for which Brendan Comiskey apologised in 1998) to express disapproval of the Catholic boycott of Protestant firms in Fethard-on-Sea in 1957. Staunton also attended the first session of the Second Vatican Council in October 1962 with McQuaid who, a year later, was one of eight bishops at his colleague and friend's obsequies in Wexford.

When Comiskey was named auxiliary bishop in McQuaid's old beat, the sentiments of Archbishop Jeremiah Kinane's famous Rockwell speech would have been ringing in his ears: 'Subject to the supreme magisterial authority of the Holy See, bishops are the authentic teachers of faith and morals in their own dioceses.' McQuaid was no stranger to the presence of abusive priests in Dublin and he was not averse to bypassing canon law when it was convenient. A chaplain to Our Lady's Hospital for Sick Children in Crumlin, known as 'Fr Edmondus' in *The Murphy Report*, sexually assaulted patients over a ten-year period. He drew attention to himself when Gardaí received twenty-six sexually explicit photographs which the priest had taken of two young girls in the hospital and had sent to England to be developed. Naturally, the Gardaí – who were alerted to the photographs by Scotland Yard – did not prepare a file for the DPP, but delegated the investigation to McQuaid, chairman of the hospital's Board of Directors. He asked Bishop Patrick Dunne for advice. Dunne believed that a crime had been committed under canon law, yet to preserve the reputation of the Church, McQuaid overruled him, noting that Edmondus had taken the photographs out of curiosity about female anatomy and did not refer the incident to the Vatican. This was in 1960. Edmondus was jailed in 1996 after decades of abuse in McQuaid's diocese.

The authority of canon law in Ireland was behind the shadow boxing between Church and government in 2002: Justice Minister Michael McDowell viewed canon law as the equivalent to the internal rules of a sporting organisation, such as the GAA. But Cardinal Desmond Connell, referencing the aforementioned spat in west Cork, argued that the Supreme Court recognised that canon law enjoyed the status of foreign law. The truth, as usual with organised religion, was somewhere in between. The *Law Society Gazette* noted: 'It is correct to say that canon law is recognised as foreign law by the Irish courts where it governs a relationship that is at issue. It would not be correct to imply that this gives canon law precedence over civil law.' Commenting in 2005, Fr Gerard Garrett, Regional Tribunal Offices, Cork, believed that there was no conflict between canon law and civil law. 'There is nothing in canon law which inhibits or prohibits the citizen's right to exercise those rights which they enjoy under the Constitution of Ireland. In fact, canon law urges the observance of civil law except where it is clear that it is contrary to divine law.'

Canon law was put to the test publicly in 1997 when the High Court ruled that the Church was within its rights to alter the sanctuary to Carlow Cathedral – the property was held subject to canon law – after parishioners sought an injunction against the Bishop of Kildare and Leighlin Laurence Ryan, to prevent scrapping the altar rails and the wooden pulpit. A wry comment on the affair was provided in the *Sunday Business Post* by Peadar Laighleis: 'At the same time as the faith of Catholic children was being undermined, a campaign was under way to ravage the Church's architectural heritage, the patrimony of all Irish people, regardless of their faith. Third-rate architects aspiring to rival Le Corbusier reckoned they could improve on Pugin masterpieces. Ecclesiastical treasures were destroyed to gratify the new iconoclastic spirit . . . despite the pleas of the faithful, whose impoverished forefathers had paid to build and upkeep their parish churches. This vandalism was justified by the line: Vatican II requires it.'

Brian Fallon in *The Irish Times* noted that there was 'a strong feeling that these changes were a clerical initiative alone and did not reflect lay opinion, which scarcely seems to have been consulted'. A letter was read in court from Cardinal Joseph Ratzinger in Rome endorsing Bishop Ryan's plans and the High Court found in favour of the Church. When 'Our Church, Our Children' was launched two months after the world had digested the contents of *The Ferns Report* in 2005, Archbishop Seán Brady clarified the canonical procedures to be followed by bishops once a suspicion of clerical abuse has arisen. 'Critically . . . we reiterate the principle of the welfare of the child as paramount and stress that care should be taken to ensure that any canonical procedure does not undermine a civil investigation.'

Abroad, fundamental to the modification of canon law was the Second Vatican Council's (1962–1965) vision of the Church as a community possessing the sacramental mission to live and proclaim the Gospel. After Pope John XXIII announced the revision of the Church's code, the first episcopal synod in 1967 gave its approval to a document – *Principia quae Codicis Juris Canonici Recognitionem Dirigant* – in which the juridical character should be preserved and not limited to faith and morals. Protracted consultation began in

Rome and was completed in 1982, when Pope John Paul II promulgated the second *Codex juris canonici* (seven books of 1,752 canons) a year later, a belated move by the Church to give practical, and some would say more conservative, effect to the theological insights of the Second Vatican Council. From an Irish standpoint, much attention was paid to the move toward decentralisation with bishops enjoying more autonomy. In 2001, the Vatican's *De delictis gravioribus* ('on more serious crimes'), written by Cardinal Ratzinger, prefect of the Congregation for the Doctrine of the Faith, published in the official gazette of the Holy See, the *Acta Apostolicae Sedis*, was a review of the much older *Crimen sollicitationis* (the crime of solicitation), which instructed a bishop how to impose confidentiality where serious crimes by priests were involved. It was a special procedural law in 1962 which imposed a code of silence on the prelate in the undertaking of managing abusive clergy, and carried the ultimate penalty for disclosure: excommunication. *Crimen sollicitationis* – procedures for handling allegations against clergy for soliciting sex while in the act of sacramental confession – was less well known during the bishopric of Brendan Comiskey and it is probable that few bishops in Ireland knew of its existence.

Crimen sollicitationis was interpreted by legal representatives of abuse victims as the Vatican's attempt to conceal sexual offences by priests or bishops and was described by lawyers in America as a smoking gun (an attempt to get the document admitted in an abuse case in Massachusetts failed after a Springfield judge ruled the document was irrelevant to a civil lawsuit). 'What is noteworthy about this document is that it included regulations that placed everyone dealing with a case falling under its norms under the Secret of the Holy Office, which was the highest degree of Vatican secrecy. Violation of the oath to keep knowledge of such a case secret resulted in an automatic excommunication, the absolution of which was reserved to the Pope. This document remained in force until 2001 and although it did not invent the extreme secrecy with which the Catholic Church has covered clergy sex cases, it is a clear indicator of the secrecy surrounding Catholic clergy sex abuse cases and the attitude behind this secrecy,' said Fr Thomas Doyle, an ordained Catholic priest in the Dominican Order, who has been an expert witness on over 500 clerical sex abuse cases throughout the world.

Four types of sexual crime, *De crimine pessimo*, namely homosexuality, solicitation for sex during confession, abuse of minors and bestiality, were identified. 'The 1922 and 1962 documents provide special norms with an added emphasis on confidentiality because of the very serious nature of the crimes involved. These special procedural norms were an expansion, with added detail, upon the procedural law of the code. The existence of this document also clearly proves that the highest Catholic Church authorities were aware of the especially grave nature of the clerical sexual crimes considered,' explained Doyle in a 2008 commentary on *Crimen sollicitationis*. 'This of course makes it difficult for any Church leader to credibly claim that the problem of clergy sexual abuse was an unknown quantity prior to 1984.' The emphasis on confidentiality was evident when, as outlined in *The Murphy Report* in 2009, not one of hundreds of allegations of clerical abuse in a thirty-year period was reported by any of the four cardinals who ruled the Archdiocese of Dublin, though John Charles McQuaid had a dog-eared copy of the 1922 version of *Crimen sollicitationis*. In reality, *Crimen sollicitationis,* viewed by Doyle as an indication of an official policy of secrecy rather than a conspiracy to stay silent, was an archaically worded blueprint to help bishops discipline priests who, in the eyes of the Church, had forsaken their chastity.

Paragraph 11 is redolent of the language and syntax of the Second Vatican Council:

> Since, however, in dealing with these causes, more than usual care and concern must be shown that they be treated with the utmost confidentiality, and that, once decided and the decision executed, they are covered by permanent silence (Instruction of the Holy Office, 20 February 1867, No. 14), all those persons in any way associated with the tribunal, or knowledgeable of these matters by reason of their office, are bound to observe inviolably the strictest confidentiality, commonly known as the secret of the Holy Office, in all things and with all persons, under pain of incurring automatic excommunication, ipso facto and undeclared, reserved to the sole person of the Supreme Pontiff, excluding even the Sacred Penitentiary. Ordinaries are bound by this same law *ipso iure*, that is, in virtue of their own office; other personnel are bound in virtue of the oath which they are always to swear before assuming their duties; and, finally, those delegated, questioned or informed outside the tribunal, are bound in virtue of the precept to be imposed on them in the letters of delegation, inquiry or information, with express mention of the secret of the Holy Office and of the aforementioned censure.

The 21st-century Church's reading of this tapestry is paramount: how the Church carried out its investigation was to remain secret, not the abuse itself. 'I congratulate you for not denouncing a priest to the civil administration,' wrote Cardinal Darío Castrillón Hoyos from the Vatican in 2001 to Bishop Pierre Pican of Bayeux-Lisieux, who received a three-month suspended sentence in a French court for not exposing Fr

René Bissey's abuse of eleven boys. Bissey, who got eighteen years in jail, had told Pican about the abuse during confession. 'You have acted well,' wrote the cardinal to his bishop, 'and I am pleased to have a colleague in the epsicopate who, in the eyes of history and of all other bishops in the world, preferred prison to denouncing his son and priest.' Nor did Cardinal Roger Mahony of the Los Angeles Archdiocese contact the police after impenitent child abuser Fr Michael Baker admitted abusing children to him in 1986: Mahony's solution was to assign Baker to different parishes for the next fourteen years. In August 2010, after plaintiffs in Kentucky dropped a six-year lawsuit against the Holy See for concealing clerical abuse, the Vatican's Fr Federico Lombardi claimed there had never been a policy to suppress sexual abuse by priests. In *O'Bryan vs. the Holy See* the plaintiffs set out to prove that Vatican officials had covered up the mishandling of abuse cases by American prelates, and that the Holy See should not have sovereign immunity from prosecution.

'The penchant for secrecy flows naturally out of the Church's feudal structure,' argued Fr Donald Cozzens. 'Think of bishops as lords of the manor who until rather recently had discretionary control of their properties, personnel and financial resources of their dioceses – in truth, their benefices.'

That the Church was pedestrian in its review of canon law articles was further borne out when it published *Normae de gravioribus delicti* in July 2010, on the back of what had been, thus far, an annus horribilis for Pope Benedict XVI. The scandal that unfolded at Canisius College in Berlin – fifty alleged cases of sexual abuse as far back as the 1970s – opened the floodgates in Germany with an estimated two thirds of the country's twenty-seven dioceses reported to have been affected. The *Suddeutsche Zeitung* alleged that the Pope, when he was Archbishop of Munich and Freising in 1980, allowed

Fr Peter Hullermann, a serial abuser of boys in the diocese of Essen, to return to pastoral duties after receiving therapy and he continued to abuse, even after a conviction for sexual abuse in 1986. Hullermann had been assessed by a psychiatrist and was deemed untreatable. The Church repatriated him to pastoral duties and he abused again until his suspension in March 2010. Roger Vangheluwe, Belgium's longest-serving prelate, resigned his office a month later, after admitting to his abuse of a boy before he was made Bishop of Bruges in 1985.

An explanation for the Catholic Church's recalcitrance in punishing sexual offenders is a twisted belief, endorsed by canon 1321,that an actual defence of paedophilia may equate with the defence of insanity in civil law. This is how it works: canon law's concept of imputation relies on the assumption of malice or culpability. A priest accused of paedophilia, and as such subject to urges beyond his control, may be excused by reason of diminished capacity. Clearly rattled by the ramification of such an outcome for someone who impulsively abused young children, *The Murphy Report* noted, as a matter of grave concern, 'a serial child sexual abuser might receive more favourable treatment from the Archdiocese, or from Rome, by reason of the fact that he was diagnosed as a paedophile.' At the heart of the Church's mishandling at the highest level of cases like Hullermann and Fr Lawrence Murphy, who abused as many as 200 boys at a school for deaf children in Wisconsin, was the involvement of Cardinal Ratzinger. He knew Hullermann personally when he was Archbishop of Munich and ignored warnings that the priest should never be allowed to work with children again. As Superior for the Congregation for the Doctrine of the Faith in the Vatican between 1981 and 2005, when he would have been inundated with abuse cases from the dioceses of Ferns and Boston, to name but two, Ratzinger was privy to Murphy's appeal not to undergo a canonical trial. In a letter Murphy sought Ratzinger's personal intervention – it is not known if he succeeded – but the canonical process was brought to a halt. Vatican policy toward abuse allegations shifted significantly in 2001: *Sacramentorum sanctitatis tutela* provided for all abuse allegations to be sent to the Congregation for the Doctrine of the Faith, Ratzinger's brainchild. Because of the unexpected torrent of clerical abuse allegations that followed, the policy was amended, as Rome could not cope with the deluge. Many serious cases of abuse in Ireland, pre-dating 2001, have not seen the light of day at the Congregation for the Doctrine of the Faith.

Prior to the disclosure of the abuse at Berlin's Canisius College, the Pope did not have time to grapple fully with the consequence of the publication of *The Murphy Report* in Ireland, which had prompted several of the country's bishops to offer their resignations. A fortnight after he wrote a Lenten letter to Irish Catholics, a rare gesture of atonement by a Pontiff, that victims' trust had been betrayed and that they had suffered grievously, the Pope appeared on the 29 March 2010 front cover of the most influential news magazine in the world, *Time*, alongside the headline: 'The Pope's Nightmare'. Nor was *Time* finished with the Pontiff. In June, Benedict again graced its cover with 'Why being Pope Means Never Having to Say You're Sorry' splashed across the back of his head. It was a veiled indictment of the papal missive to the Irish faithful at Easter, with *Time* reporting that the Pope had apologised for errors committed by the Irish hierarchy, and not the Holy See. Were officials in the Vatican fearful that a blanket apology by Benedict might diminish the papal magisterium, the authority of the Pope to be God's mouthpiece on earth? Worldwide publicity greeted the publication of *Normae de gravioribus delictis* on the back of the severest criticism of the papacy by *Time*: the Vatican had to be seen to respond with determination to the unease throughout America and Europe to the almost weekly revelations of clerical abuse among the planet's 1.2 billion Catholics. It extended the statute of limitations for abuse cases, ruled that civil law must be complied with by Church personnel and opened up the canon law trial process to lay people.

The decision to connect canon law procedures for confronting clerical child abuse with canon law procedures for concelebrating the Eucharist with Protestant ministers appeared to diminish the gravity of the former. The Vatican disagreed and relied on semantic word play to differentiate the two *Delicta Graviora*: sharing the Eucharist with ministers who do not have apostolic succession is a sacramental crime (like chucking the consecrated host in the bin, according to a bemused letter writer to *The Irish Times*), child abuse, however, is criminal. Before the summer of woe in 2010 for the Church had passed, the Vatican doubled its own statute of limitations on the prosecution of clergy from ten years to twenty when the correct alternative would have been to abolish any impediment to an investigation of abuse. Benedict pressed ahead with a visit to Britain in September which, to the surprise of his critics, was successful. He emerged from behind the ephemera of newspaper headlines and revealed another side to his character: less officious, more warm-hearted. He became the first Pontiff to meet victims of clerical abuse.

What is ironic about the Church's mishandling of abuse cases, from Bonn to Boston, is that a faithful adherence to canon law would have helped chastise offenders within its rank and file, while also igniting a light at the end of the tunnel for victims. Curiously, the hierarchy in Ireland exploited the rigidity of the legal advice at its disposal to shield the abuser and prolong the suffering of the victim. Neither *The Murphy Report* nor *The Ferns Report* came across one case where canon law was used to provide justice or reparation for the victims of abuse. It is impossible for the Church to reconcile polar opposites: confidentiality at all costs or justice by civil law. 'The penal process of canon law was for a period of years set aside in favour of a purely pastoral approach which was, in the Commission's view, wholly ineffective as a means of controlling clerical child sexual abuse,' noted *The Murphy Report*.

That the Vatican acted with the urgency of a snail in addressing sexual abuse scandals in its midst is not an issue for the Church because as Fr Colm Kilcoyne pointed out a decade earlier: 'The media lives off the fresh and the novel. The Church operates in time but its thought frame is eschatological – all is seen in terms of eternity.' Brendan Comiskey's period of incapacity in Wexford, his somnolence at a time when children and teenagers were being abused by priests on his watch, is explained as the bishop being in over his head; that he was clueless in the face of a rising tide of abuse allegations; that he was unfamiliar with the ugly convolutions of clerical paedophilia and did not know what to do; that, instead of giving him directions, the gobbets of canon law text left him disorientated amid a legal maze and that he was at heart a good man, held over a barrel by reprobates like Seán Fortune. It is an explanation whose currency may have had some plausibility in the aftermath of his resignation. The publication of *The Murphy Report* in 2009 alters these perceptions: many of the auxiliary bishops were intimate with cases of clerical abuse and Laurence Forristal, Donal Murray and Comiskey were aware, 'for many years', of complaints and suspicions of clerical sexual abuse in Dublin. Their primary loyalty, concluded the report, was to the Church itself. When Comiskey arrived in Ferns in 1984, he simply brought the Dublin Archdiocese's way of doing things with him, and his judicious instinct was rendered subservient to obscure canons, which left him isolated from a society sickened by the abuse of children by priests. Deputy Brendan Howlin, leafing through *The Ferns Report*, found that the Church, its institutions and its priests in Wexford existed in 'a separate world' of accountability and responsibility. 'In the fog of debate about canon law versus state law, there must be no doubt that the State has the prime responsibility to protect its citizens, most especially its children,' he added. 'While the prime responsibility lies with the perpetrators of these awful criminal acts, what is revealed is a powerful institution incapable or unwilling to deal with the terrible truth. The response of Bishops Donal Herlihy and Brendan Comiskey is spelled out in detail [in *The Ferns Report*]. While it can produce a false result to judge the actions of people up to forty years ago through the prism of today's state of knowledge and understanding, the failure to act effectively when actual knowledge was received beggars belief.'

10

Bishop Brendan Comiskey: His Rise And Fall

'In those days, it took considerable wealth to put a boy through Maynooth, and they looked and acted as if they came from a line of swaggering, confident men who dominated field and market and whose only culture was cunning, money and brute force. Though they could be violently generous and sentimental at times, in their hearts they despised their own people.'
John McGahern, *The Guardian*, 2006

Brendan Comiskey's reign as the Bishop of Ferns began in celebratory style – bunting fluttering and local bands playing – in Wexford town on a beautiful Monday afternoon in May 1984, when he was the guest of honour at a reception hosted by the Corporation, the day after he was installed at Enniscorthy Cathedral. Comiskey became the first Ulsterman since St Aidan to occupy the See of Ferns, with responsibility for 98,000 Catholics in 58 parishes and 141 priests serving 103 churches. Departing from his text at St Aidan's Cathedral (where the commentator at the installation was his successor, Fr Denis Brennan) following the formal presentation of the Apostolic Letter, Comiskey said: 'I will do all in my power to be worthy of your trust.' Ten thousand turned out in Wexford to see the young and handsome successor to Donal Herlihy. During the next eighteen years, Comiskey enjoyed a personable relationship with the Corporation and its elected members. In 1990 he became the twenty-sixth person to receive the Freedom of the Borough: he rubbed shoulders with the Mayor of the day, Oireachtas members and the local glitterati at the annual opening night of the Wexford festival – when Dublin came Slaney-side to pay homage to the cheerful merry-go-round of champagne, gossip and opera – and when he resigned his post in 2002, a vigil outside the bishop's palatial home was organised by a former mayor, but to little avail. A small crowd assembled. Comiskey's star had streaked across the dull firmament of Wexford provincial life like a meteor, but Ireland had changed and he was no longer wanted. He came in the spring and he left in the spring.

His appointment as Bishop of Ferns was the apogee of a star of the Church in the making. Head of his order, the Congregation of the Sacred Hearts of Jesus and Mary in Ireland and Britain, at thirty-four, Auxiliary Bishop of Dublin at forty-five and Bishop of Ferns at forty-seven. He admitted to his media friends that he did not know the Diocese of Ferns. 'I feel a bit like Pope John Paul – like a man from a far country. I intend to listen a lot and to pray a lot. I intend to meet and talk to every priest and member of a religious order. I will talk to every lay member who wants to talk to me.' If he had a moment to reflect on his early life during those two hectic days on 20 and 21 May, his promotion was light years removed from his humble introduction to the world, the youngest of ten (eight boys and two girls) in Tasson in the parish of Clontibret, located between Castleblaney and Monaghan, in 1935.

'You were in border land there,' recalled the bishop in an interview to celebrate his fortieth anniversary as a priest. 'Where I grew up, our house was about a mile from the border. In very scarce times we would smuggle, a little. We weren't into the smuggling business but we were into the food, for example. The children would run across the border and get a pound or two of tea. We would bring that into the South and we would get four pound of butter and then you would run across the Border again, maybe the next day, and you take two pound of butter and get four pound of tea and you would multiply. There would be no money. It was all bartering. We had a little barrel reinforced and buried in the little garden at the front. The bread, the tea and the butter were kept there because the Customs would raid the house now and again.' The precarious financial circumstances of raising ten children were described by the bishop as dire. 'My father [Patrick] was a motor mechanic and there were no motors in the 1940s as there was no petrol around after the War. Because of that, we were quite poor. We had no farm or that. The ten children and two parents were depending on the income of one man who worked as a mechanic when there was petrol and, when there wasn't, worked at a bicycle shop.'

In spite of the deprivations, Comiskey had a loving and happy childhood and there was always enough food to feed a dozen mouths. Pocket money was earned by the children picking blackberries to sell across the border near Keady in County Armagh. He was considered such a chatterbox as a child that his mother, Claire, used to swear that he had been injected with a gramophone needle instead of a syringe at birth. He achieved the then rare feat of attending both primary and secondary school. 'At the time, in my townsland, there were only two people who ever went beyond primary school into secondary education.' Due to his mother's indomitable will and business nous, most of the Comiskey brood attended secondary school. She made extra money by leasing land or buying and selling cattle. All of Brendan Comiskey's siblings had successful careers: Genevieve (ward sister), Kevin (postmaster), Sean (teacher), Paddy (motor trade), Peter (chief agricultural officer), May (nurse), Joe (garage proprietor) and Maurice and Edmund were businessmen. After primary education at Annyalla National School and Castleblaney Boys' School, and secondary education at St Macartan's College, the youngest Comiskey, in 1954–55, completed a spiritual year at Sacred Hearts' Novitiate, Cootehill, Cavan, where, among other pursuits, he farmed, built roads and played football as often as he could, before embarking on the first of many great adventures abroad.

With twelve other students, he sailed on the SS *New York* from Cobh to New York in 1955, and from there to the Sacred Hearts base at Wareham, Massachusetts, where he studied philosophy. The seminary was the home of a former ambassador, situated on 200 acres and looking out onto the Cape Cod Canal. 'We had a boat house and boats. It was heaven,' said Comiskey. 'We lived like lords. Coming from Ireland, thinking, if this is the seminary, Lord, let me stay here forever.' Forever lasted two years, and Comiskey next attended Jaffrey Centre in adjacent New Hampshire, where he spent his leisure time among eighty-five Irish seminarians ice-skating, boating and climbing Mount Monadnock. The Congregation of the Sacred Hearts, abbreviated to SS.CC. after its Latin name, *Sacrorum Cordium*, was more than just a spiritual home and an alma mater for Comiskey. After his resignation from Ferns, Comiskey found solace at the provincial home of the

Ireland–England province of the SS.CC. in Ranelagh, Dublin, and became active in parish and missionary support activity.

The SS.CC. maintained a community house near Cootehill – birthplace of Archbisop John McQuaid – where it had a base since 1948, with a pastoral outreach to Cavan and Monaghan. As recently as August 2010, a fit-looking Comiskey, whose photograph appears several times on the official SS.CC. website, both in clerical and lay garb, was flagged as a well-known member of the Congregation, and he was the preacher at the annual USA East Province Retreat in Wareham.

Comiskey's academic year as a young student was divided between studying theology at Jaffrey Centre and in summer, Greek and Latin at the Catholic University in Washington. Leaving America in 1961, departing Boston not on a liner but on a Boeing 707, Comiskey was ordained by Dr Eugene O'Callaghan at the Congregation of the Sacred Hearts at Tanagh, Monaghan, in June 1961. 'It was a small place that used to be a henhouse and was converted into a beautiful little church,' he recalled. He was twenty-six, one of eight of the original twelve who set out from Cobh across the Atlantic six years earlier. Together – now as priests – they left Ireland for America again, destined for the West Coast and California, teaching Latin and English at Damien High School at La Verne. 'It was magic when I look back on those years,' said Comiskey. 'We were like greyhounds, we were so well trained in the seminary. I have nothing but great memories. I was vice-principal, dean, athletics director and chairman of a couple of departments. We worked around the clock.'

Other pupils came from broken homes, or were teethed on poverty, and it was part of Comiskey's ministry, which he enjoyed, to help young people who came from the wrong side of the tracks. To make education and school more inclusive, he played a pivotal role in introducing soccer to Southern

California. Teaching was hard work. Unlike the American priests who quit early in the afternoon, the young Comiskey's day began at 8 a.m. in the school and finished when it got dark. He made a favourable impression on his pupils and their families and maintained links with them throughout his life. 'I left my heart there. To a certain extent, you always leave your heart to your first assignment as a priest, unless you have a bad experience. That's magic to look back on.'

Comiskey, coming from a loving family background, did not need America, then in the tremendous flux of social change, to realise that a close-knit community with a common goal is a precious resource. The close entwining of colleagues, of pupils, of families in pursuit of a common goal – education – gave him a personal sense of fulfilment and achievement. He was a natural teacher. His affection for America never ceased and he maintained strong links with Irish–American groups, like the New York St Patrick's Day Committee, which would have appreciated his advice when fending off criticism of its anti-homosexual policy. Journalist and author Niall O'Dowd felt that, after the passing of Comiskey's friend, Cardinal Tomás Ó Fiaich, the Bishop of Ferns had become the strongest connection between the Church in Ireland and the Irish community in America. 'Having worked in the US, he understood how the political game was played and the importance of the media to get the Church's story out. He was also viewed as a man of rare humour, one of the few bishops from Ireland who would go to a pub for a pint and a chat – before he stopped drinking,' said O'Dowd. 'In an era when the leaders of the Irish Catholic Church, such as Cardinal Connell and Archbishop Brady, are effectively unknown in the US, Comiskey was very much the public face of the hierarchy.' After California he moved to Rome to study and he received a Licentiate in Theology. He returned to America to teach Moral

Theology at the Washington Theological Union and served as Chairman of the Moral Theology Department. He was elected Provincial of the Anglo-Irish province of the Congregation of the Sacred Hearts in 1969 and Secretary General of the Conference of the Major Religious Superiors in 1974.

Karol Wojtyła's election as Pope on 16 October 1978, making him the first non-Italian Pope since the Dutch Adrian VI (1522–23), was to have a seismic effect on Comiskey's career. During Pope John Paul II's visit to Ireland a year later, the new Pontiff referred to the absence of order priests among the Irish prelates (Comiskey, once bishop, was unusual in being a member of an order rather than diocesan). Whenever the next episcopal vacancy arose in Ireland, the Vatican suggested that it went to a member of an order. In January 1980, Comiskey was installed as an auxiliary bishop of Dublin under Archbishop Dermot Ryan in the country's second most powerful see, and was based in Bray. It was not long before the voluble Comiskey, a natural communicator with a neat turn of phrase, began to have his name suffixed as a go-between of the Church and the different governments that were in and out of office during his four-year tenure. The year 1980 began with his ordination as bishop at St Andrew's, Westland Row. At this time, as *The Murphy Report* made clear, Comiskey was among a group of archbishops in Dublin that was 'aware for many years of complaints and suspicions of clerical child sexual abuse in the Archdiocese'. The isolation of living in Bray coincided with his first serious bout of drinking.

His appointment as Bishop of Ferns in 1984 removed his slim chance of succeeding Archbishop of Dublin Dermot Ryan, who was promoted to a senior position in the Vatican. Ferns would have been an opportunity for Comiskey to groom himself for future promotion, and indeed his predecessor in Ferns had been on a terna (a shortlist of three candidates to succeed a bishop) as a likely successor to Archbishop John McQuaid. Having rubbed shoulders with Charles Haughey and broadcasters like Gay Byrne and Marian Finucane in the nation's capital, was it not galling for Comiskey to see his public profile as a commentator gradually diminish the farther south from Dublin he moved? He must have struggled for a bigger role whenever the nitty-gritty of parish-pump politics in Wexford could not satiate his intelligence, but he was never again an official spokesperson for the hierarchy.

Undaunted, he put his considerable academic intellect to a good and steady use, commentating on the affairs of the State at will, and stayed active within the Church outside the diocese: he was appointed Chairman of the Bishops' Commission for Communications, President of the Catholic Communications Institute of Ireland, a member of the Bishops' Commissions for Ecumenism and Education, was a founding member of the Irish Churches' Council for Television and Radio Affairs and was appointed chaplain to the International Council of the Alliance of Catholic Knights. As Auxiliary Bishop of Dublin, and from his home at Cluain Mhuire in Bray, County Wicklow, Comiskey became a regular contributor to *The Irish Catholic* and *The Furrow*, submitting essays throughout the 1980s and 1990s on all matters religious, and it is in the pages of *The Furrow* that we encounter the innate conservatism of a personality thought to be liberal in outlook. In 'The Church in the Eighties', he wrote that a legacy of the visit to Ireland of Pope John Paul II was 'a hunger for the holy' among the Irish; in a speech, 'Twenty Years with the Irish Media', which he originally delivered to the Religious Press Association of Ireland at All Hallows College, Dublin, in 1994 – the twentieth anniversary of his engagement with the media, a prelude to the battles that lay ahead – he described himself as an optimist without illusion; in 'The Media and the Churches', an address at St Anne's Cathedral in Belfast in 1984, he acknowledged that the Irish 'are far better at imputing culpability than we are at accepting responsibility', and, in his contribution to a series of articles about the priesthood at risk in *The Furrow*, Comiskey argued that integration and integrity are essential for the spiritual life of the modern priest.

Comiskey invested considerable effort and research into his many speeches, which could be brief (his homily at Knock in 1988 was of moderate length, a mere three pages) or protracted (an address to the Laurentian Society in 1986 was nine foolscap pages), but he had a gift for being argumentative without being disputatious, for drawing on both secular and religious sources at home and abroad to support a moral standpoint, and could empathise with the other side. The guiding principle in his life, his theological and philosophical *raison d'être*, which is manifest in speech after speech, and which must have served him well after standing down as Bishop of Ferns, is that the principal part of the pastoral response of the Church in modern life is evangelisation.

A flippant and cantankerous Comiskey, who found it easy to swallow the bait proffered by the media when it went looking to the hierarchy for a sound bite, is absent from the scholar of theology and philosophy, the learned sage who was able to namecheck John H. White, Dr Dermot Keogh, John Courtney Murray, Cardinal Joseph Bernardin, John O'Connor, Congressman Robert Drinan, Richard John Neuhaus, Mandred Vogel, Clyde Manschreck, Garret FitzGerald, Bishop Donal Murray, Deputy John Kelly, Martin Luther King, Lord Devlin and Edmund Burke in a single speech, as he did in November 1986, on the vexatious subject of the Church and State, in which he both began and ended with a lengthy quotation, neither of which was his, which intimates that Comiskey was more comfortable paraphrasing people he admired. Nor was his derivative didacticism reserved for the great and the good in Dublin and Belfast, and he was more than willing to share his musings with the laity in Wexford: 'The Future of Work' given in Seán Fortune's parish, Fethard-on-Sea, in 1987, lasted fifteen minutes, and his speech launching a booklet, *Supporting the Family*, in Wexford a year later, spanned five pages.

Whereas he owed his ubiquity in the press during the 1980s to his cogitations on the spats between Church and State, during which he had a walk-on role, the 1990s proved more pugilistic, with Comiskey hounded by a truculent media, which was less reverential after the Eamon Casey affair. All aspects of Comiskey's private life – his drinking, his travelling, his socialising – became fair game until, spirit broken, he found refuge in exile, only to return triumphantly to the scene of his installation as Bishop of Ferns – Enniscorthy cathedral. His profile is inseparable from the landslide that was *The Ferns Report* but it was not, naturally, always so. And when you consider the many times he was cross-examined by the media, especially at an unprecedented press conference at St Peter's College after he returned from America, you can admire how he could summon, even with the briefest of smiles, the bellicose natural defence of a sandstone cliff jutting into hostile waves.

But the demarcation between tragedy and farce was sand shifting in an hour glass, and forces outside his control, such as the endgame being played out by Gardaí and Seán Fortune, would hasten the end of his tenure in Ferns. His residency as suffragan bishop began with the mixture of illumination and shadow that was to characterise his next ten years in Ferns: he was the beneficiary of the Freedom of the Borough of Wexford, following in the footsteps of Charles Stewart Parnell and Comiskey's hero, President John F. Kennedy. (After Kennedy's assassination in 1963, many of Comiskey's friends contacted him to console him, so aware were they of his affection for the late President. 'To me he is quite special. His charisma and the magnetism of his personality, his communication skills and of course his Irish connection,' recalled the bishop thirty years later.)

One of the few people not surprised by *The Irish Times'* revelation in 1992 that Bishop Casey had fathered a child, Peter, with Annie Murphy, eighteen years earlier, was his close friend, the Bishop of Ferns. Comiskey was one of a small circle within the Church whom Casey contacted about his love child. Comiskey was amazed and quite shocked by the disclosure, and it took some time for it to sink in before he could give the 65-year-old Casey what he was seeking, advice about resigning. Since January that year *The Irish Times* had been investigating Murphy's claims that Casey had been her lover, and though Casey eventually resigned in May, he had tipped off Comiskey in early April during Holy Week. Whatever transpired in the conversation between the two prelates, bearing in mind that Comiskey was still trying to cope with Casey's bombshell, the Bishop of Kerry had decided by Easter Sunday that resignation was the only course of action open to him.

The Church in Ireland, bloodied and bowed, had little time to recover from the scandal of Casey, banished to Ecuador, when another Dublin publication, *The Phoenix*, revealed that Casey's brother in arms when Pope John Paul II visited Galway, the late Fr Michael Cleary, the singing priest and the most vocal of his tribe to oppose contraception, had fathered a child with his housekeeper and lover, Phyllis Hamilton. 'The fundamental moral contradiction embodied by the Casey and Cleary affairs left many in Irish congregations questioning for the first time the gap between preaching and practice,' wrote Robert Savage and James Smith in *Sexual Abuse and the Irish Church: Crisis and Responses*.

These two events rocked the Catholic Church to the core and, in the words of the former editor of *The Irish Times* Conor Brady, 'shook the confidence and belief of a traditionally loyal flock', which resulted in a dissipation of the hierarchy's power. Casey's love child and Michael Cleary's secret family gave the national media a licence to pursue the merest hint of scandal, and the Bishop of Ferns had enough smoke about him to warrant a firestorm of interest. 'I had the overwhelming sense of the Church as an authority institution that was unable to square up to awkward facts even when they were staring it in the face. Inevitably, that put it on a collision course with the news media,' reflected Brady.

In March 1995, Comiskey was interviewed by a reporter for *The Wexford Echo* and a future RTÉ correspondent, Aoife Kavanagh, for a weekly series, *Public Face . . . Private Life*. In the course of the interview, in which the bishop professed to be irritated by 'woolliness or floundering around' in lively debates, he was questioned about celibacy, which he had raised three years earlier in *The Irish Press*. 'The loneliness of celibacy is sometimes almost unbearable. I know everybody feels lonely every now and then, but this life can be particularly so. I do love the life, and love the Church which gives me great freedom, but the loneliness is hard.' When the interview was published, the comments did not generate any extraordinary publicity and, emboldened thus, Comiskey in the months ahead would be audacious on the subject of celibacy, calling for a debate on its future in the *Sunday Tribune* in June, overnight injecting an unprecedented note of subversion that would overshadow the celebration of Maynooth's bicentenary. He would have read in an American Church journal, *The National Catholic Reporter*, that forty bishops there had urged a debate on many issues, including contraception and celibacy. It was no secret in Wexford that Comiskey found women fascinating. 'I'm

181

unashamed of it and I refuse to be parted from the other half of the human race. I never made any vow or promise not to spend time enjoying the company of women and men.'

It is unlikely that he anticipated the furore which his reflections in the *Tribune* unleashed, or the wallop he would receive from another bishop's crozier. In the eyes of the media, 1995 was the Catholic Church's summer of discontent, made glorious by a bishop's solo run, buoyed by the support he received from almost all of his clergy in Wexford. 'I consider it a very important function of my teaching office as bishop to listen to the experience of our priests and people. My listening tells me that our priests are greatly distressed, and in some instances demoralised, by a series of sexual scandals involving the clergy and by the legitimate, if extremely painful, questions coming from a confused and bewildered laity,' said Comiskey. He denied that he was attacking celibacy or celibate priesthood, but that as issues relevant to the future of the Church, they should be carefully studied on an ongoing basis. His call may have been motivated by other issues closer to home: the premature deaths of two colleagues, which Comiskey believed were hastened by the Church being overwhelmed by paedophilia scandals, such as the conviction that year of Fr Brendan Smyth, and the priestless parishes that he would have come across in America (vocations in Ireland had fallen by 85 per cent since the mid-1960s).

Reason is the slave of emotion, and there is little doubt that at this juncture in his life, Comiskey was experiencing frustration, not helped by the realisation that he would never become Bishop of Dublin or Armagh. He felt isolated within the hierarchy without the close and convivial friendship of Casey and Ó Fiaich. His remoteness from his fellow bishops was to be exacerbated that summer, once an internecine squabble between him and Cardinal Daly was played out in the media, who were ever happy to provide a platform for warring prelates, as two bishops putting on the boxing gloves had not been seen since Cardinal Cullen and Archbishop McHale fell out over nationalism in the mid-nineteenth century. Comiskey's epistolary record up until 1995 did not point to a man capable of flirting with pluralism or of becoming a firebrand for reform, but he was flirting with danger on two accounts: he stood accused of being openly critical of Pope John Paul II and he may have, unintentionally, established a link between celibacy and child abuse. 'Vatican officials could not think of a senior bishop in any country who had taken such a public stance in favour of discussing celibacy in the face of the Pope's repeated statements that the debate in the Church on the issue was closed,' observed Andy Pollock of *The Irish Times*.

Comiskey appeared to enjoy the developing spat, which spawned a feast of opinion columns where it mattered most to him – Dublin – and he backed his call for ongoing perusal of priestly celibacy arising from his argument that where there is no priest, there is no Eucharist, and where there is no Eucharist, there is no Church. By mid-July, the Vatican had heard enough, and summoned the free-spirited bishop to Rome for what observers assumed would be a mauling by Cardinal Bernardin Gantin, prefect of the Congregation of Bishops, who had written to Comiskey asking him to 'correct his erroneous views'.

Comiskey and his advisers (diocesan spokesperson Fr Walter Forde believed celibacy ought to be a voluntary option) considered their next move. In a disjointed newspaper interview, he defied the Church's age-worn tradition in its dealings with the Irish media, where it preferred to co-exist with suppression of information, not spillage. The welling-up of frustration in a bruised Comiskey resulted in an explosion of petulant anger and exaggerated hurt, and his only target, much to the amusement of atheists and agnostics, was the Catholic Church. He accused Cardinal Daly – who had publicly rebuked Comiskey at Knock – of being behind the summons to Rome; he implicated the Papal Nuncio in Daly's plot; he likened the hierarchy to the three monkeys who see no evil, hear no evil and speak no evil; he said Daly had no jurisdiction over the Diocese of Ferns; he alleged that Daly was misrepresenting what he said about celibacy and he said Daly was the cause of the controversy that had tongues wagging from Dublin to Rome. (The Catholic Press and Information Office, in a terse statement, confirmed that (a) Daly did not confer with the Papal Nuncio about Comiskey and (b) Daly made no request to Rome. Daly had said that Comiskey's views were personal but did not have the weight of his office.)

Abruptly, after the mildly incoherent and strongly incongruous interview, an overwrought Comiskey hightailed it to a hotel in Kenmare owned by a friend, leaving his disciples in Wexford to throw jaundiced titbits to a scavenging media. Slowly but surely, however, the accusations against Cardinal Daly began to unravel: Daly said he did not report Comiskey to Rome nor did he misquote what Comiskey said about celibacy. While Comiskey was publicly admonishing the hierarchy for not doing enough to deal with clerical abuse scandals, he could not escape the insuperable management problems of his own: he had recently presided over the egregiously pretentious funeral of Canon Martin Clancy, whom he suspected of interfering with young girls; he had sent Fr Donal Collins to the Granada Centre for treatment after he admitted indiscretions with teenagers; he had been informed by Daly (of all people) of an allegation of abuse against Monsignor Micheal Ledwith; Fr James Doyle, who had been shipped by Comiskey to England after abusing a boy, was back in Ireland; and the interminable concern over Fr Seán

Fortune, who was given administrative leave by his bishop in March, was becoming intolerable. Comiskey's strident call for a debate on celibacy, and his willingness to be a rebel prelate with a cause, had the desired effect of becalming the circling sharks in the media, but only briefly. Nor were his priests all singing from the same hymn sheet. Comiskey was admonished by Fr Thaddeus Doyle in *The Curate's Diary*. 'We should also be slow to accuse someone unless we have proof that our accusation is well founded. And if we publicly accuse someone in the wrong, we should apologise. The accusation was that the cardinal was responsible for the intervention by Rome. He denies this. I believe him. Bishop Comiskey further accuses the cardinal of starting all this by attacking him. Well, he didn't start all this nor indeed was his treatment of Bishop Comiskey any harsher than Bishop Comiskey's treatment of a lay person who wrote in to *Sounding Out* supporting celibacy.'

Doyle was precipitous in advising Comiskey to attend to more pressing concerns, such as the danger of a division in the diocese. But Comiskey could not, because he was playing truant in Kerry and was incommunicado, occasionally firing a missive from the Kingdom from his bracken-clad bunker, via Walter Forde. One statement, on 9 August 1995, in response to a request for an interview from fifty media organisations, began with the no longer omnipresent bishop observing that 'I have said what I wished to say, no more, no less,' before clarifying his position in a 1,000-word rambling commentary.

Throughout August the Church kept its counsel in the expectation that common sense within the family would prevail: it did not. Comiskey, who had apparently mended fences with Daly in a telephone conversation and had attended a dinner hosted by several bishops in Clonmel, was scheduled to address the Humbert Summer School in Ballina on 28 August and, clearly angry and upset, he let fly, but the cardinal was not his target. Accepting that the Pope was not interested in summoning him to Rome in the immediate future (though Comiskey later met Cardinal Gantin in the Vatican for a cordial exchange of views) or in requesting his resignation, which took the sting out of the bishop's invective, Comiskey felt that he had been humiliated by the Church's unfair treatment of him and, looking to the near future, addressed two issues on the horizon, child abuse and the upcoming divorce referendum. On the latter, he predicted that the government would be defeated in November – he was wrong, though Wexford voted no – and on the former, he said bishops were being judged by the standards of the 1990s on events that occurred in the 1980s. 'No lawyer or psychologist we consulted at the time told us to "go and report that".'

But when Comiskey was asked three times in 1995 by the Gardaí to give a statement about Seán Fortune, he declined. Comiskey, though in all likelihood stressed, was in good enough health to contemplate leading the Irish national pilgrimage to Lisieux in France in late September, but a sabbatical, and not a pilgrimage, was foremost in his mind when he suddenly disappeared from the diocese. He had served fifteen years as Bishop of Ferns and diocesan policy was that the prelate should take a three-month break every ten years. The bureaucracy of diocesan business, which he disliked, would have drained him further. That Comiskey, now sixty, was due a rest was not begrudged but the manner of his departure was. It had not been flagged and neither the clergy nor the laity had any inkling that he was going.

On 17 September the diocese released a statement at Sunday Masses explaining for the first time Comiskey's decision to take a three-month sabbatical, with immediate effect, to America. 'The purpose of a sabbatical is one's personal and professional growth and renewal through study, work, prayer and rest,' he said. Inexplicably, he added that he had been contemplating and planning the break 'for some time', which begs the question why he had publicly committed himself to the onerous task of leading the pilgrimage to Lisieux.

Comiskey's flight, surreptitiously quick though sanctioned by the Papel envoy Archbishop Jorge Mejia, and apparently on medical advice from a consultant physician at Wexford General Hospital, made himself and the diocese open season for the media, which descended upon Wexford town like Byron's Assyrian on the fold: in the absence of any meaningful explanation from the bishop and his advisers, who had spent the summer sermonising on the rights and wrongs of the modern Church, journalists foraged on every scrap of information and gossip they could glean. Monsignor Richard Breen was left in charge of administering the diocese until Christmas but, at seventy-five, he was no media virtuoso. Comiskey's wooing of journalists in his deadly summer had been long, but in his absence their disposal of him was swift and ruthless. Matters deteriorated when word slipped out that the bishop had fled to Rochester, Minnesota, to receive treatment for alcoholism (Comiskey had often looked to America for spiritual renewal, going on retreat at St Benedict's Monastery at Snowmass in Colorado, where four hours of silent meditation was common) though newspaper reports suggested that he had skipped town to avoid having to deal publicly with an insurmountable clerical abuse problem on his doorstep. The besieged diocese had to do something to control the conflagration, and issued a statement two weeks after his departure confirming that not alone was the bishop receiving treatment for his alcoholism, but had done so before. Comiskey's benders, which seriously affected his health in 1994–1995, divided episodes of tremendous creativity and prolonged depression.

'We would like to point out that it was the bishop's own

decision to go and that he had personally made contact with a clinic in the USA and that a few days prior to his departure from Ireland, he arranged for himself to be admitted at a later date. This was not a sudden decision and had been given careful thought and preparation,' explained Forde. By then, the floodgates were open, and Comiskey's personal lifestyle – his trips to Thailand, his ownership of property, his love of female companionship, his friendship with priests under investigation – was flavour of the month in the tabloids, relying on an intravenous drip of information from sources, not always verifiable or reliable, from the Diocese of Ferns.

Help for the embattled bishop was at hand, but from the unlikeliest of quarters – Wexford's most senior politicians, including its Oireachtas members. Sparked by comments in *The Irish Times* by Fintan O'Toole ('nobody deserves the kind of assassination by innuendo that Brendan Comiskey's reputation has undergone') and Andy Pollock ('Bishop Comiskey is 3,000 miles away, somewhere in the US, trying to get over a near nervous breakdown and a serious alcohol dependency'), a pamphlet, *Natural Justice*, was published by the Chairman of Wexford County Council, Rory Murphy, and distributed throughout the county. 'May we suggest that natural justice demands that we defer judgement on this man until he is well and back in our midst. Until then, perhaps those who have experienced this goodness would speak well of him,' said Murphy. The move was a personal initiative by Murphy, a former Fianna Fáil general election candidate, and did not have the official imprimatur of the County Council, but the 'we' in his missive was signed by Ivan Yates, Brendan Howlin, Avril Doyle, John Browne, all deputies, and Senator Michael D'Arcy. It was a peculiar intervention because the admonition to the media was to back off. Three of the signatories – Howlin, Yates and Doyle – were ministers in the Rainbow Coalition government that had assumed office a year earlier. Yates was Minister for Agriculture, Doyle was a Minister of State and Howlin was Minister for Health, the department which, under his successor Micheál Martin, would commission a preliminary report into clerical abuse in Ferns in 2002. But probing Comiskey in the autumn of 1995 was furthest from the minds of the three ministers: 'I am happy to reaffirm my personal support and encouragement for Bishop Brendan Comiskey in the context of his very fine qualities as a person and as a bishop, not least because of his role in promoting ecumenism within the Diocese of Ferns,' said Yates.

If Howlin was more circumspect ('reports of many kinds abound in public life, and it is a basic right for every individual to have the opportunity to vindicate his or her good name. No less than anyone else, Bishop Comiskey deserves that right.'), Doyle was less so, remarking that Comiskey's 'frank and informal statements on matters of public morality or social need and his ability to communicate to his people make him a great Christian teacher.' Senator D'Arcy from Gorey offered his 'fullest support to Bishop Comiskey and I have absolute confidence in his ability to lead the Catholic Church in Ferns for many years to come'. Writing in the November edition of the *Ferns Diocesan Bulletin*, Professor Mary McAleese, a friend of the bishop's (who had visited St Peter's before she became President of Ireland), asserted that keeping faith with the Church when its skeletons are falling out of closets is not easy and certainly not comfortable. 'Much easier to be on the outside with the rabble throwing brickbats just like Peter.'

The problem for the laity and the 'rabble' in the diocese was that the 'great Christian teacher' had left the classroom and had not been replaced. 'The media coverage that followed his leaving took the clergy by surprise and they were completely ill equipped to deal with it,' reflected *The Ferns Report*. Coinciding with the publication of the endorsement of Comiskey by Wexford's three government ministers, an arrest warrant was issued for Seán Fortune after the DPP had directed prosecution in relation to multiple abuse of eight victims. Donal Collins was charged with sexual assault in December and remanded on bail by Wexford District Court. Comiskey had already been interviewed by Gardaí about Collins earlier in the year. 'High minded commentators have attacked their colleagues in journalism for indulging in an orgy of speculation and innuendo regarding bishops who go away with no word of farewell, leaving not a trace left behind,' wrote Declan Lynch in the *Sunday Independent*. 'Of Comiskey, they say that they should have loved him better, didn't mean to be unkind. You know that was the last thing on their minds. Yet speculation is a very natural response to Church statements which have something of a game show quality themselves. Do you open the box, or take the money?'

Espousal of the bishop's Christian calibre was not confined to politicians from across the political divide in Wexford. Canon Nigel Waugh, rector of Bunclody, suspected that many would be delighted if Comiskey stumbled. 'I do not know if Bishop Comiskey will be back at Christmas. I hope he will and that he will stand up to all the begrudgers, rumour mongers and reactionaries. But if he is gone forever, it will be a long time before we in the Church of Ireland see his like again.' The bishop was not gone forever but he would not be back, as promised, by Christmas.

In sync with the probable state of affairs behind the scenes in Wexford was Gay Byrne, who had known Comiskey since the 1980s. On his morning RTÉ radio programme, he aired the view that he did not believe that Comiskey had gone to America because of stress or a dependency on alcohol. 'I think there is something other. I haven't the faintest idea what it is, but I think there is something else, and I think it is something dreadful, and I'm almost afraid of what it might be. That's my personal reaction.' A lone voice among the clergy in Wexford was, yet again, Fr Thaddeus Doyle. 'It's not a time for evasions nor for glossing things over with religious clichés. Personal responsibility will need to be taken for the hurt and damage that has been caused, and the making good of that damage must be seen as an overriding priority.'

Comiskey himself put an end to speculation about his return when he sent private letters to the clergy in the diocese on 12 February 1996, apologising that his sudden departure had upset so many priests but, because of media interest, he was reluctant to be more specific. 'I can see clearly now that, in addition to acting upon my doctor's advice, I found it quite impossible to admit publicly to my alcoholism prior to treatment.' His apologia was not the wholehearted *mea culpa* that his clergy deserved, but that would have to wait. This was the bishop corresponding as paterfamilias. 'I am only too aware of the stress that the media coverage has caused you and will continue to do so for a while. It has been a period of great suffering for all of us.' His convalescence was over.

The latest instalment in the dramatic life and times of Ireland's most colourful bishop was choreographed to give him as warm a homecoming as possible in the diocese, and St Aidan's Cathedral in Enniscorthy, a town with demonstrably more fidelity to the Church and its troubled bishop of late than Wexford, did not disappoint. Comiskey's reappearance at evening Mass on 17 February was not intended to be a secret; in the attendance was a large scattering of journalists, fidgeting uncomfortably and awkwardly among the faithful with notebooks and pens drawn, photographers, television cameras, friends, family members and representatives of the other Churches, including the Church of Ireland Bishop of

Cashel and Ossory, Noel Willoughby. Several outbursts of applause from the congregation during Comiskey's scripted homily, but from which he often wandered, helped dissipate whatever apprehension he may have harboured. Buoyed by the benevolence from sections of the congregation, he addressed some of the more pressing issues off the cuff: his treatment in America had not cost the diocese £8,000 a month; he had never considered not returning to the diocese and he had never put at risk a child's safety to protect a priest. To the assembled Fourth Estate, he had this warning: the callousness of allegations in the media overrode all journalistic confidentiality and he intended to hear the bearers of the allegations repeat them under oath. 'The sound-bite-conscious prelate's use of symbolism was masterly,' observed John Cooney, biographer of Archbishop McQuaid. 'Several times the Bishop beat his breast, with a contrite admission that he had made mistakes in his handling of child abuse allegations against priests.'

A day later, Temperance Sunday, the bishop took his message to Wexford's Rowe Street Church for 12.30 Mass, but the tidal wave of goodwill in Enniscorthy had been reduced to a trickle of isolated well-wishers, and his shortened homily received a polite applause. 'We had very little in Tasson, where we were brought up, but we had our good name. Where do I go to get that back?' he asked. The answer was in a response his friends and confidants were putting together to answer his critics, including devout Catholic and solicitor Noel Smyth, whose estimated wealth at the time was in excess of £10 million, and PR consultant Barbara Wallace, the former chairperson of Wexford Festival Opera, whose clients included Wexford County Council and the South Eastern Health Board, and who had been critical of aspects of the press coverage of the conviction of Fr James Doyle in 1990.

Comiskey's team knew it had to act quickly, and it did: a press conference by the bishop was scheduled for St Peter's College on 28 February, just ten days after his return, all the better to harness the goodwill that was much in evidence in Enniscorthy. In the interim, commentators, never in short supply in Ireland, responded to the bishop's return, but the positive far outweighed the negative. 'Everyone who wants to see this whole situation cleared up quickly will wish the bishop well as he makes his return,' commented an editorial in the *Irish Independent*. In an open letter in the *Sunday World*, Fr Brian D'Arcy wrote: 'Bishop Comiskey made mistakes, the same as each and every person reading this. And the same as the guy who's writing it. Brendan admitted his mistakes in a moving homily last Sunday.' Days before the press conference, the bishop met with a delegation from the Council of Priests, promising to deal systematically with every allegation made while he was out of the country, and he attended his first AA meeting in Wexford.

The much anticipated showdown began when Comiskey's thirteen-page statement was handed out to the large media pool, which took thirty minutes to digest the contents, divided into three sections: an overview of the allegations, diocesan finances and child sex abuse. Comiskey cut an isolated figure walking on the lawn – hands behind his back – under a clear blue sky, as reporters hunched over his statement and rummaged through the entrails of the most chewed-over life in the country.

The day had started ominously for the media when a section of local and national reporters, including Veronica Guerin, had an early breakfast meeting in a Wexford hotel to organise the grilling of the bishop: the plan to spread questions among the journalists did not translate to St Peter's, however, because others, like Vincent Browne, who were not at the rendezvous and therefore not party to any agreement, quizzed

Comiskey as they saw fit. After the press conference, the bishop's team was visibly delighted at how Comiskey, contra mundum, had equipped himself. At one level, his explanations were articulate, bullish and extensive. Not a single journalist managed to land a blow and his performance, boosted by his exposure of the many inaccuracies published about him in the tabloids, was such that Michael Foley in *The Irish Times*, comparing the encounter to a football match, put the score at Bishop Comiskey 3, the media 1.

To counter criticism in the media in the preceding days that the meeting was finely tuned by professional public relations experts, Fr Peter O'Connor stepped forward to chair his first ever press conference. The bishop, who sat vulnerably on his own at a table and invited questions on any topic, played the proverbial blinder, and his accessibility caught those journalists who feared he would issue a terse statement and leave, completely off guard. He had come to run the gauntlet on his own and when it was over two hours later, he walked away the happier of the two camps. In the process, he addressed those issues that had been the fodder of excessive coverage in both the tabloids and broadsheets. Comiskey had never obstructed any Garda or Health Board investigation into child sex abuse; he had never refused to be interviewed by Gardaí; he had never misappropriated diocesan funds; he had never been treated in the Hazelden centre in Florida (as alleged in a front-page scoop in the *Sunday Independent*); he had never been arrested or jailed in his life and he had never paid for a first class airline ticket.

'A pretty horrific list of things, all of which I have been accused of, every one of which is simply untrue,' explained an exasperated Comiskey. But in his heart the bishop must have realised that his record on child sex abuse in the diocese was poor. He stressed that he had never obstructed any

Garda investigation, but *The Ferns Report* showed that he was requested by the Gardaí to give a statement on three occasions during their investigation of Seán Fortune, and he declined. His cooperation had limitations. He began his defence of the clerical abuse allegations by insisting that 'there has never been a single case of child abuse in this diocese which has been brought to my attention which I have failed to act upon.' Comiskey's definition of action was to encourage priests under suspicion in his diocese to move abroad (James Doyle), get treatment (Donal Collins), take a holiday (James Grennan) or go to another parish (Seán Fortune and Martin Clancy).

'I never ignored an accusation,' he said, but in the Monageer case, he did not lift a finger. On reflection, his press conference was replete with explanations but not motivation: what did he like about Thailand to warrant repeat visits? Ought a bishop, with a thickening dossier on abusive priests, be so keen to return to a country synonymous with the sex trade? 'The bishop had to face the dens of Bangkok and the meadows of Monageer. Maybe the two should be twinned,' quipped columnist Nicky Furlong. He was, admittedly, not alone among Irish bishops with a need to exoticise themselves occasionally. Comiskey was criticised for his handling of abuse cases in *The Ferns Report*, published almost a decade after the famous press conference at St Peter's. Knowing what we know now, his performance was akin to a whirlpool, where facts and fiction collided in the shadow of semi-disclosures and half-truths. It was window dressing at its most professional. He bridled at the sloppy reporting by some journalists, and rightly so, but his verbose staccato of excuse after excuse was negated by himself years later when he resigned: he could not control Seán Fortune who wrecked countless numbers of young lives. On paper, his defence of his record in Ferns in 1996 is impressive, but excusable circumstances abound ('It took all of us to arrive at today's guidelines') and his pretence at having done all he could ('I have never ever tried to sweep under the carpet any child sex abuse allegation') is paper thin.

He began the press conference by reiterating that he had always called for a more open Church, but not once did he mention, amid the plethora of figures he quoted during his probe of diocesan finances, how the Church had taken out a policy to insure itself against abuse claims. What *The Murphy Report* revealed in 2009 is that Comiskey was not dissimilar to any other prelate in the Dublin archdiocese: canon law may have proved improvident for the moral welfare of bishops with dark secrets to keep, but their failure to act to protect children arose from an indentured servitude to the Catholic Church.

In the years following his return to the diocese, Comiskey maintained a low profile, only rarely, but to good effect, putting his head above the parapet: in June 1998, the bicentenary in Wexford of the 1798 insurrection, Comiskey apologised for the Catholic boycott of Protestant firms in Fethard-on-Sea in 1957, organised by a priest and supported by local clergy. His apology was, in great part, personal. 'When I most needed support, no one of any religious persuasion was more generous and forthcoming than members of the Church of Ireland in this diocese, people like Ivan Yates, Bishops Noel Willoughby and John Neill, the Rev. Nigel Waugh and so many others, clergy and laity.' Two months later, Norman Ruddock, Chancellor of Ferns, publicly nominated Comiskey as the most important Irish Churchman of the twentieth century. 'At our Ferns Diocesan Synod he came as an invited guest and said: "I am an alcoholic". A numinous spirit descended on the gathering that I had never experienced before,' recalled Ruddock. Comiskey and Bishop Willoughby had instigated an ecumenical committee to examine the issue of mixed marriage in Ferns years earlier, producing a report that broke new ground in the relationship between the two Churches. Comiskey's generosity to the other Churches in his diocese and empathy for ecumenism was noted by Canon Waugh in 1995: 'In the difficult area of inter-Church marriages, it is not uncommon for a couple to be left waiting until the day of the wedding itself for a dispensation to marry. Occasionally documents get lost and must be reapplied for. Sometimes there is a worry as to whether or not a Roman Catholic priest will be present in a Church of Ireland church to give the marriage canonical form. But these problems do not occur in the Diocese of Ferns, where the bride is married in her church, regardless of denomination, and the wedding proceeds without administrative hitches.'

After the advent of local radio, Comiskey was instrumental in establishing Christian Media Trust, which produced religious programmes for South East Radio in Wexford, and offered seats on the Board of Directors to representatives of other denominations. 'The Church of Ireland and Methodist Churches were not in a position to fund any of the considerable costs involved, nor were they asked to,' added Waugh. Between 1998 and 2001, the bishop suffered the bereavement of four brothers – Edmund, Kevin, Sean and Joe – heartbreak for a man who was extremely close to his immediate family, a sequence of tragic personal events he never referred to publicly.

Comiskey's other successes before his world imploded included his pivotal role in bringing the relics of St Thérèse of Lisieux to Ireland, which were seen by 75,000 in the diocese alone, in April 2001, followed a few months later by a well-received address to the Humbert School in Castlebar. The diocese, on the surface, was in rude health: Ferns had 144 diocesan priests in 2001, compared to 138 in 1951. 'Those who speak of a crisis of vocations to the priesthood in the diocese are not only ungrateful to God for the many priests he had given us, they are also not too good at their sums,' boasted Comiskey, who had clearly forgotten a statement he had published in *The Forum* three years earlier: 'I have one very serious concern I wish to share with you in this letter. I do so, not out of an alarmist sense but out of a desire to tell the truth to the people of this diocese while there is still time to do something about it. The truth is that, unless the trend of vocations in the priesthood is reversed in this diocese, our parishes will be served by fewer and fewer priests.'

The opening scenes of the BBC documentary *Suing the Pope*, which was first broadcast on 19 March 2002, evolves as follows:

> Irish Catholic priest, Father Seán Fortune was a bullying, serial paedophile who preyed on young boys . . . His boss, Bishop Brendan Comiskey, knew children were at risk but failed to protect them . . . These men have been denied justice . . . (Sarah MacDonald confronts Comiskey outside Rowe Street Church) . . .
>
> 'I just wanted to know why didn't you stop Seán Fortune,' she asks . . . 'I'm going to have Mass at half past six. I, I, I . . .' he replies . . . she continues . . . 'abusing young boys?'
>
> Bishop Comiskey won't give them answers. Now they're suing the Pope.

The screening of *Suing the Pope* on BBC2, and again on 2 April on RTÉ, after a special edition of the current affairs programme *Prime Time*, is the defining moment in the relationship between the diocese and the laity, the bishop and the laity and between Church and State. If it can be said that a single cathartic incident prompted the State inquiry into diocesan handling of abusive clergy that was to follow, it was the broadcasting of

Suing the Pope, which could not be observed with the mindless passivity that had so long persisted among the Catholic faithful in Wexford. Patsy McGarry, reviewing it in *The Irish Times*, was in no doubt. 'Printed words cannot compete with the impact of victims on camera. Years of excellent investigative print journalism on paedophile priests in Ferns was unable to achieve the same impact as 50 minutes of victims and their families telling their stories to camera.'

With Fortune out of the picture permanently, the shackles came off. Angriest among the victims was Colm O'Gorman, who was serially raped by Fortune and who was later to become a household name as an articulate and brave spokesperson for abuse victims. His words, rooted in decades of pain, had a searing intensity. 'And you have, frankly, bastards like Brendan Comiskey, hiding in his nice palace in Summerhill, behind his alcoholism and his regret and his, you know, his inability to understand or to do anything about it. It's not good enough; it's not good enough. It's not good enough any more. People have died. People are dying. People are hurting.'

In chilling detail, Pat Jackman recalled Fortune's abuse of him. O'Gorman and Jackman belonged to highly respected Wexford families: O'Gorman's father was an elected councillor who once ran for the Dáil, and Jackman's father was a successful businessman and a loyal servant of the Church. When both young men spoke of being assaulted and raped by a man of the cloth on national television, the blinkers were removed from a community that had refused to assimilate the full horror and terror of sexual abuse. Their accounts were graphic and harrowing. The rape portrayed was far removed from the docility of a red-faced priest rubbing up against a student during a woodwork class. Unfortunately for Comiskey, his impromptu rendition of Gloria Gaynor's 'I Will Survive', as Sarah MacDonald asked him why he had done so little to protect Fortune's victims, condemned him in the eyes of many as having little empathy for O'Gorman, Jackman and the other young victims. It also indicated that he was now out of touch with his brief, whatever that was. He might, looking back, have been wiser to have sung 'What a Difference a Day Makes' because *Suing the Pope* began the countdown to his resignation as Bishop of Ferns.

According to Norman Ruddock in *The Rambling Rector*, the bishop's senior clergy made it clear that he would have to resign.'He had rocked the boat and caused them embarrassment,' added Ruddock. 'They gave him little loyalty. The knives were out. He was never happy among the conservative phalanx in his diocese, and always seemed drawn to the younger priests with new ideas and fresh thinking.' Comiskey had a sharp sense of audience, as media interlocutors tend to, and he sensed the disavowals even among those who had stood by him in the past.

After fifty minutes of compelling though shocking viewing, the scales fell from the eyes of ordinary Catholics throughout Wexford. The local Rape and Sexual Abuse Services Centre was inundated with calls from the public: almost 200 in a 48-hour period. 'In the past there have been situations where communities have not been sensitive,' said Yvonne Pim, director of services.'They just could not believe that these things could happen. All these revelations will give a greater sense of understanding.'

A survey carried out by *The Wexford Echo* a week later found that 62 per cent of participants polled wanted the bishop to resign and 92 per cent believed the bishop had not done enough to remove Fortune from the diocese. The poll was published on 27 March, Comiskey tendered his resignation to Pope John Paul II the next day and, after spending the Easter weekend behind closed doors, he resigned on 1 April. Comiskey had lasted fifteen days since the broadcast of *Suing the Pope*, which was repeated by RTÉ a day after he stood down. Coincidentally, and entirely fortuitously, the Catholic hierarchy had commissioned an independent research agency to examine the effects on the public of child sex abuse by priests, and was halfway through its data collection period when *Suing the Pope* was first broadcast. The agency (the Health Services Research Centre at the Department of Psychology, Royal College of Surgeons in Ireland) was ideally placed to gauge an instant public reaction to the programme, and their findings were illuminating.

'Post-screening participants were less likely to be satisfied with the Church and with priests, less likely to trust the Church to take care of its own problems, less likely to look to priests for moral leadership, less likely to believe the Church would safeguard children entrusted to its care, less likely to accept abuser priests to work in their communities under supervision and less likely to see the Church's response as adequate.'

When details of the survey were made public in November 2002, three in four people felt that the Church's response to the abuse of children by its clergy was inadequate, and less than half believed the Church could safeguard children entrusted to its care.

After *Suing the Pope* the diocese began a rearguard action of sorts, publicising the contents of a reply by Comiskey in February to an invitation by the BBC to participate in the documentary, a last-ditch effort at damage limitation: 'I have found that my engaging with this issue in the media has been too often misrepresented as arguing in public against the survivors and as refusing to acknowledge and apologise for the great damage that has been done to vulnerable children. This, I think, has brought more hurt than healing.' But the genie was out of the bottle. He had refused to take part. His statement was issued by the diocese's new Director of Communications, Fr John Carroll, who added: 'it is to be regretted that Ms MacDonald chose to ignore this statement.' Bizarrely, though there is no accounting for the logic that emanated from the court of Comiskey, the bishop felt himself permitted to write to the four abuse victims in *Suing the Pope* once they had gone public. 'This is a course of action which the Bishop has – to date – not felt free to take lest it be misinterpreted as seeking to dissuade them from the legal route to justice, which is their natural right,' added Carroll.

The mind boggles. It was as if Comiskey and Carroll could not quite register the rancour. *Suing the Pope* and Comiskey's refusal to accept an invitation from the BBC to counter the criticism of his inaction proved a public relations disaster for him. (The faux pas was not repeated when Sarah MacDonald did a follow-up documentary to *Suing the Pope*, which was broadcast in February 2003. Eamonn Walsh consented to a short interview. In reply to her suggestion that the Church was not accepting liability for the damage done, Walsh said: 'There will be compensation. We don't have a bottomless pit but we will do what we can with the resources that we have and that's what I communicate.) *Suing the Pope* was not without a silver lining for Comiskey. He took his cue from the demonisation of Fortune, and when he read out his resignation statement shortly after noon on Easter Monday, 1 April appropriately, he blamed most of his troubles on Fortune, whom he scapegoated as 'virtually impossible to deal with'. The bishop had spent the morning among advisers and friends, many of them in tears, a scene described by Rev. Norman Ruddock as akin to 'a long wake'. The media waited in a loose knot until Comiskey emerged from his house: if he looked up he would have picked out the high tower of St Peter's College. Behind him gathered a rookery of acquaintances: the vicar general of the diocese, the local rector of the Church of Ireland, Rev. Ruddock, his personal doctor and, by his right shoulder, the Ferns diocesan press secretary, Fr Carroll, suitably grim, and the man who would succeed him as Bishop of Ferns, Denis Brennan.

His seventeen-paragraph statement, in which he ascribed his downfall in part on the 'very grave wrongs' of Fortune, was read succinctly; he declined to answer any questions and hastened back inside. The rain ceased and the clouds cleared. There was an expectation that, with Fortune's removal from the scene, his absence would help cauterise the diocese's gaping ulcer, but he proved more destructive to the bishop dead than alive. The diocese had escaped a trial by the State with Fortune's suicide, but had not allowed for a trial by his victims, particularly Colm O'Gorman, whose adamantine spirit found flight in an uncommon articulacy from a wounded soul.

The bishop had been given the Freedom of Wexford by the local Corporation, and a member of that assembly, a former mayor, organised a vigil on the evening of his resignation outside the closed gates of the palatial home. The small group was convinced that their bishop had been horsewhipped by public opinion for his failed vigilance. When *Suing the Pope* was finally broadcast on Irish television, Comiskey was no longer Bishop of Ferns. He did not have sufficient yardage for the redemptive possibility, however slim, of rectifying his misjudgements, and Fortune cannot be blamed for that. Comiskey's complacency in the jaws of tribulations eventually backfired. Toward the end of his career, when a series of mis-calculations like his involuntary appearance on *Suing the Pope* had reduced his inflated reputation to tatters, his drawn visage at the moment of his resignation clearly showed a very human stress and fatigue. He was a broken man. And yet, for one so hesitant as to make Hamlet appear decisive, his resignation shocked and disappointed those who needed him the most: Pat Jackman said Comiskey's head on a plate was not what victims wanted, but answers. 'I have to go to Mass next Sunday and half of the parishioners are going to be looking at me and thinking I was responsible for the bishop resigning,' he said.

All roads, inevitably, lead to Rome, and that was where Comiskey was off to in furtherance of the resignation process. 'I ask for the prayers of my people as I begin this journey.' With that last line, the bishop bade farewell to his flock. The diocese scotched rumours that Comiskey had been asked to resign. He had met with the Prefect of the Congregation of Bishops in Rome, Cardinal Giovanni Battista Re, who counselled him to take more time before making any decision.

Comiskey may have been the highest-ranking prince of the Catholic Church in Ireland to resign over his mishandling of deviant priests, but his downfall was mirrored abroad, adding substance to Colm O'Gorman's analysis that clerical sex abuse is not about one man or one country, it is about an institution. Four days before Comiskey fell on his own sword, Archbishop of Poznan in Poland, Juliusz Paetz, stepped down after fending off reports that he had repeatedly molested seminarians.

Before the year was over, heads of prelates would roll in Argentina (Archbishop Edgardo Storni: alleged to have abused seminarians), Australia (former Anglican Archbishop Peter Hollingworth: allegations of abuse in his diocese), Germany (Auxiliary Bishop Franziskus Eisenbach: accused of assaulting a woman during an exorcism) and America (Auxiliary Bishop James McCarthy: had affairs with several women; Archbishop Rembert Weakland: tried to assault a man; and Bishop Anthony O'Connell: repeatedly abused a young boy).

The exposure of extensive abuse by many priests in the Boston diocese throughout 2002 claimed the scalp of Cardinal Bernard Law that December: he had offered his resignation to Pope John Paul II about the same time as Comiskey, but it had been rejected. Similar to Comiskey, once the extent of Law's protection of convicted paedophile priests like John Geoghan became known, senior clergy demanded his resignation. With Comiskey in ecclesiastical limbo, the majority of Ireland's bishops went to ground. Just three – John Buckley, Willie Walsh and Leo O'Reilly – responded to questions about the handling of sex abuse allegations in Ferns advanced by the *Evening Herald*.

In Wexford, the fight to address the plight of other victims of clerical abuse was far from over. It had just begun. O'Gorman, who accused the hierarchy of leaving Comiskey to sit out in the cold on his own, called for a full State inquiry. A week after Comiskey's departure, Minister for Health Micheál Martin, following a meeting with O'Gorman and other victims of Fortune in Kilkenny, agreed to instigate an inquiry into what took place in Ferns.

In 2003, Martin announced the establishment of a non-statutory inquiry into the handling of complaints about priests in the diocese, chaired by Mr Justice Francis Murphy, and assisted by Dr Laraine Joyce, deputy director of the Office for Health Management and Dr Helen Buckley, Department of Social Studies, Trinity College, Dublin, who had worked on *Child Protection Practices in Ireland: A Case Study* in the mid-1990s for the South Eastern Health Board. The terms of reference had nine key points, including whether the response of the Diocese of Ferns was appropriate to alleged incidents of abuse that took place before Comiskey's resignation.

The Ferns Inquiry would probe over 100 allegations against 21 priests between 1962 and 2002. Between 1932 (the ordination date of the first priest against whom an allegation was made) and 2002, the number of priests ordained in the diocese stood at 248. It had, however, taken an English-made television documentary about an Irish problem to set the wheels of reparation and justice in motion for many of the victims of clerical abuse in the Diocese of Ferns.

11

Comiskey and the Media

'The best obtainable version of the truth is about context. And this is perhaps the greatest single failing of our journalism today. Far too much of it, maybe even most of it, is utterly without context.'
Carl Bernstein, Trinity College, Dublin, 1993

On 20 January 1980, the day Bishop Comiskey was ordained Auxiliary Bishop in the Archdiocese of Dublin, a party was held in his honour and among the attendees were many journalists and union officials. 'I had battled with practically all the organisations represented there,' remembered Comiskey in an address to the Religious Press Association at All Hallows College in 1994, 'and yet we were able to distinguish being in disagreement from being disagreeable. We could be friends and differ. I shall never forget that night, that message and those friends.' The honeymoon, the bishop admitted, since his arrival in Ferns, was over, and he accepted that he was 'a little less innocent, a little more bloodied, but forever, I hope, an optimist without illusions'. The optimism was shattered by the events of 1995, when he fled the diocese, the events of 1999, when Seán

Fortune took his own life, by the events of 2002, when *Suing the Pope* brought about his resignation and the events of 2005, when *The Ferns Report* put his stewardship in the diocese under an unforgiving microscope, from which he did not emerge favourably.

Two years after the media tore into Brendan Comiskey for quitting the Diocese of Ferns overnight in late 1995, a unique event took place also at All Hallows when journalists and representatives of the Churches met to examine the tense relationship between both. Up until the resignation of Bishop Eamon Casey in 1992, a cosy partnership had prevailed between the national media and the Catholic Church in Ireland, which explains why hundreds of cases in the Dublin archdiocese uncovered by *The Murphy Report* never appeared in the print media until priests began to appear before the courts. 'For most of this century,' Fr Colm Kilcoyne told the All Hallows conference, 'the Church held all the cards. The Protestants had *The Irish Times*, the Catholics had the *Irish Independent* and *The Irish Press*. Local papers were firmly committed to rocking no boats. Radio was respectful. Critics were oddities or communists or both. The most powerful symbols of identity and the rituals for expressing it were in the hands of the Church.'

Though *The Murphy Report* and *The Ferns Report* were initiated by the State in response to any number of allegations that first surfaced in the broadcast media (*Cardinal Secrets* on RTÉ and *Suing the Pope* on BBC), *The Murphy Report* uncovered much that was new whereas *The Ferns Report* expanded on what was already suspected, because journalists in Wexford had been pursuing the Diocese of Ferns since 1988. The media operating within the diocese – two weekly newspapers and local radio – had reported on the activities of Seán Fortune, Donal Collins, James Doyle and James Grennan long before the publication of *The Ferns Report* in 2005. The obeisant press in Dublin had a laissez-faire approach to clerical abuse and high-ranking Church misdemeanours until Casey's resignation altered the landscape forever, though editor of *The Irish Times* Conor Brady has admitted that some of his staff journalists did not want to touch the scoop.

'One or two newsroom reporters, apprised of the story, initially refused to have anything to do with it – to the irritation of [John] Armstrong [news editor] and myself.' Print journalists have never acknowledged that the revelations about clerical abuse, for which they took the credit, were the culmination of the daring reportage of television documentaries made by Mary Raftery for RTÉ and Sarah MacDonald for the BBC.

Much of the extensive print-media reporting in Dublin of events in Ferns was almost entirely sourced in Wexford, though not always with convincing or satisfactory results. More often than not allegations in the national media against Comiskey in late 1995 when he was on sabbatical in America relied on third-rate and unverifiable sources within the diocese and were invariably inaccurate and were recycled without any diligent checking of facts. It was the first time that the Irish media had decided that hard news should be displaced by 'infotainment' in its coverage of the behaviour of a prelate. The tabloids became adept at discovering other ways of saying something about Comiskey when there was often nothing new to say. A pitiless pursuit, according to Cardinal Cahal Daly, 'where fact often jostles with innuendo and insinuation, hint and suggestion which, where the dead or absent are concerned, is obsessive, some would say malicious.' The hostile reporting of Comiskey's private life and the allegations that he had moved an anonymous serial clerical abuser from parish to parish was not unconnected to the criticism of the Church's handling of Fr Brendan Smyth, who was arrested in 1994. 'When this anticlerical atmosphere was at its height, I felt I was being something of a deviant if I put in a good word for the Church among my fellow journalists,' Andy Pollock told the media–Church conference at All Hallows. 'I found it difficult for a period to interest my editors in any religious topic other than the ramifications of the latest twist in the clerical child sex abuse scandal. And if it was like that in *The Irish Times*, how much more extreme must have been the situation in the tabloid papers.'

That the tabloids went to town on Comiskey is indisputable, specifically the *Daily Star*. There are two factors worth considering in the tabloids' lively and seething coverage of Comiskey in 1995: they didn't have a monopoly on racy headlines ('Bishop Come-and-Kiss-Me flees flock' – *The Sunday Times*) but they demonstrated their capacity to generate acutely more heat than light. The *Daily Star*, drip fed old and new tittle-tattle on a daily basis from the damaged diocese, surmounting the paucity of dependable sources by the ingenious device of not identifying any. The *Star's* full frontal attack on Comiskey was relentless: 'Child Sex Storm Hits Comiskey Diocese' (20 September); 'Thai's The Limit' (26 September) and 'Comiskey's Thai Choice' (2 October). Fr Brian D'Arcy, writing for a newspaper which ironically had Comiskey in its cross hairs, the *Sunday World* ('Police held Bishop in Vice Capital' alongside the prurient 'Father Cleary's secret affair broke my heart'), was asked by a colleague to give him a list of Comiskey's enemies because stories were landing on his desk at an alarming rate. 'I doubt if anybody could have made the number and kind of alleged mistakes attributed to him by Church people, news bulletins, magazines, papers, scandal rags and gossip columns this past six months,' wrote D'Arcy in early 1996. 'All of them were written as fact and all of them attributed malicious intent to him. He has been treated abysmally.' Andy Pollock in *The Irish Times* attributed what he saw as a drop in journalistic standards to the aggressive marketing in Ireland of British tabloids. 'There is now less concern for accuracy; more prurient interest in people's private lives, particularly their sex lives and more indulgence in the kind of feeding frenzy in which the whole media descend on one event and attempt collectively to squeeze the last drop of sensation value out of it.'

As a consequence of the failure to report accurately what was taking place in Ferns throughout 1995, Bishop Comiskey at his press conference at St Peter's the following March was able to list inaccuracy after inaccuracy in the national media. The grave issue of the bishop's handling of priests accused of clerical abuse was lost amid the hysterical headlines of the *Sun's* 'I didn't Bang in Bangkok' and 'What the Bishop missed in Thailand' alongside a photograph of prostitutes sitting at a bar. He was let off the media hook – by the media and its sloppy distortion of facts that were readily accessible in the diocese. The abandonment of normal adherence to editorial accuracy and balance was sacrificed for two reasons, one emanating from the other: the Irish penchant for malicious gossip and the increased pressure on Irish dailies to compete with their British counterparts. Speaking in Wexford in 2010, Geraldine Kennedy, editor of *The Irish Times*, opined that 'some sources' motives may not always be so pure: they may be driven by vindictiveness or revenge. It is always up to journalists to determine in so far as they can the reliability of the information they receive.'

Unfortunately, the relentless spinning of half-truths and rumours about Comiskey while he was receiving treatment for alcoholism in America to sate a circulation war among the broadsheets and the tabloids left the credibility of investigative journalism in the country in tatters.

The diminution in accuracy during the feeding frenzies occasioned by the Diocese of Ferns – Comiskey's sabbatical,

Seán Fortune's death, *Suing the Pope* – was a by-product of both a failure to identify sources – essential for accountability and motivation – and simple verification. Gradually, the corrections and the apologies started to mount: the *Sunday Independent* falsely claimed in 2005 that Chief Superintendent James Doyle had destroyed documents in relation to the Monageer probe; The Ferns Inquiry dismissed reports in the *Irish Independent* in 2005 that there was organised child procurement by clergy in Ferns; a report in *The Sunday Times* that a clinical psychologist had been asked by the diocese to steel priests for the publication of *The Ferns Report* was inaccurate; the *Sunday Tribune* apologised in 1995 for claiming that former Bishop of Derry Dr Edward Daly had been interviewed by the RUC about allegations of sex abuse; in 2003 the *Daily Mirror* apologised for claiming that a sex offender was being housed by the Dominican Order in Tallaght, when he was in fact abroad; *The Ferns Report* rejected a lead story in the *Irish Independent* in 2004 that a gay sex ring was in operation at St Peter's College Seminary and the *Evening Herald* in 2002 claimed that the Dublin Archdiocese had paid €100,000 hush money to a sex abuse victim of Seán Fortune. It never happened.

Carl Bernstein, one half of the celebrated duo behind the Watergate exposures in *The Washington Post*, accurately foresaw how dwindling accountability was infesting the media when he addressed a conference at Trinity College, Dublin, in 1993. 'We're not doing the basic work of our profession, the hard business of reporting and searching for the truth, for relevance, for context, for accuracy, for the best obtainable version of the truth.' Certainly, in the autumn of 1995, the Irish media were more than happy with the best available version of the truth in their reporting of the intricate and never less than interesting life of Brendan Comiskey. He was not expected to stay on as Bishop of Ferns and he was not expected to return from

America, so the media's mugging of Comiskey was an ageing mutt's last go at a retiring postman. But Comiskey did return in early 1996, later than he said he would, but much sooner than the Irish print media anticipated.

In the aftermath of his threat during his first homily after his return to consider legal action for defamatory reports, the media's response was instant: it backed off, though the continuing antagonism to Comiskey by some journalists was manifested by other means. The *Wexford People*, the first newspaper to accuse Comiskey of fleeing the diocese because he could not cope with the abuse charges being brought against one of his priests (Fortune), excised the bishop from every photograph of confirmation classes it published by deleting the first row where Comiskey sat. 'This is pathetic and only serves to illustrate the vindictiveness and the small mindedness of the people responsible,' said a comment in the St Senan's Parish Newsletter. The *Wexford People,* with an original aphoristic tartness, replied that it was respecting the bishop's plea for privacy. The *People* and the bishop had been playing a media tennis match for years, occasionally to the mutual benefit of both, such as when the bishop gave his only interview during the celibacy debate the previous summer to the *People*, a newspaper for which he had often expressed a public dislike. Why the change of heart? Nobody knows. Every earthquake begins with a tremor and Comiskey blamed the mauling he received by the tabloids while he was on sabbatical on a claim first made by the *People* ('Bishop's desperate bid to overcome abuse case shame') which was recycled in the Independent News and Media daily papers owned by Dr Tony O'Reilly. The *People* next commissioned a poll on the eve of Comiskey's impending return from America and produced its findings across a lead banner headline: 'Majority now want Bishop to resign'.

The poll was subsequently rehashed by the next day's *Irish Independent,* but as an exercise in undermining Comiskey, it backfired spectacularly.

Reviewing the poll in the *Sunday Tribune,* Oliver O'Connor said 'the media's reporting of the poll on the bishop was an example of varying degrees of shoddiness, misleading inferences and downright untruths.' The *Wexford People* and RTÉ's *Morning Ireland* reported that 309 people were polled (MRBI usually sampled over 1,000 in 1996), the *Irish Independent* twice reported 500 were polled, *The Irish Times* first reported no figure but arrived at 371 in future reports. 'Human error creeps in everywhere, even on simple, easily ascertainable facts. It could happen to a bishop,' quipped O'Connor. His conclusion was damning: 'It seems that there is disquiet over Bishop Comiskey's reported handling of money, clerical child sex abuse allegations and his own movements. The attempt to quantify that disquiet has shown up, at best, shoddy and inaccurate reporting.' When Comiskey returned from America to a crammed St Aidan's Cathedral, he could not resist a dig at the *People's* poll. 'If you continue clapping like that I'll be accused of getting all the nine per cent who supported me into the cathedral.' Chastened, and with its tail between its legs, the *People* retreated to the long grass to sulk, to bide its time and to consider its riposte, which didn't take long: the bishop was expunged from the confirmation photographs it published a month later.

Engaging the local media was not, of course, the exclusive preserve of the bishop. He was always served with skilled communicators, such as Fr Walter Forde, who on many occasions in 1995 had to step into Comiskey's shoes whenever the most communicative bishop of his generation found it hard to explain to his laity why he was lying low. Forde – a former chairman of the Religious Press Association of Ireland

– took exception to a series of articles in *The Wexford Echo* in July 1995 that tapped into the unease within the diocese about certain aspects of the bishop's episcopacy. Slating the reports as 'inaccurate, unbalanced, snide and negative', Forde complained not to the newspaper's editor, but to the chief executive, adding that *The Echo*'s coverage 'could be seen as ridiculing the Bishop and taking from his good name and standing'. Forde said his comments did not in any way restrict or prejudice Comiskey in any action he might take. In other correspondence to the newspaper, Forde accused *The Echo* of 'adopting the tone and approach of the published pieces and private comments of journalists from the *Sunday World* and the *Sunday Independent*,' and that 'never in twenty years have I felt that any coverage was as unbalanced and negative as that contained in your last issue'.

Taking up the cudgel on the bishop's behalf when Forde moved sideways was Fr John Carroll who, after 2000, was both Diocesan Secretary and Diocesan Press Officer. Carroll, while editor of the Ferns diocesan bulletin, *The Forum*, raised eyebrows in 2002 when he postulated, not withstanding the increase in revelations of clerical abuse worldwide, that the 'scapegoating' of the Catholic Church indicated that 'we are in denial of the truth that the great majority of abuse cases takes place within the family, the last sacred cow remaining in Ireland', an opinion somewhat similar to Cardinal Oscar Rodriguez Maradiaga of Honduras, who claimed that Church abuse scandals were being deliberately exaggerated by a hostile media. Senator David Norris argued after *The Ferns Report* that the small percentage of abuse cases attached to priests in Ireland, 4 per cent or 5 per cent, was statistically anomalous. 'For that to be representative of the general population, one would have to have 200,000 priests in the country, and we do not have that many.' Carroll contacted *The Echo* on 21 November 2001 seeking to get in touch with a woman who had written a letter about the Church, which was published. Her contact details, on her request, had been withheld from publication, and for good reason. 'Perhaps you would be so kind as to forward to me [the correspondent's] address and contact number. She raised many points, some of which I may choose to address. As you will understand, it would be necessary to establish her identity prior to such an exercise.' *The Echo* politely declined. Six days later Carroll, noting that both the editor and the Managing Director had refused point blank to give him the correspondent's contact details, replied: 'This is the second time that the Diocese of Ferns has had occasion to raise such a matter with management in the past number of years. Any remaining confidence one could have with *The Echo* newspapers has now been extinguished.'

The Echo pointed out that it was the correspondent's prerogative to remain anonymous, much to the chagrin of Carroll, for whom the letter was a forgery and the management's response was 'nothing short of a cover up of a forgery'. Carroll, as Director of Communications, was prepared to burn his bridges with one of only two newspapers in his diocese, all because of an editorial decision to protect a source, which he believed to be a fake. On the eve of the most turbulent trial by media in Comiskey's ministry, which would be resolved only by his resignation in four months, the relationship between the diocese and at least one half of the local media had reached its nadir. On the surface, a disregard for the Church was a mark of virtue for the media, and a disregard for the media was a mark of virtue for the Church. Comiskey once said that if he had not followed his vocation, he would have become involved in the media: after his mugging by reporters in 1995–96, he surprised many by agreeing to write a weekly column for *Ireland on Sunday* a year later. Though he had 'a deep conviction of the crucial part media play in a free society', he frequently was a source of friction for reporters going about their daily job. Within days of *The Ferns Report*, a headline screamed across the front page of the *Irish Independent*: 'Bishop Comiskey threatened to rape me'. Reporter Justine McCarthy regretted that she had not written the story when the drunken threat by Comiskey happened eleven years ago, but she had been dissuaded by her editor, Vinnie Doyle. The comments as reported by McCarthy (that if she wrote about his house and his clothes, 'If you do that, I'll come up to Dublin and I'll rape you,') occurred during a lunch in Wexford, just months before Comiskey's address to the Religious Press Association. The claim was buried by the *Irish Independent* and then resurrected in the wake of *The Ferns Report*. Why? McCarthy said she had no right to hold onto her secret after reading about the allegation in *The Ferns Report* of an alleged drunken assault by the bishop on a young woman. 'I wish I had written this story of Comiskey's rape threat against me 11 years ago. Maybe it could have saved a child from the horror of Ferns.' Unlikely, as the alleged incident involving Comiskey and the girl occurred five years before McCarthy's interview with the bishop, and *The Ferns Report* did not record a single incident of abuse of a young child, if any, after 1994. The report was an example of the depth to which the bishop's working relationship with journalists had plummeted.

Perhaps he had only himself to blame: within the profession, certainly in the late 1980s and long before he became besmirched by the clerical abuse scandal in Ferns, he was known to enjoy sparring with journalists. He addressed this in Wexford in 1989. 'Far from wishing to appear as a media basher, my comments spring from a deep conviction of the crucial part media play in a free society and from a genuine appreciation of the journalist's profession.' Really? Within a year Comiskey was having stand-up rows with journalists over the coverage given to the trial of Fr James Doyle in Wexford, the first priest in Ireland to be convicted of the sexual assault of a child. Comiskey was never a shrinking violet under the glaring light of the media. After his name became linked with a businesswoman in 1992, he warned newspapers that he would sue to clear his name if unfounded sexual allegations surfaced about him. Brenda Power remembered an equally pugnacious bishop when a television reviewer in *The Irish Press* light-heartedly expressed the hope that the singer Madonna's first child wouldn't cause as much trouble as the son born to the previous Madonna. 'Bishop Comiskey considered this remark to be blasphemous and used the might and prominence of his role to demand a boycott by all God-fearing Catholics of the Irish Press group newspapers,' recalled Power. 'At that time the group was in serious difficulties and, indeed, closed not long afterwards with the loss of hundreds of jobs and hardship for many families.'

Fr Kevin Hegarty was removed as editor of *Intercom* after four years in the post, solely because the hierarchy believed some of the articles in the magazine were lowering morale within the Irish Church. As Chairman of the Bishops' Commission on Communication, Comiskey was effectively the editor's boss. Hegarty had revived the magazine by including stimulating and relevant articles, including one in December 1993 that posed tough questions to bishops on their handling of emerging clerical abuse cases. It was his undoing. 'The efforts to cover up clerical sexual abuse were in one sense disturbing. I joined [*Intercom*] in June 1991 and when I began raising questions like clerical sexual abuse and questioning compulsory celibacy and the issue of women priests, I began to experience questioning from various bishops.' An editorial committee was set up by the bishops to keep an eye on *Intercom,* and they dismissed Hegarty in late 1994.

Another journalist who fell foul of Comiskey was Kieron

Wood, author of *The Kilkenny Incest Case*. Appointed religious affairs correspondent by RTÉ three years into Comiskey's episcopacy in Ferns, Wood's relationship with the Catholic bishops became uneasy after he revisited the Fethard boycott of the 1950s and did reports about Bishop Eamon Casey, prompting the Bishop of Galway to try to have him blacklisted. Cardinal Tomás Ó Fiaich requested Comiskey to resolve the problem the Italian way – over dinner. 'Comiskey regaled me with stories about his native Monaghan and we parted on good terms,' recollected Wood in *The Sunday Business Post* in 2002.

'But the uneasy truce did not last long.' After Wood did a speculative piece on the likely successor to the late Archbishop Kevin McNamara, which turned out to be accurate (Monsignor Desmond Connell), RTÉ's director general Vincent Finn (1985–1992) received complaints from the Catholic Church. Comiskey was forced to scotch rumours in the media that he was behind a move to shaft Wood. After Wood reported on 26 June 1990 how Connell had to clarify a number of points about a series of articles by the Bishop of Ferns in *Intercom*, Comiskey immediately contacted Wood by fax. 'This is not the first time you have indulged in this type of reporting and that is your right. It is also my right to reply and, in the very near future, I intend doing just that.' After Wood reported on the visit of an American witch to Dublin – a day later – the Catholic Communications Institute (of which Comiskey was president) complained to Finn that Wood's reporting was 'consistently mischievous and inaccurate'. Finn's solution was to inform the Catholic Communications Institute that Wood would be reassigned, though that in itself did not placate Comiskey. He sent Finn a three-and-a-half-page missive outlining his objections to Wood's reporting, describing the report on the *Intercom* issue as 'truly a nasty piece of work', leaving Finn with no option, in his eyes, but to carry out an internal inquiry. However, Wood's reports were proven to be correct and accurate, but this in itself did not prevent him from being reassigned to legal affairs.

The relationship between the media and the Catholic Church continues to be irksome, and two columnists with *The Irish Catholic* took potshots at their colleagues in the secular press in 2010, and in doing so dispelled the myth of unbreachable solidarity among journalists, which was undoubtedly prevalent a decade ago. Ronan Mullen accused *The Irish Times* of running a campaign to unseat the Bishop of Galway after *The Murphy Report* 'because they knew he had handled an abuse case badly or that he had some knowledge that the Church was failing to report cases or something equally serious. But they didn't. And he hadn't.' David Quinn took umbrage at the analysis by RTÉ and the *Irish Examiner* of Pope Benedict's visit to Britain later in the year. 'Right to the bitter end, RTÉ allowed the scandals to predominate its coverage with the report on the Sunday evening intoning that the Church's reputation still hung by a thread. The contrast with what we were watching and hearing on the BBC and Sky and reading in the British press couldn't have been starker. Meanwhile, over at the *Irish Examiner,* Shaun Connolly was just about able to admit to himself and his readers that the visit fell short of a "disaster". We know what we saw, and it's not what much of the Irish media saw, or wanted to see.'

The collation of the Ferns, Murphy and Ryan reports in a five-year period has challenged the Irish media, which has not failed to be assiduous in its coverage of the sexual abuse of children by the religious. The Catholic Church, in a state of dazed forbearance, cannot expect journalists to relax their scepticism, while the routine tests of good journalism, vigilance and credibility, in short supply in some quarters during the drive-by character assassination of the Bishop of Ferns in the autumn of 1995, might ensure that neither titan will abdicate its responsibilities in the years ahead. In an unprecedented gesture and perhaps a peace offering to the Fourth Estate, Archbishop Diarmuid Martin, speaking in the Pro-Cathedral, Dublin, in November 2010, recognised 'that the recent shattering revelations about abuse would probably never have come to full light without outside intervention'.

Epilogue

'The Church acted like a family within a family. Instead of reaching out to the wounded she gave her first and sometimes exclusive support to the offending priests. In that way the Church created a family within a family. In doing so the Church allowed other innocent children to suffer sexual abuse later on.'
Bishop Eamonn Walsh, 2005

Eamonn Walsh appeared to be the ideal replacement for Brendan Comiskey – businesslike, straight talking, a safe pair of hands – and was parachuted into the Diocese of Ferns by the hierarchy without fanfare in 2002. He had a mission to straighten out Ferns and set about the colossal task with energy and alacrity.

His public record by 2002 was solid: he had served as secretary to three bishops – McNamara, Carroll and Connell – from 1985 to 1990, when he was ordained Titular Bishop of Elmham and Auxiliary Bishop of Dublin with pastoral responsibility for the deaneries of Blessington, Tallaght and South Dublin, among the most populous in the country. During his time as secretary, he was not always party to discussions between archbishop and priest (there was no clear job description for an auxiliary bishop), a lapse with future repercussions. As Walsh admitted:

> If I was approached on a matter of a confidential nature, or if I had a concern which had been expressed to me, I brought this to the attention of the Archbishop. Archbishop Connell took a very conscientious line in respecting a person's reputation and on any other matter he deemed confidential. Information given in this way was not shared at meetings with others present. The result was that discussions were often held where the full facts of the subject under discussion were not known to all participants. Sometimes the Archbishop himself would not have full information. It is very regrettable that clear pathways of communication were not effected until after the introduction of the Framework Document in 1996. Poor communication led to long-term disastrous consequences.
>
> (Statement issued by Bishop Walsh in 2009)

Offending priests in Dublin were given appointments on the basis of medical assessment that suggested they were fit for ministry, with appalling consequences for their victims.

Long before Walsh was settled in Ferns in unenviable circumstances, bringing order to the most disreputable diocese in the western world after Boston, he had established a singular response to clerical abuse that was out of sync with others in the Church.

Though the Archdiocese of Dublin committed itself to improved reporting of abuse in 1996, Walsh had advocated this response six years earlier, a time when – he accepted – bad decisions had been made because of an absence of understanding of paedophilia. He was made Chairperson of the Irish Bishops' Liaison Committee on Child Abuse in 1999, establishing a National Child Protection Office and commissioning 'Time To Listen', a research study on clerical sexual abuse. The favourable response to the report helped his appointment as Apostolic Administrator in Ferns.

He rapidly made his presence felt: he got to know the priests in the diocese, he visited parishes, he talked to secondary school pupils, he addressed congregations, he met abuse victims, he was accessible to the media, he studied decades of diocesan files and invited, in record time, a number of accused priests to seek voluntary laicisation. If they declined, they were defrocked. He ruffled feathers among the clergy. There was criticism about the late discovery of some documents submitted to the Ferns Inquiry, but the fault lay with human error rather than the withholding of cooperation. The diocese had on record correspondence from Bishop Herlihy explaining that a priest had to be moved from the diocese because of his relationship with a girl ('Fr Iota') but the existence of the letter was not made known to the inquiry until an advanced stage. When *The Ferns Report* was published, Walsh told the people of Wexford that the Church had no excuses and no place to hide. He accepted that because some priests had remained silent out of blind loyalty to colleagues, children were abused. 'Some priests who were ordained for the diocese should not have been ordained, and would not have been, had those who had made complaints or expressed suspicions been heard.'

In June 2003, the diocese instructed clergy to display a new interim policy ('The diocese undertakes to do all in its power to create a safe environment for children and young people and to ensure their protection from physical, sexual and emotional abuse') in the porches of churches. This policy reflected a hardening of attitude by Walsh to ensure that all parishes within Ferns became safe environments 'where risks are minimized, where those affected by abuse are supported, where offenders become accountable for their actions and where all allegations are dealt with justly and promptly'. In November, the first meeting of the Ferns Advisory Panel – which would review all abuse allegations before the diocese – met after Walsh ensured its membership represented a variety of disciplines, including canon law, psychotherapy and business. The Child Protection Committee set itself an ambitious target of instructing clergy in good practice guidelines in every parish and curacy before the end of 2006. In preparation for the publication of *The Ferns Report*, staff at St Peter's College – dubbed sensationally as the 'cradle of evil' by the *Irish Independent* – finally benefited from a crash course in child protection guidelines in August 2005. It may have been forty years too late, but it was a start. The college, generations after its students knew better than to be left on their own with Seán 'Flapper' Fortune and Donal 'Paws' Collins, operates a child protection policy and has a code of conduct for staff: teachers cannot be alone with a pupil; teachers should avoid becoming a parental figure to a particular pupil; taking photographs of pupils in changing areas is prohibited, and illegal drugs and alcohol cannot be given to pupils.

The future of the seminary was in doubt in Bishop Herlihy's time: in June 1977, the Council of Priests called a meeting of clergy to discuss the seminary's future because of falling vocations, but by October Herlihy was happy to confirm the intention to keep it open. Its death knell had been adjourned, but not before its most distinguished alumnus, Cardinal Tomás Ó Fiaich, returned to celebrate Mass once more in the College Chapel. In 1994, James Maxwell became the first lay principal of the school and Fr Oliver Doyle was appointed the last ever College President. Owing to the development of an outreach of Carlow RTC on the ecclesisatical wing in 1995, the seminary was relocated to rooms near the College Chapel, before closing for good, along with the boarding school, three years later, its seminarians transferred to Maynooth and Fr Doyle to Montana in the United States. St Peter's celebrates its bicentenary in 2011 and it is hoped that a new generation will give fresh impetus to the legend on the college coat of arms: *disce prodesse* – strive to be of service.

Some of the correspondence Bishop Walsh received from victims concerned allegations of abuse by religious in the diocese other than clergy. A man who attended the Christian Brothers' School in Enniscorthy in 1961 detailed a litany of abuse perpetrated by a Brother on him and others when he was a young boy in fifth class. 'It was then the fashion for boys to wear short trousers and he would place his right hand on the inside of my right leg just above the knee. He would then start massaging my leg and moving his hand upwards in under my trouser leg. He would try to touch my genitalia.' The boy related the incidents to his father, who approached Fr Joseph Ranson, a legendary figure in the town, responsible for St Aidan's becoming the first cathedral in the country to display the Irish tricolour. Ranson met a senior Brother in the CBS and repeated the boy's allegations. The offending Brother was summarily removed from the school, but not before the senior Brother expressed his displeasure to the boy's father that Ranson had been informed before him. In the correspondence to Walsh in January 2003, the man remembered a specific incident of physical abuse by the aforementioned Brother:

> One day he brought two boys, first cousins I think, from fourth class in front of our own class for disciplining, which had never happened before. Boys were normally dealt with by their own teachers in their own classes. The

Brother was unhappy with the note written by a parent which gave the reason for their absence from school. He held the note disdainfully between his forefinger and thumb above his head and verbally ridiculed it. He then procured a polished wooden implement used in callisthenics and proceeded to beat the boys with it, mocking them as he did so. My recollection is that he gave each boy twenty slaps on each hand. He would say 'now for the first round', and we watched two little boys literally being tortured before us, and they were screaming like you cannot imagine . . . all the spit dried out of my mouth.

A week after *The Ferns Report* became the talk of Catholics throughout the world, Eamonn Walsh addressed a packed congregation at St Aidan's Cathedral in Enniscorthy, the scene of Brendan Comiskey's rapturous and sycophantic homecoming after his sabbatical in America and, in a twelve-minute sermon, pointed out that 'priests were ordained to bring people to God and to reach out to the most vulnerable children. Instead of doing that, some priests did the unthinkable and people were left destroyed, wounded and scarred.'

Local history was made a month later in November 2005 when Ferns diocesan personnel – Fr Gerry O'Leary, Sr Helen O'Riordan and Ms Isabelle Flynn – were among a group of nineteen nationwide to become the first ever child protection trainers: they were instrumental at an inaugural public meeting organised by the Child Protection Committee of the diocese in a Wexford hotel, which simulated scenarios to help people identify potential abuse.

But before *The Ferns Report* saw the light of day, there was disquiet among the clergy in Wexford over Walsh's manner of asking priests about whom allegations had been made to step aside. Walsh acted because of the parmountcy of putting the protection of children first. In particular, priests were concerned by the case of Fr John Kinsella, erstwhile curate of The Ballagh parish, who stood down pending an investigation into allegations of abuse against him.

The allegations against Kinsella were not new to the diocese or the Gardaí, but the DPP decided not to press charges. As the diocese was still investigating the incidents, Kinsella was not reinstated. This prompted priests to worry that the right to be innocent until proven guilty did not extend to clergy. 'The most notorious criminal enjoys the privilege of being considered innocent until proven guilty, whereas, it seems, a priest or religious is regarded as guilty until proven innocent, especially regarding matters of sexual nature,' claimed Fr James Curtis, the parish priest of Clongeen in 2003. But Walsh was not for turning.

The affair continued to simmer both before and after *The Ferns Report* and next surfaced in the media in the most unexpected of outlets, the front page of *The Irish Catholic* under the headline: 'Bishop Under Fire from Ferns Priests.' The gist of the priests' complaints was the reluctance of Walsh to communicate with them about the diocese's response to the imminent publication of *The Ferns Report*. Diocesan Communications Officer Fr John Carroll, who had survived the purge of the Comiskey court, accepted that some clergy were more informed than others.

Was revolution, among Wexford's priests, in the air? If it was, an attempt was made to stifle it when the Vicars of the Diocese attended a meeting convened by the Vicar General, Monsignor Lory Kehoe from Gorey: the priests, Fr Denis Lennon, Fr Paddy Cushen and Fr Joe McGrath, representing the deaneries of Wexford, Enniscorthy and New Ross, gave their full public support to Walsh, a pledge of loyalty that had already been made at a day-long gathering of clergy. 'At that time hard decisions had to be made and Bishop Eamonn took these decisions with courage and with sensitivity to the pain of all involved,' recalled Bishop Denis Brennan.

In February 2006, Fr John Littleton, president of the National Conference of Priests in Ireland, called on the hierarchy to consider allowing priests under investigation for sexual misconduct to continue ministerial work. 'The problem is, when people are removed in such a public way from their office, there is never any possibility of them having their good name restored and it doesn't matter who goes to the parish afterwards to correct the information given out which proved to be misleading some time ago.'

He might just have been referring to Fr Nicholas Marshall (a seminarian at St Peter's from 1968 to 1974) who was requested by Walsh to step down as parish priest of Rathangan, even though the man who made the complaint subsequently retracted it. Two years had passed and there was no sign of Marshall's reinstatement, much to his irritation and anger. He went public a month before Littleton's remarks, once the diocese announced that he was to be replaced by Fr Tom Dalton.

Despite the support of the Vicars of the Diocese, ordinary clergy throughout the county were aghast at the chasm developing between them and Walsh: their views and fears were articulated in an article in *The Furrow* by an eminent source: Fr Bill Cosgrove, parish priest of Monageer and former Dean of Discipline at St Peter's College, opined that it was unsurprising that some bishops were of the opinion that the relationship with priests had been damaged by the manner in which the accused were dealt with. 'A thorough and prompt investigation must be carried out in relation to any and all allegations by qualified investigators. It will be essential that this be totally independent of the bishop and his advisors.' Another article in *The Furrow*, 'Accused but Innocent – What Should a Priest do?', advised priests not to step aside if requested until the preliminary investigation had been concluded and, if further investigations were warranted, the priest should not enter into discussions with his prelate until he had received both legal and canonical representation.

There is a scene in an episode of the hard-hitting New York-based television drama *Law & Order* where a lawyer remarks, after a judge allows prosecutors to charge a diocese after it had compensated an abuse victim, that 'all the jury has to hear is sexual abuse and priest in the same sentence, and it's all over'. Fr Eddie Kilpatrick could empathise with the sentiment. In 1992 his world fell apart when he was informed by the Diocese of Derry that allegations of abuse had arisen from twenty years earlier. Kilpatrick protested his innocence. In 1994, the RUC carried out an investigation and the Bishop of Derry, Seamus Hegarty, gave Kilpatrick no option but to leave Murlog forthwith. He did, but not quietly. He wrote to every priest in his diocese, protesting his innocence, contacted the press and informed his parishioners of developments. Then he gathered his belongings and, because the diocese had made no provision for him once he departed, travelled first to London before returning to the Inishowen Peninsula. The police believed that the evidence against Kilpatrick was admissible, substantial and reliable, and his case went to trial five years later. The jury delivered a unanimous verdict of not guilty.

Kilpatrick first learned of the allegations in 1992, a file by the RUC was prepared in 1994, he was asked to leave his parish in 1995 and his name was finally cleared in 1997, but the damage to his reputation and his health had taken its toll. For five years he received regular exposure from the print media – none of it flattering – and made about twenty personal appearances in court, so often was his case adjourned.

Who now remembers the name of Nora Wall, the shy and retiring former Sister Dominic of the Sisters of Mercy who, after her conviction for raping a girl in a child care centre in Cappoquin on a date unknown in 1987, was pilloried by the tabloid press as evil incarnate? In 1991, 51-year-old Wall became the first person in Ireland to receive a life sentence for rape and the first to be convicted on repressed memory evidence. She endured the most venomous media and public opprobrium upon her conviction. Her conviction for rape was certified a miscarriage of justice by the Court of Criminal Appeal in 2005 after questions arose regarding non-disclosure by the prosecution of evidence from one of the witnesses, who had admitted lying in evidence.

In 2010, David Rice, a former Dominican-turned-journalist, articulated the feelings of many priests left isolated by new Church guidelines. 'Nowadays the Church has gone to the opposite extreme. It protects itself by presuming guilt and removing the priests on the merest accusation, which means that every priest in the land lives in perpetual fear of a false accusation.'

Bishop Walsh, in applying the 2001 papal directive *Sacramentorum sanctitatis tutela* to all cases of allegations of abuse against clergy that had the semblance of truth, acted in a manner that, if not always allowing the benefit of doubt, was decisive. The diocese firstly communicated any determination it received with the accused priest; it never became party to a settlement without the consent of the accused and it never requested confidentiality clauses with either party to a settlement. Canon law traditionally permitted a bishop to move a curate for a 'just reason' and a parish priest for a 'grave reason'. A bishop can issue a penal precept requesting a priest to stand aside, appealable by the priest to the Congregation for the Doctrine of the Faith. Walsh's criterion was more direct: a credible allegation was enough to warrant a removal from ministry of any priest. During Walsh's tenure in Ferns, all priests requested to stand aside voluntarily from ministry did so. In 2004, Walsh learned that the South Eastern Health Board in 1990 had received an allegation of inappropriate behaviour from a teenage girl against Brendan Comiskey. The Board did not report the allegation made by the girl's parents to the Gardaí, and Comiskey himself was unaware of it until after his resignation in 2002. Pending an investigation, in which Comiskey stood aside from active ministry, a report was prepared by Monsignor John Dolan, Chancellor of the Archdiocese of Dublin, at the request of Archbishop Desmond Connell, Metropolitan for the Diocese of Ferns. 'The report concluded that a delict – a canon law offence – had not been committed as regards the behaviour alleged but the fact that under the influence of alcohol, Bishop Comiskey was alleged to have acted in such a manner, was something that needed to be addressed to ensure that no repetition of such behaviour could take place,' found *The Ferns Report*. After the probe, Comiskey agreed to refrain from high-profile acts of episcopal ministry. The allegation first surfaced when the Health Board was interviewing a victim of Fr James Doyle.

Vocations to the priesthood in Ferns were in steady decline: 91 priests in 2005 compared to 157 in the early 1980s. Walsh had little room to manoeuvre when he made as many as twenty clerical changes that summer, with at least eight parishes or curacies losing their full-time priest. Nine months after the publication of *The Ferns Report*, in which the diocese confirmed that it was not in receipt of any allegation of child sexual abuse involving a priest about which it had not informed the Gardaí or the Health Board, the new bishop, Denis Brennan, introduced another set of transfers to the clergy *in situ*, affecting fifteen priests.

The cataclysmic impact of *The Ferns Report* reinvigorated the vexatious debate about the Church's guidelines on child abuse. The ink in the report had little time to dry when the Irish Episcopal Conference, the Irish Missionary Union and the Conference of Religious in Ireland (CORI) published their new child protection policy, 'Our Children, Our Church', neatly paraphrasing an often-repeated expression by Bishop Walsh in *The Ferns Report*, that the welfare of the child is paramount. But was it? Archbishop Seán Brady stressed that it was the Church's intention to ensure that Irish society could have the utmost confidence in the commitment of the Church to the protection of children. 'We want children to feel that they have been treated at all times with the dignity, respect and care they deserve by the community of the Church,' Brady added.

Critically, 'Our Children, Our Church' proposed replacing the two existing offices operated by CORI and the Irish Episcopal Conference with a single national office for child protection under the auspices of a new National Board for Child Protection, chaired by Justice Anthony Hederman. What was a small step for Ireland but a giant leap for the Catholic Church was the concession that a lay professional, such as a psychiatrist and not a bishop, would decide how to proceed with an allegation of, or suspicion of, child abuse. Undoubtedly, the Church expected flak, and the flak throwers did not disappoint.

Margaret Kennedy of the London-based Minister and Clergy Sexual Abuse Survivors, made clear that there was no policy in the United Kingdom that allowed organisations to make their own inquiries into abuse allegations before informing the police. 'Most secular organisations have a child protection officer, but that officer's role is to make sure that all allegations are handled quickly and efficiently with immediate referral to the proper authority – the police.' The only role the

Church has in this area, she argued, is to report all allegations of sexual abuse to the police with the utmost urgency. 'Ambiguity of role and process would be vastly clarified if there was a simple policy of mandatory reporting,' she added. Mandatory reporting, of course, was the elephant in the room for both the Church and a succession of governments. Fergus Finlay, Chief Executive of Barnardos in Ireland, insisted *The Ferns Report* clarified that abuse is facilitated by a close and secretive environment, and that secrecy must be replaced by the introduction of mandatory reporting. 'What is most disappointing about the Catholic Church's new child protection guidelines, is the insistence on retaining within the Church the final decision on whether or not to report alleged child abuse to the civil authorities.'

'Our Children, Our Church' was wholly at odds with the spirit of *The Ferns Report* and (according to a Barnardos press release) 'allows the Church a space for discretion, which is utterly unacceptable'. One In Four director Colm O'Gorman accused the Vatican of having never engaged with the scrutiny *Crimen sollicitationis* was subjected to in *The Ferns Report*, the first Vatican document the inquiry believed gave directions to bishops on the secret handling of abuse claims. 'The Vatican has never responded to this finding and other findings in the report which found that it had failed in its responsibilities to properly address the sexual abuse of children by priests.' O'Gorman was critical of the Vatican's failure to introduce 'meaningful and mandatory' child protection policies across the Catholic Church worldwide.

The closest Ireland came to introducing mandatory reporting was as a direct response of 'Putting Children First, A Discussion Document on Mandatory Reporting' in 1996, when Minister of State at the Departments of Health, Education and Justice Austin Currie was persuaded by the following statistic to make a decision one way or another. The number of cases of reported child abuse in Ireland, from 1987 to 1994, had increased from 1,646 to 4,600, an increase of over 180 per cent. He was not helped in his deliberations by the divergence of opinion between the Law Reform Commission (reporting only child sexual abuse) and the Kilkenny Incest Investigation (reporting of all forms of child abuse). Explained Curry: 'Mandatory reporting could challenge the whole aim of our therapeutic counselling services. If reporting were to lead to legal action, then victims may have to confront their abuser and possibly even their abusers with the attendant risk of trauma which such an encounter might provoke.' Currie was also mindful that in America, where mandatory reporting was introduced in 1960, there was, besides a substantial increase in the number of cases reported, an increase in the number of unsubstantiated cases. A draft White Paper was prepared in 2000 but mandatory reporting was not pursued by the government after the introduction of 'The Protections for Persons Reporting Child Abuse Act 1998'. Between the resignation of Brendan Comiskey and the publication of *The Ferns Report*, the government established the Garda Central Vetting Unit (vetting employees of agencies funded by the Health Service Executive (HSE) where the work involves access to children) and appointed the first Ombudsman for Children, Emily Logan.

Having decided not to proceed with mandatory reporting, the government introduced fresh guidelines, such as the 'Child Protection Guidelines for Post-Primary Schools' in 2004, which made it easier for someone to report a suspicion of child abuse. Immunity from civil liability was extended to any child abuse whistle-blower in 'The Protection for Persons Reporting Child Abuse Act 1988', though false reporting could result in three years in prison.

'Why is it that, despite the very clear guidelines, many of us working with children and adolescents have difficulty in knowing how to respond to the issue of abuse? Yes, we know what we should do – we should report our concerns and let the designated liaison person and the professionals working in the health boards and the Gardaí determine if there is justification for our concerns. Knowing what we should do, is very different from knowing how to respond,' wrote clinical and educational psychologist Dr Claire Hayes. Throwing its tuppenceworth into the debate, *The Ferns Report* felt that maximum confidentiality should be extended to the victim, 'consistent with achieving protection for other children at risk'.

Stung by the criticism that it had not learned crucial lessons from the 271 pages of *The Ferns Report*, the Church received a further blow in July 2007 when a government-commissioned review of 'Our Children, Our Church' highlighted a lack of integration between it and guidelines produced by various State organisations. For example, Dr Helen Buckley of TCD's social studies department, who prepared the review, noted that the wording in 'Our Children, Our Church' made it a difficult document to navigate for those who were most in need of clear guidance on child protection procedures. 'Our Children, Our Church' was in danger of being an independent document rather than derivative of State guidelines.

The laity in Wexford issued a collective sigh of relief when Denis Brennan was installed as the eighty-first Bishop of Ferns in April 2006. Brennan was educated at St Peter's College in the early 1960s and was ordained at the seminary in 1970. He became a member of the Missionaries of the Blessed Sacrament at the House of Missions, Enniscorthy, and was its last Superior before its closure in 1992. Appointed Administrator of St Senan's Parish, Enniscorthy, from December 1986, he became parish priest of Taghmon in 1997.

Brennan served as Vicar Forane for the Wexford deanery and as the diocesan delegate with child protection responsibilities.

He was a popular, if surprising, choice, the first Wexford-born bishop since William Codd in 1917, but it was evident that the hand of recent history lay firmly on his shoulders during his episcopal ordination: delivering the homily, Fr Joseph McGrath referred to the 'shadow of shame' that had shrouded the diocese, which 'will not be forgotten, ignored, airbrushed out or unrepented for'. Principal consecrator Archbishop Diarmuid Martin, his co-consecrator Apostolic Nuncio Giuseppe Lazzarotto and the diocesan Apostolic Adminstrator Bishop Eamonn Walsh, were among those who heard the new bishop define what his ordination to the episcopate meant to him, and he did not forget the victims of clerical abuse. 'Today is about their struggle to be listened to and believed, their ongoing pain and their search for healing.'

The decades of abuse in the diocese was top of the agenda when Brennan – in Rome with other Irish bishops on an *ad limina apostolorum* (an obligation on bishops to visit the Pope) visit – had a private audience with Pope Benedict in October 2008. Expressing his 'personal anguish and horror', Benedict accepted that priests had 'devastated human lives and profoundly betrayed the trust of children, young people, their families, parish communities and the entire diocesan family'.

This was strong language – coming from a Pope – and unprecedented. The occasion marked also a personal triumph for the new bishop: Brennan, beneath the revered icon Salus Populi Romani, gave the homily at the Mass in the Basilica di Santa Maria Maggiore. He warned his fellow bishops 'against despair in the face of trial'. Storm clouds, however, of an ominous nature, which would test the mettle of the bishops 'in the face of trial', shadowed the Irish Church throughout 2009. The onslaught commenced in January when a Health

Service Executive audit found that the Diocese of Cloyne had breached existing child protection guidelines by failing to alert authorities to an allegation of child sexual abuse; the HSE also disclosed that bishops throughout the country had declined to submit detailed information on allegations of abuse for legal reasons. Section 5 of the HSE audit, eight questions in total, was not addressed by a single bishop, apparently because of confidentiality reasons, which, to paraphrase Minister for Children Barry Andrews, detracted from the value of the audit. Andrews' response was to ask the Dublin Archdiocese Commission of Investigation, established by the government, to look at the child protection policies of Cloyne (though the HSE had felt the referral was not warranted).

Meanwhile, Monsignor Charles Scicluna, the head of a department of seven within the Congregation for the Doctrine of the Faith in Rome charged with investigating allegations against priests, revealed that out of the 3,000 priests reported by bishops for sexual misconduct in ten years, 300 involved paedophilia. Against the tide, Ferns was doing what it could to inspire confidence in its active clergy: it had decided to dispense with the celebret system – a letter that said the priest was of good standing – and issued identity cards instead. The oldest Christian artefact in the Diocese of Ferns, the broken Cross of St Fintan's, which adorns the diocesan vestments, is near the entrance to the Church of Ireland in Taghmon, one of four crosses setting the boundary of the monastery founded in the sixth century: its desecration was attributed to Cromwellian soldiers, who sacked Wexford with brute force. A carving of the restored cross, symbolising Bishop Walsh's efforts to restore the diocese to better health, was presented to him before he returned to the Dublin archdiocese, where more trouble was brewing.

The Commission to Inquire into Child Abuse, which

investigated the abuse of children in sixty residential Reformatory and Industrial Schools, managed by Catholic Church orders from 1936, published *The Ryan Report* in May 2009. It reported that the religious treated children like prisoners and slaves, encouraged ritual beatings and shielded their abusers. The abuse was described by *The Ryan Report* as 'systemic, pervasive, chronic, excessive, arbitrary, endemic'. Children lived with the daily terror of not knowing where the next beating was coming from. The role of the government, particularly administrations led by Éamon de Valera, indifferent to the welfare of poorer children under their noses, was addressed. Consider the performance of the Department of Education: it rarely applied the standards in its own guidelines to young children when confronted with complaints by parents, but obstinately protected the religious congregations and the schools. Sexual abuse, ignored in the department from the top down, was endemic in boys' institutions. Perpetrators were able to operate undetected for long periods and, if caught, were transferred to another school, where they could abuse again. (The Department of Education never investigated the allegations of abuse by a school chaplain against confirmation-age pupils in Monageer, reported by one of its employees – the principal – to the South Eastern Health Board.)

An RTÉ *Prime Time* programme, *Cardinal Secrets*, in 2002 (by Mary Raftery, who had investigated abuse in industrial schools in *States of Fear* a decade before *The Ryan Report*, and Mick Peelo) so troubled Justice Minister Michael McDowell that it lay the groundwork for the Commission of Investigation Act 2004. Two years on, the Commission of Investigation, Dublin Archdiocese, was established under the chairmanship of Ms Justice Yvonne Murphy. The report of the commission, known worldwide as *The Murphy Report*, disclosed in November 2009 that the State had facilitated the Church in hushing up thirty years of child abuse by the religious in the Archdiocese of Dublin, incorporating four counties.

'There was little or no concern for the welfare of the abused child or for the welfare of other children who might come into contact with the priest. Complaints were often met with denial, arrogance and cover-up and with incompetence and incomprehension in some areas. Suspicions were rarely acted on.' Not once, during the 1960s, the 1970s or the 1980s, did four archbishops – John McQuaid, Dermot Ryan, Kevin McNamara and Desmond Connell – report a single incident of clerical abuse to the authorities. It was 1995 before Connell brought seventeen priests to the attention of Gardaí, such as Fr Ivan Payne, against whom thirty-one people made allegations and Fr William Carney, alleged to have abused over thirty victims.

'The Dublin Archdiocese's pre-occupations in dealing with cases of child sexual abuse, at least until the 1990s, were the maintenance of secrecy, the avoidance of scandal, the protection of the reputation of the Church, and the preservation of its assets. All other considerations, including the welfare of children and justice for victims, were subordinated to these priorities,' said *The Murphy Report*. Auxilary bishops, like Comiskey, who would have observed at first hand how the archdiocese did its best to undermine Irish law, were then sent further afield to run and effectively mismanage a diocese of their own.

The disclosure that auxiliary bishops would have been informed, as a matter of course, of allegations against priests, and would have been responsible for assigning troubled priests to new parishes with the consent of the archbishop, sealed the fate of some. Bishop Donal Murray (1982–1996) and Bishop James Moriarty (1991–2002) offered their resignations, which were accepted by Pope Benedict. Bishop Martin

Drennan (1997–2005) resisted calls to resign as Bishop of Galway, while both Bishop Eamonn Walsh (1990 – present) and Bishop Raymond Field (1997 – present), both belatedly offered to resign on Christmas Eve 2009, though Benedict, ten months later, refused to accept their resignations, a source of considerable embarrassment for Archbishop Diarmuid Martin, who was 'shocked by the level of disassociation by people from any sense of responsibility'. In the aftermath of *The Murphy Report*, Dr Vincent Twomey, professor of moral theology at NUI Maynooth, maintained that resigning was the only option available to the five auxiliary bishops. 'It comes down not to conscience but to moral courage. We've smothered our conscience, maybe we don't have the moral courage to stand up and be shot down.'

Walsh – whom Martin had initially deployed as a diocesan spokesperson even when he was familiar with the report's contents – had his supporters, both within the Church and the media, and there was empathy for his contention that his guilt was by way of association, not complicity in a cover-up. He hinted that his attempt to report allegations of abuse was thwarted by the diocese. Walsh was a lesson in how to fight a rearguard action. In a detailed letter to priests of the diocese on 17 December 2009, he outlined his record, placing special emphasis on the inter-agency meetings that he piloted in Ferns with the HSE and the Gardaí. In a stinging riposte to Archbishop Martin, Walsh concluded: 'The question of resignation has been raised on the grounds of guilt by association. However, guilt by association only arises when someone is complicit in a decision or action, or is silent when to speak would have made a difference. Present in a room or proximity to a decision-maker of itself is not guilt by association. If anyone attributes such guilt to me, he or she does so without foundation, and against the findings of the Dublin report [*The Murphy Report*].'

For good measure, he concluded that Martin had confirmed his public confidence in his auxiliary bishops at a meeting of priests five days earlier: Martin's clarification that he meant confidence in their ministry sparked Walsh's offer to resign. That the Pope rejected his resignation polarised opinion: Nuala O'Loan, former Police Ombudsman for Northern Ireland, having looked at the references to Walsh and Field in *The Murphy Report*, felt that the resignations would have been an injustice. Colm O'Gorman remarked that, as a barrister and canon lawyer, Walsh had not challenged the prevailing culture and Benedict's decision was beyond the point of reason. Was there an animus between Walsh and O'Gorman? Asked by Jackie Hayden, in a questions-and-answers style interview for the book *In Their Own Words*, why nobody in the diocese had asked people to refrain from verbally abusing O'Gorman, Walsh's response smacked of aloofness, even indifference. 'If they've been personally abusive of Colm I certainly wouldn't stand over them. I've heard the most outrageous things said on late night Dublin radio programmes, but it would be a full-time job trying to dissociate yourself from all those type of comments. Maybe I've become so used to having abuse hurled at me and my colleagues that we just remind ourselves that the truth will out in the end.' Interviewed on RTÉ radio days after Benedict's decision, Mary Raftery believed Walsh knew enough about what was going on in the archdiocese to warrant his resignation.

The response of the Church in Dublin was in contrast to the Archdiocese of Chicago, which created the Commission on Clerical Sexual Misconduct with Minors in 1991, to learn how to become more effective in addressing abuse allegations. Within a two-year period, the recommendations of the commission's report were adopted and implemented, including the reporting of allegations of child abuse to the

Illinois Department of Children and Family Services, and the reporting to the appropriate State's Attorney whenever the diocese removed a priest from ministry, which it had to do nineteen times. Chicago was a rare example of how a diocese could be proactive rather than reactive: policies initiated by Joseph Cardinal Bernardin in 1992 were reviewed ten years later by Cardinal Francis George. 'Building on the premise that no child should be at risk of sexual abuse by a cleric, the policies have been strengthened over the last decade,' said the report. Presaging the changes that Walsh would bring to Ferns, and for which he would be criticised by clergy, the Archdiocese of Chicago left no priest in ministry against whom a substantiated allegation of abuse was made, and all allegations were reported to relevant authorities. 'We have done our best to ensure that victims are treated sensitively, forthrightly, and been given the respect they deserve,' said Diocesan Chancellor Jimmy Lago (there was 'reasonable cause' to suspect that clerical abuse occurred in fifty-five cases, dating back forty years, and involving thirty-six priests. Eight were dead, nine resigned and nineteen were removed).

The Irish bishops met with Pope Benedict and senior curial figures again in the Pontifical Irish College in Rome in 2010 to discuss what the Vatican referred to as 'the serious situation which has emerged in the Church in Ireland', described by Bishop of Clogher Joseph Duffy, Chairman of the Communications Commission of the Irish Bishops Conference, as not a cosmetic exercise, an understatement as the Pope was in despair over the burgeoning clerical sex abuse scandal in his native Germany. *Der Spiegel*, a week earlier, reported that almost 100 priests in the country's 27 dioceses were suspected of child abuse.

For two days, Benedict listened as each of the twenty-four Irish bishops offered his own observations and suggestions.

According to a Vatican statement: 'The bishops spoke frankly of the sense of pain and anger, betrayal, scandal and shame expressed to them on numerous occasions by those who had been abused.' However, it was abundantly clear to most observers outside the inner sanctum of Benedict and his Irish bishops that the questions that mattered most in Ireland – why the Pope had not offered to meet abuse victims, why the Papal Nuncio, Dr Giuseppe Leanza, would not appear before a Dáil foreign affairs committee, why the Holy See had failed to cooperate with the Murphy Commission – remained unaddressed. Vatican policy is that apostolic nuncios do not appear before parliamentary commissions, but this did not stop Alan Shatter, Fine Gael's shadow spokesperson on children, calling on the hierarchy 'to engage in constructive, transparent dialogue with regard to the manner in which the Church has dealt with the issue of clerical child abuse'.

The bishops left the Vatican not entirely empty handed: they had an opportunity to look at Benedict's pastoral letter, due to be delivered during Lent to the Catholics in Ireland, and suggested emendations. In a lengthy address, Benedict was set to admit that among the contributing factors that created the conditions for priests to abuse children were inadequate procedures for determining the suitability of candidates for the priesthood; insufficient spiritual formation in seminaries and novitiates; societal favouritism toward authority figures, such as the parish priest, a priority by the Church to protect its reputation at all costs and a failure to apply canonical penalties.

A legacy in Ireland of decades of abuse, covering up and being economical with the truth, is how those active within the Church – laity, priests, bishops – who would rather forget acts of criminality by the few who were protected by the powerful, are forced to live with those who cannot, such as two children, aged ten and fourteen, both brutalised by a paedophile and asked by another priest to commit to a vow of silence. Cardinal Seán Brady, who as 35-year-old Fr Brady in the 1970s was merely implementing what he understood as Church protocol, in silencing the two victims as part of a canonical inquiry into Fr Brendan Smyth, said it was not fair to judge his actions of thirty-five years ago by the standards of 2010. There was not the remotest possibility of Brady resigning after the revelation, which came to light a week before Benedict's unprecedented Pastoral Letter was circulated in Ireland. Days after Comiskey's resignation in 2002, Brady had issued a statement as President of the Irish Episcopal Conference. 'The sexual abuse of children by priests is an especially grave and repugnant evil.' He added that Comiskey's stepping down came out of context of deep human suffering, both of victims of abuse and himself.

'Hiding behind a legal technicality does not sit well for a man of the cloth, and adds to the public's lack of faith in the Catholic hierarchy in Ireland,' wrote Marie Parker-Jenkins, Faculty of Education and Health Sciences, University of Limerick. 'Out of respect for the victims, it would be more honourable for Brady to resign.' But he did not, and he proved that the values of his Church, well meaning on paper such as Benedict's Lenten missive, are empty formulas when not applied in practice. Brady's only misdemeanour in his own eyes was his adherence to a duty of confidentiality.

Ferns, out of the limelight for so long while the Church imploded elsewhere in Ireland and in Europe, never lost its aptitude for shooting itself in the foot, and the arrogance with which it had conducted its affairs for decades surfaced in a very public display of ineptitude and insensitivity. It appealed to its laity, and by extension the victims of clerical abuse, to help pay its legal costs. By 2005, the diocese had paid out €2,792,118 in settlements with abuse victims, (including €200,000 to a Catholic priest who had been abused as a seminarian at

St Peter's), 90 per cent of which had been raised from the Stewardship Trust (Church & General had paid Irish bishops €10.6 million to release it from having to deal with abuse claims before 1996), which was diminishing. The diocese had paid €199,850 from its own almost exhausted sources, and there was a suggestion that fixed assets, like the bishop's substantial house, would be sold to raise money. Priests in the diocese, both serving and retired, had already ploughed €75,000 into the St Ibar's Trust to help bail out Ferns.

A year on, the diocese confirmed that it had paid a total of €4.7 million in respect of twenty-nine cases settled, but another twenty were still pending, and expected to cost a further €5 million. Ferns had submitted an application to the government for recovery of legal costs (€2.68 million) arising from its cooperation with both the preliminary investigation into the diocese by George Birmingham SC, and then the Ferns Inquiry, chaired by Justice Francis Murphy. The diocese had paid €300,000 towards these costs but still owed around €2.3 million for legal representation, and had secured €760,000 through borrowings to finance the treatment and monitoring of offenders. Ferns would receive a once-off payment of €650,000 from the government.

By 2009, the figures being bandied about within the diocese were staggering: forty-eight settlements had been made, to the tune of €8,120,775 (€2,138,692 of which were legal fees), and there were still thirteen civil actions pending. The costs for treating its abusive priests had risen to €836,000, though Fr John Carroll confirmed that the retention of the diocese's fixed assets would not 'get in the way of finding a lasting solution in the area of child sexual abuse'. Bishop Brennan, addressing the diocesan AGM in 2009, made no secret of the fact that the laity would have to consider ways of contributing to the coffers. 'As we look to complete this road [of justice], it will be necessary to invite the parishes to become part of the process financially.'

As nobody, however, appeared to be paying any attention to his warning, he reiterated his appeal a year later, but this time it did not fall on deaf ears, and all hell broke loose, not only in Ferns, but throughout the country. Innocuous interviews by Eugene Doyle, Chairman of the Finance Committee for the diocese, on RTÉ radio and Newstalk, suggested Brennan wanted parishioners to pitch in to help offset €10.5 million in legal bills arising from cases brought against priests in his employ. The backlash was immediate and immense. 'In asking for funding from your own parishioners you are asking the abused to pay for costs associated with their own abuse,' commented Evin M. Daly, CEO of One Child International. 'How absurd. It reinforces the perception of contempt that you – the Church – have toward the victims.' Daly added that there was more to the debt to victims than just financial. 'There is a moral and ethical obligation to provide recompense from within the halls of the Church proper for the incomprehensible crimes committed against the innocents. There can be no other way.' Attempts by Doyle to clarify the diocese's position only served to add fuel to the flames of derision. He told Newstalk's Eamonn Keane that the diocese had its protection measures in place, but that 'life has to keep going on'. An incensed Christine Buckley, director of the Aislinn Education and Support Centre in Dublin and an abuse survivor of Goldenbridge Industrial School, reminded Doyle that 'life didn't move on for many of our people, many committed suicide, many are incarcerated in psychiatric hospitals, many are literally lost souls'. Stung by the virulence of the antagonism, three days later Carroll confirmed the diocese's change of tack: going to the parishes for money was but one option. 'It may very well be that a decision will be taken to dispose of one of the diocesan assets.' However, following deanery meetings in September to discuss the difficulties in fund-raising, Bishop Brennan asked each priest to contribute €1,000 annually to a new Friends of Ferns Diocesan Fund, as it was felt that the clergy should take the lead and contribute first themselves. There were ninety-two active priests in the diocese, so it was hoped that the fund, which would commence in January 2011, would realise €92,000 at first. The diocese included a standing order with the summons for the donation.

The number of men beginning formal studies for the priesthood in Ireland since the publication of *The Ferns Report* has been pitifully low: thirty in 2006, thirty-one in 2007, thirty in 2008 and thirty-six in 2009. Late in August 2010, just sixteen seminarians chose a life as a priest, spread between the national seminary at St Patrick's College, Maynooth, St Malachy's College, Belfast, the Irish College in Rome and the Royal English College, Valladolid, Spain. They came from dioceses throughout the country, from Down and Connor, from Cork and Ross, from Kildare and Leighlin, but not among the eleven dioceses to supply seminarians was Ferns.

Finally, that the Catholic Church in Ireland equivocated in the past with serial clerical offenders was emphasised once more with the delayed publication of Chapter 19 of The Murphy Report in December 2010: there subsisted, with the Dublin Archdiocese's governance of Fr Tony Walsh and the Ferns Diocese's governance of Fr Seán Fortune, a common miscalculation of the appropriate and proper response to the prevention of their crimes. Like Fortune, Walsh – who abused children for sexual gratification once every two weeks for eight years, and admitted as much to the Church – was moved from parish to parish and attempts to corral him were interspersed with sporadic bouts of counselling in Ireland and in England. Between 1978, when allegations of abuse were made known to the archdiocese, and 1996, when he was defrocked, Tony

Walsh was just another case handled by no fewer than half a dozen bishops. Their power to arbitrate was compromised by the bounds of their oath of secrecy.

A proposal by Bishop Eamonn Walsh in 1991 that the archdiocese report Walsh to the Gardaí was rejected as 'an outrageous suggestion' by Monsignor Gerard Sheehy. Nor was the paralysis in deed confined to the Irish bishops. Archbishop Desmond Connell succeeded in removing Walsh from his apostolate in 1993, but Walsh appealed the decision and it was overturned by the Vatican, if Walsh entered a monastery for ten years. However, no monastery would take him and, as criminal charges had been brought against him, he could not be sent abroad. Connell, one of the first prelates in Europe to initiate a canonical trial, personally petitioned and begged Pope John Paul II in 1995 to dismiss Walsh and a decree to that effect was issued by Cardinal Ratzinger. The apoplexy among Tony Walsh's victims at the revelation in Chapter 19 that the first complaints against him were treated in a desultory manner by the Archdiocese was intensified three days after its publication by Pope Benedict's contention, in his Christmas message to cardinals, that paedophilia was not considered an absolute evil by society as recently as the 1970s, a misdiagnosis that raises grave concerns about the Vatican's ability and willingness to confront what Bruce Arnold has described as 'the great crime of the third millennium'.

Appendix 1

Transcript of interview given by Bishop of Limerick Donal Murray on 27 November 2009, following publication of the Commission of Investigation report into Child Sex Abuse Allegations in the Archdiocese of Dublin (*The Murphy Report*), to Joe Nash on Limerick's Live 95FM.

JN: Bishop Murray, good morning to you.

BM: Good morning.

JN: Thank you for joining us in the studio. Let me quote directly from the report to begin with: 'Bishop Murray was another long-serving auxiliary bishop from 1982 to 1996. He handled a number of complaints and suspicions badly. For example, he didn't deal properly with the suspicions and concerns that were expressed to him in relation to Fr Tom Naughton. When a short time later factual evidence of Fr Naughton's abusing emerged in another parish, Bishop Murray's failure to reinvestigate the earlier suspicions was inexcusable.' What's your response to that?

BM: Before I say anything, the whole focus has to be in all of our minds on the children, innocent children who were abused and whose lives were destroyed and I want to offer my sympathy and my apologies to anybody who was abused in Dublin and above all to anybody whose abuse might have been mitigated or prevented if I had acted in another way than I had. My prime concern here isn't to respond or defend myself. Could I say about that particular case, what the Commission says first of all, one could misunderstand what the Commission says. The Commission criticised me in three cases. In none of those cases did I receive an allegation of sexual abuse. What happened in the case that they are referring to was that two people came to me, they expressed concern about the closeness of Fr Naughton to the altar boys. Obviously I questioned them. I asked them whether there were any particular altar boys they were concerned about; they said no, they weren't suggesting anything wrong was going on and I thought that was a good sign as at the time I would have said that if he wasn't isolating altar boys that was a good sign. Now I'm not so sure that would have put my mind at rest. Then I asked them was there any particular kind of behaviour that they were concerned about and again they said they weren't suggesting there was anything wrong going on; they just wanted him to grow up and that I should tell him to have less to do with the altar boys. If I was trying to cover up I would have stopped there. I didn't stop there. I went to the parish priest and asked him what did he think, had he heard anything. He was very sceptical that anything was going on. I said to him, look you have to go now – I wouldn't have known people in the parish – and said I want you to go to sacristans, teachers, people who might be in a position to have heard anything if there was any suspicion and I would come back in a few days and you could tell me what you found. When I came back he said you can put your mind at rest, there's nothing wrong going on. I was actually surprised at how positive his report back was as I knew they didn't get on well, himself and the curate. Then I called Fr Naughton to my house and I asked him about it.

He denied he was doing anything wrong and I said to him look, no matter, even if these things are unfounded or if there are misunderstandings, you have to be very careful about anything you are doing that is causing parents to be concerned. If the altar boys come to celebrate Mass, you must deal with them as far as the celebrating of Mass is concerned, and don't have anything more to do with them. And then I went to the Archbishop and told him what had happened. I was only eighteen months a bishop at that stage and wanted to see if there was something else I should have done. I also wanted to be sure there wasn't something else in this man's file that would make two and two add to four. So that's really what happened. So I accept that afterwards . . .

JN: What happened to him then?

BM: Nothing happened to him because we hadn't an allegation. The other thing going in that parish was I was getting complaints about his manner, that he was abrasive. Even though the PP said there was nothing going on and he said it would be better to move this man and give him a new start somewhere else. It was decided that would happen at the end of the year. That was the reason he was moved. It was not because of any allegations. We hadn't received any allegation.

JN: He was moved simply because of his manner?

BM: He was moved because he had offended so many people in the parish so really it would be better that he would start somewhere else.

JN: A lot of parish priests offend people in different parishes, including in this diocese and they are not moved.

BM: We can't move them all but this was one where there seemed to be a particular kind of difficulty about his popularity in the parish.

JN: He was moved and pretty quickly evidence emerged of abuse on his part?

BM: That's right. That's right. That's when we should have gone back.

JN: The Commission says that your behaviour there was inexcusable.

BM: I would accept we should have gone back and I think, in fairness one should say it was the diocese that should have gone back because it would have to have involved the people who had specific evidence.

JN: When did you become aware of the second set of allegations that appeared to have more facts behind them?

BM: I became aware of them, actually, before they came in, in the sense that I became aware there had been a fight in that parish and that there was some rumour that it had to do with his relationship with children. When I heard that, I immediately reminded the Archbishop and the other bishops of what I had told them, whatever it was 18 months or two years before.

JN: Why didn't you and others in the Archdiocese go back to those earlier allegations at that time?

BM: I don't think we were thinking in those terms at that time. We should have, we recognise we should have. I think it is important to say that it is a question that couldn't arise now as the people who would be doing the investigation now would be the Gardaí.

JN: *How many complaints of sexual abuse would you have handled in your time as an auxiliary bishop?*

BM: Handled complaints in the sense that I would have received the original complaint? Very few. You could say I was the first person to hear concerns of any kind about Fr Naughton but I was not the first person to hear allegations and there were two or three cases but sometimes I heard allegations of abuse against somebody who was already out of ministry or we were already aware that there were allegations against.

JN: *You are mentioned reasonably frequently in the report as being involved at some level in the enquiries into a number of cases, Fr Horatio for example.*

BM: I have forgotten what all those names mean. I think I know that one. I think that's the one where they say I wasn't given the information I needed in terms of previous medical assessments and so on. I don't think it criticises me in that case.

JN: *Did you say to the Commission that the ultimate responsibility here was the Archbishop's?*

BM: Well, of course, that's certainly the truth. I wasn't saying so much that it was the ultimate responsibility of the Archbishop; I was saying that the system, flawed as it was, implied that the person who would have all the information would be the Archbishop. Priests would move around between one bishop's area to another and so on so it was very important that there was something fed into the central administration.

JN: *What does it say to you that an Archbishop in the mid-1980s was looking for insurance cover for the archdiocese against these allegations of potential claims of child sexual abuse by priests?*

BM: I wasn't involved in that decision. I think it was simply that the Archbishop at the time was being told by various American bishops that you should have this insurance, maybe we should, but I don't think at that time there was any appreciation of the scale of the problem.

JN: *This may seem like an odd question, it is worth asking, but did you know clearly in your own mind that child sexual abuse was a sin and a crime?*

BM: Yes, of course. Yes, of course. But I think . . . as I say, there was a kind of culture in the Church and I suspect in other places too of not involving the Gardaí in this sort of thing. I think that was a mistake. It was all wrong.

JN: *Where did that come from?*

BM: I don't know. I don't know. I certainly didn't initiate it but I think I can see clearly it was wrong. I didn't see clearly then when I was a very short time a bishop, I didn't see it.

JN: *Most of the people listening this morning would come to the conclusion that if somebody came with a complaint, particularly in an organisation or elsewhere, the very first step you would take alongside any internal investigation, would be to report it to An Garda Síochána?*

BM: Well in fact, no. There would be very little in the way of internal investigation now. Very little. We would establish basic facts – was the priest in the place at the time? – that sort of thing.

JN: *That's now.*

BM: Investigation isn't our job. That was part of the problem, I think. We had no way of doing investigations really in the forensic way the Gardaí can do them.

JN: *Exactly, and that would still have been the case in the early 1980s.*

BM: It was indeed.

JN: *But then the question comes to mind, why simply not hand over the information in the file to Gardaí and then, with clean hands, you can say . . .*

BM: Absolutely, absolutely that's what should happen and it does happen. And thanks be to God it happens. People are talking about a cover-up but it was also a huge burden and a huge anxiety. I mean it's the most difficult thing of all, to be face to face with somebody whose life has been destroyed by somebody who was supposed to be bringing them peace. It's a dreadful experience but the whole thing, our experience is nothing compared to theirs obviously and the pain that they have.

JN: *Marie Collins, who is a survivor, and the Minister for Justice Dermot Ahern said yesterday, and you used the word yourself, that there was a cover-up within the Archdiocese of Dublin involving senior people, Archbishops and auxiliary bishops. You were one. Was there a cover-up and were you involved in it?*

BM: No. I certainly never was involved in a cover-up. The other two cases I was involved in were cases that had begun long before I was involved at all. I was asked to do certain things in them, in connection with them, but I was not involved in covering up. I think that if one covers up it is really something, that is, you see, there was an extraordinary idea, I think, that they almost saw parents and children as not being part of the interests of the Church. When the Commission talks about protecting the interests of the Church, protecting the interests of the Church means protecting the interests of the people, especially the children.

JN: That didn't appear to be the case.

BM: Yes, that's what I'm saying.

JN: You are saying you weren't involved in any cover-up but do you accept the characterisation by the current Minister for Justice as a cover-up?

BM: Oh yes. There are certain things . . . I would have to go through the whole report in detail but there were certainly things. There were talks about trying to persuade the Gardaí to drop cases and all that sort of thing. I certainly would . . . there's no excuse for that.

JN: Are you concerned that there may be a criminal investigation into that cover-up and that you might get dragged into it?

BM: No I'm not. Because I don't think I was involved in any cover-up that I am aware of . . .

JN: Could you be brought in on the periphery because obviously you had an involvement in certain cases in the way that you have outlined yourself?

BM: Yeah. Well, I mean, if I am I am. I don't believe I was involved in covering up anything. Like I said, if I was involved in trying to cover up that case in Valleymount I would not have gone any further than the fact that the people who came to me said they weren't suggesting there was anything wrong going on.

JN: Another reference that was made even by yourself was in the context of where the Archbishop stood in all of this in the hierarchy of the Church, was a respect for canon law. Were you and others respecting canon law over the civil law of the Republic?

BM: No, I think actually what the report is saying is that canon law wasn't being observed in the same way. There seemed to be a period from about the 1960s on, before that period there were a number of canonical investigations that took place so I mean obviously it still didn't justify not approaching Gardaí but these priests were dismissed having followed a canonical investigation but that didn't necessarily do anything much for the children.

JN: *It is interesting there are headlines all over the papers and one of them is from today's* Irish Examiner *and they quote from the report: 'The archdiocese's preoccupations were the maintenance of secrecy, the avoidance of scandal, the protection of the Church's reputation and the preservation of its assets – other considerations, including the welfare of children and justice for victims were subordinate to these priorities'.*

BM: I think there's truth in that and I am not aware, as I said in that case in Valleymount, I had not got any allegation. I had not got the name of any child. I had not got a description of any kind of behaviour.

JN: *Did you become the go-to person in certain cases of allegations of abuse? In other words, was the Archbishop and others saying to you, 'Well, Dr Murray, you've dealt with a number of these'?*

BM: I hadn't dealt with that many of them compared to most of the other bishops, I'd say, at the time. No, you would be involved sometimes if the person who was accused was living in your area, maybe out of ministry, maybe in semi-retirement, or whatever, you would be asked to deal with some particular aspect of the case.

JN: *What about the suggestion in the report from a woman who said that she approached you at a confirmation and you dismissed her?*

BM: I certainly didn't dismiss her. I only vaguely remember that. She was asking me, as I understood it, was he [Fr Naughton] going to be moved. I knew he was going to be moved in six weeks or so but he hadn't been told so I didn't really feel I could say it straight to her but I thought I said something fairly encouraging that we were looking at it or we were dealing with it. I think that it might be interesting to say too, and this doesn't prove anything except to me, but when the concerns arose in the second parish, I immediately remembered the two people who came to me.

I didn't remember that; I didn't remember any other approach because none of the other approaches to my mind had to do with sexual abuse of children, had any reference to children.

JN: Could you have prevented, Bishop Murray, certain instances of abuse if you had acted differently?

BM: Well, when I discovered, and I think that's again about the case in Valleymount, when I discovered around 2001 or 2002, that there were in fact allegations of abuse circulating in Valleymount, that people had said they had gone to the parish priest about it; that people had said that a schoolteacher was aware of it; I obviously said to myself, was there some way I could have got that information, perhaps from the two people who came to me, if they had all that information? You ask yourself that and you say is there another way of asking the question or was there some way maybe I could have made it clear to the parish priest that it was absolutely essential that if he heard anything that he would pass it on and so on I tried to do all those things and I say to myself, could I have done it differently?

JN: Did you believe at all times that when you had taken the information back to the Archbishop, your boss, that he was going to make the decisions and you would have to live with them regardless of what they were?

BM: Well, I don't think so in the sense that I would have to, that we would certainly have to discuss some of these things, not that none of these issues the Commission can criticise me on, but we would have discussed some issues on how to handle accused people and so on. We would not always have agreed.

JN: Did you believe, and I know that your gut instinct is not evidence, but did you believe in your heart that Fr Naughton was a child abuser?

BM: No I didn't, I'm afraid. That was the mistake. I was very concerned that that might be what was behind what the two people . . . but after talking to the parish priest and after getting all this feedback from him and so on, I'm afraid that the parish priest told me to set my mind at rest and I'm afraid that's what I did. It remained in the back of my mind and that's why when the accusations arose in the next parish, I immediately, I immediately remembered the two people who came to me.

JN:*When you and others within the Archdiocese communicated with each other over that, and there were a lot of allegations and a lot of complaints coming in, at any point did you think to yourselves, are we really doing the right thing here? There are a lot of things happening under the surface, there are a lot of complaints happening – they are individual, I accept that – but they were certainly building up to a critical mass and yet it is hidden from public view.*

BM: I think yes, in a sense, that's one of the great things that has happened in the last, you know, ten, twelve years, is the number of lay people who are now involved in this whole question of child safeguarding and the whole question of dealing with . . .

JN: *But can you understand how that would lead people to the conclusion that there was a deliberate conspiracy or cover-up?*

BM:Well, yes, of course I can, but I think it's worth saying that the report also says that communication at that level was poor, in other words the individual auxiliary bishops did not know.

JN: *But it says the documentation was excellent.*

BM:Yes, yes. But that documentation wasn't shared by the auxiliary bishops. I think there was a sense, and it wasn't entirely wrong but it led to terrible conclusions, but there was a sense that when a person was accused, that you shouldn't be destroying his good name until something was established against him. And so information was shared by the Archbishop on a kind of need-to-know basis and that need to know was drawn far too narrowly in my view now.

JN:*Were you conscious of the need to protect the Church's reputation at all costs?*

BM: I don't think I would have wished to protect the Church's reputation at all costs. I would not, I mean, I think, I suppose the real intense understanding, growing in understanding of what abuse does to people only comes when you've spoken to and listened to and talked to victims.

JN: *But Marie Collins says the report debunks that view, that it was a learning curve. Her view, and she says it is backed up by the Commission, is that you were all highly educated men and you knew exactly what it was from the first instance?*

BM: Well, I don't like to disagree with the Commission but I would say that I hope we are all on a learning curve. I think the worst thing that would happen would be that we would become complacent and say we know all about this now and say we have it all covered. In some senses we have to remain learning about best practice about how to be most effective in dealing with these things.

JN: Just to quote again from the report, 'Many of the auxiliary bishops also knew of the fact of abuse, as did officials such as Monsignor Gerard Sheehy and Monsignor Alex Stenson, who worked with the chancellery; Bishop James Kavanagh and Bishop Dermot O'Mahony, Bishop Laurence Forristal, Bishop Donal Murray and Bishop Brendan Comiskey were aware for many years of complaints and/or suspicions of clerical child sexual abuse in the [Dublin] archdiocese.' What's your response to that?

BM: Well, that's true. I don't think I was aware of the scale of it. I have to say that when I saw the report first there were cases that I knew nothing about and horrified at the scale of it, I have to say. But I did know that there were a number of cases, of course, yes.

JN: Do you think that if women had been in more senior positions in the Roman Catholic Church in that period that the cover-up would ever have happened?

BM: I don't know the answer to that. We certainly have a lot of women involved in our child safeguarding and protecting in Limerick now and they do a great job and, I think, have added a great deal to our work but I don't know the answer to that.

JN: Archbishop Diarmuid Martin, the current Archbishop of Dublin, says you and others must ask (a) if you did the right thing and (b) if your current ministry in Limerick, and to the other auxiliary bishops around the country, is the right one for you?

BM: Yes, indeed, and, you know, I have asked myself that question very often, especially since and, indeed, long before this Commission was set up. But I think I have concluded that I always acted in the best of faith; I always did what I thought was the best. There are occasions such as the one in Valleymount where I say to myself could I have done it differently? Would there have been a different result? I don't know whether there would or not. I would do it differently now and certainly report to the Gardaí now.

JN: Fr Naughton was convicted only in the last year, if I am correct?

BM: I am not sure about that. I think there were some cases in Valleymount and there was a civil case long before that though. When I was talking about when it came, when I began to discover there were things going on in Valleymount, there was a civil case in 2002.

JN: Are you considering your position as Bishop of Limerick?

BM: I have been considering for a long time and I have come to the conclusion that I have learned a lot of lessons, both from my own experience and from what I have seen around me, and I think I should implement those lessons and I think we have been implementing them, lessons that are reinforced by the report but lessons that we were implementing before the report came at all, ever since I came to Limerick.

JN: Will you resign?

BM: No.

JN: Is your position tenable?

BM: I believe it is but the question of whether I remain, as far as I am concerned, is a matter for the people of Limerick and the priests of Limerick but I believe we have put very fine child safeguarding structures in place and I think that our record for reporting allegations and so on is 100 per cent.

JN: Are you dealing with complaints of sexual abuse within the diocese of Limerick?

BM: You mean at the moment? There is no priest under investigation at the moment.

JN: Are you dealing with any historical cases from before your time?

BM: There are historical cases. But obviously people who are dead are not under investigation but we are trying to deal in a number of cases with the people who are victims of priests of up to forty years ago maybe.

JN: What assurances can you give parents listening, Catholics listening, that you are a credible arbiter if such a complaint arises again because, I think, what's that old saying, every bishop is a pope in his own diocese?

BM: I believe I have. I suppose I am not the best judge of it. I believe we have dealt correctly and conscientiously with every complaint that I have received since I came to Limerick.

JN: *Do you believe that your behaviour in all of those cases, other than what you talked about in the Fr Naughton case, was exemplary or did you make mistakes in other cases too?*

BM: I think the other cases revealed a certain failure of structures. I mean, there was one case in which I was criticised because there was no proper monitoring system in place. There was a question of who was supposed to be doing that, there was also the question of what monitoring system will really work. But the monitoring system that was in place was not established by me and it wasn't adequate but I don't think any monitoring system is adequate, to be quite honest. I think that's a question we still have to address.

JN: *You are saying you are not going to resign. Two questions: is it possible that you will be moved or forced out if the media storm grows over this and is the Catholic Church in Ireland dead?*

BM: I don't think the Catholic Church in Ireland is dead. I think . . . that . . . One of the phrases that keeps coming to me during all this period, I think, has been the phrase of St Paul: 'God's strength is made perfect in weakness' and 'when we are weak then we are strong'. I think the Church thought it was strong in the past, and it's a terrible situation to be in actually. We are far truer to ourselves when we know we are weak.

JN: *Could you be forced out?*

BM: I have no idea. I have no idea. If I felt my ministry was not the best – was not good – for the Diocese of Limerick, I wouldn't have to be forced.

JN: *I am sorry; I have to finish it on that.*

BM: Could I just say one thing? The worst thing that abuse does in some ways is that it undermines the faith of people. As I've said in the letter that I have sent out to the priests, the people who are abused are closer than they realise to the Lord on the Cross, saying 'my God, my God, why have you forsaken me'. They are closer to him than we are, I'm afraid.

Appendix 2

Interview with Colm O'Gorman in December 2003 by Brendan Keane, which was published in *The Wexford Echo*.

BK: When did you first become aware that you were being treated in an inappropriate manner – which of course is putting it very mildly?

CO'G: When it was happening there wasn't a moment when I had a chance to think about whether or not it was appropriate. It was just a case of dealing with, coping with it and getting through it.

BK: But how did you deal with it – how did you rationalise what was happening?

CO'G: It was my fault . . . I was doing something wrong. It was me . . . I'm bad. Seán Fortune was very quick to act on that one – I mean he was great at switching into the priest after something had happened, saying 'Oh I'm worried about you, you've got a problem'. The number of people that we've talked to at One in Four who talked about being abused and then sent for confession by their abuser! The intention was always [to give the impression] it's your fault . . . you need to confess. You've done something wrong. In Ireland of the time it was very easy to believe it was my fault. That was a lot easier to believe than to believe I was being raped by a Catholic priest because there was no way that you could hold onto that piece of information and continue to live in that society anyway because it just couldn't happen. Either the impossible is true or it's your fault; and 'it's my fault' is a lot more comfortable because if it's my fault I don't have to do anything about it. I'm just bad.

BK: When did you decide you had to stop it from happening and how did that thought occur to you?

CO'G: It was 1994 and I had been living in London since 1986 and I suppose my life had to some degree begun to settle down for the first time. I still didn't have any kind of sense of myself in lots of ways but I think things were beginning to kind of come up for me. I'd started to talk to friends about it and it had just started to emerge for me. I wasn't able to put words to it yet – or language to it. There was just something that wasn't ok and it was the first time in my life that I had been in a place where I'd had enough time to just stand still for that to even occur to me. Life had been very chaotic . . . I'd left Wexford when I was 17 in January 1984. I hitched to Dublin and I was homeless then . . . on and off for six to nine months. I started to put things back together again to try and cope and live someplace and then I went to London in '86. Then it was just about trying to find out a bit more about who I was in the world and what I was about.

BK: I presume at that time you were also finding it extremely difficult to figure out who you were as a person?

CO'G: I hadn't a clue who I was. All the time I was living in Wexford I just believed I was sick, that I was foul, that I was perverted, that I was wrong, that I was awful and that's all there was – there was no other way of dealing with it other than that. For a long long time it was like that. Even in 1994 when I started to think about doing something about what had happened . . . didn't come in a way that said I needed to do something about what had happened to me because that was wrong, it was like it could still be happening and that would be wrong. What happened to me wasn't wrong – that was my own fault . . . I deserved that!

The first thought about reporting it was because it might still be going on. I talked to my partner and I talked to my sisters about it . . . at one point I was going to write to Brendan Comiskey about it and I didn't – I stayed with it.

There were a whole series of ironies about it that year. My father and my sister Deirdre were meant to go to a family wedding and the wedding was in Ballymurn. Seán Fortune was going to be the celebrant of the Mass and she told me . . . that was just too much to think about. My father didn't want to go because he had some sense of what had happened . . . he'd never been able to talk about it but he knew that something wasn't ok. My sister went to the wedding with her partner and she told me afterwards that he had kids all around him and in particular young boys . . . 12- or 13-year-old boys. That just made me feel like there's no way that it's stopped – I was going to have to do something.

BK: *How did you make the distinction between it being wrong – if it was still going on – but in your own case it was your fault? There's a contradiction there.*

CO'G: There's a paradox there, I know . . . it's a complete contradiction. The only way to deal with what had happened was to believe it was my fault so I fundamentally and completely believed that. Most people when they first go to report it have no real connection with the impact of it on themselves. It's usually about their fear that it might be happening to somebody else. It really needs to be about the fact that it happened to them. There's a huge amount of work that needs to happen therapeutically and in many other ways to get people . . . and it was important for me to realise that it didn't matter just that it might be happening to other people but at the most basic level it mattered that it happened to me!

BK: *But that's true of a lot of things. People can forget that they are a person themselves.*

CO'G: If I accepted that I mattered then it was that bad. If I accepted that it wasn't my fault then I was really raped. If I accepted that I was a boy . . . that I was 14, 15 and 16 years of age [when it happened] and that he was a Catholic priest and an adult man, and that I didn't have a choice, and that even when I tried to say no and when I tried to get away that I wasn't physically allowed to get away . . . and there was no space . . . that's too much to bear. That's too shattering. I couldn't even begin to think first of all I'm a man . . . men are not meant to be victims and they're not meant to be sexual victims particularly. I can't deal with that – there's no way I want to go there – so you don't. So you do something else – it's my fault, grand – but it's ok to see other people as vulnerable but your own needs don't have to exist and you must not be vulnerable yourself.

BK: *At this stage to compare the way you look on it now as opposed to then do you think it's stronger now because you can look on yourself as being a victim?*

CO'G: The most important thing that happened for me was to realise that I had been a victim and to be able to connect with the devastation that resulted from that. It took a long time to do that. I mean it was two years after I went to the Gardaí before I even began to get a sense of what I'd been through and what that meant. It took a huge amount of work and support from people who were very important to me – people who supported me through that.

Therapists in particular who just really stayed with me until I was ready to confront that ... but I just couldn't. I mean I didn't feel anything about anything. The only feelings I ever had in the world were about other people; they weren't about myself. I related to the world through other people and at that point I had only existed in relation to other people. My only value was in what I was worth to other people and what I could do for them. None of it had anything to do with myself because I just wasn't worth it and also because I just didn't feel. Don't get into feelings – I'd rather not feel anything. Just make everything [about me] not matter and then it's ok. It was a huge job – I was a nightmare of a client even to get to the point where I could recognise what had happened to me and what that meant. To connect to the devastation of that and the hurt of that was huge. It was February 1995 when I first went to the Gardaí and my father was very instrumental in that because he finally acknowledged that he couldn't live with it any more. He knew that something had happened – my sister told him that something had gone on – and he hadn't slept in 12 years. He just couldn't live with it – it was killing him. That was the real key – that was the last piece. Never mind the fact that it might be happening but now it's affecting him, which was what I was always terrified of. Seán Fortune used to always threaten to tell my parents and that's what I couldn't cope with – the idea of what it would do to them and what it would do to my father.

BK: Some people within the last few years – for example when they ring in to discuss your case on radio programmes – have said that at 15 or 16 you should have been old enough to fight him off and you should have known that what was happening was wrong. I have my own view on that – which wouldn't necessarily be in agreement with them – but do you think they just don't understand the enormity of the abuse?

CO'G: I think they don't understand . . . I think they need to believe, just like I did, that it's not true that a Catholic priest could rape a teenage boy. I think they need to believe that boys and young men are not victims and can't be victims. I think it's all about their own stuff . . . it's about their inability to recognise maybe even their own vulnerability. The first time I was in a friend's house in London — about two years after I'd gone to the Gardaí – her 15-year-old son came and sat down at the table. It was a real shock . . . I nearly fell off the chair because he was so young – he was a boy! That really shocked me because I suddenly realised, well, so was I . . . I was a boy [when the abuse happened]. I was just a kid – I had no clue. I don't know how much things have changed but I was particularly naive as well in lots of ways.

BK: At the time it happened people growing up were very different [to nowadays] . . . One would certainly get the impression that a 15-year-old then and a 15-year-old now would have a bit of a gap between them [in terms of maturity and naivety] which is probably something that people now don't realise.

CO'G: The only piece of sex education we ever received in school was at 16 when we told by a priest that having sex with a condom on was like having a bath with your socks on and that 95 per cent of boys masturbated and the other 5 per cent were liars. That was the total of our sex education all the way through school. Our science teacher in third year at the time the abuse had started flicked pass the sections on human reproduction and wouldn't even go into it. That's the level of naivety that we were being kept in and that was the level of ignorance and naivety that we possessed at the time.

BK: Do you think that was something that possibly came from the Church and highlighted just how much power the Church had?

CO'G: Well, the only sex education we ever received was from a priest. I went to a Christian Brothers school.

BK: There was an irony in that itself?

CO'G: Absolutely. The Church controlled education and that had very positive impacts for Ireland and I also think it had very negative impacts for Ireland.

BK: Where people couldn't accept that this could happen do you think that had a lot to do with the fact that the Catholic Church was what they believed in and it was essential to their very existence – it gave them a purpose?

CO'G: It was central to our lives – it doesn't just give us our faith ... it didn't just give us meaning. I don't think we can just blame the Church for this – I don't think that's good enough. I think we need to look at our part in it [as a society]. There was a contract between us and the Church and from them it was: give us undying and unquestioned obedience and do exactly what we tell you to do and what we'll give you instead is a complete moral blanket. You'll live in a comfort zone – you'll never have to think about right and wrong, you don't have to think about personal morality. You don't have to bother your little heads with any ideas about sexuality or love, or hate, or right or wrong – we'll tell you! Just do whatever we tell you to do. You can do whatever you like to people by the way just as long as you go to Mass every Sunday and as long as you confess. As long as you kneel down at the front of the church every weekend – it doesn't matter how you go out and behave towards other people then because if you confess anyway and if you're good and give your contributions to the Church then you'll go to Heaven and everything's grand. That's a fantastic comfort zone – why would anyone want to give that up? That was the contract and we bought into it. We all bought into it – I did.

BK: Maybe that's another reason why people find it so hard to accept – if this happened and it's wrong then that's saying society let it happen?

CO'G: Yeah, but we did. I think the point is that I'm not pointing the finger at society – I'm part of that – we all did [let this happen]. We all allowed that to happen. I was down in Killarney at the Labour Party conference and I was talking down there about this in some regard and I remember that whole concept of Ireland as a Republican democracy and that part of the Constitution that says all the powers of the government are derived from the people – the judicial, executive and legislative powers are derived from the people. That's the power with which children are being raped and abused. It's our power that has allowed that to happen and we need to accept that – it doesn't mean that we're to blame. It doesn't mean that we're all at fault individually but we're responsible for it and we need to own that. Maybe we also need to let ourselves off the hook a bit and stop beating ourselves up about it. It's not about fault, it's not about blame – it's about responsibility and it's about facing the truth of our own actions, or inactions, and deciding what we're going to do from now on and what we're going to do to put right what's already happened. That's the key part.

BK: *Do you think that a lot of people have a misconception about you and the organisation [One in Four] – that your sole aim is to bring down the Church?*

CO'G: Yeah . . . but the reality of the organisation is that 75 per cent of the people that we work with – and we're now seeing 60 to 70 people a week – have not been abused by clerics. The organisation is not a clerical abuse group – we're not a lobby group. We're not a campaign group – we're a therapeutic and support service for people who have been sexually abused – wherever it may have happened. Three quarters of the people we see have not been abused by clerics – they've been abused in their families, in their schools, by professionals like doctors, dentists or whatever and by both genders. We're seeing a significant number of people who have been abused by women as well. That's an area we're seeing much more of now and I think on one level it's difficult but it's also a positive thing because I think it's emerging and we are beginning to deal with it a little bit. The organisation has never been about clerical abuse, it has never been about campaigning and lobbying – it's been about supporting people on an individual basis.

People [who] have that fantasy about what we're about – well, that's their fantasy. It's got very little to do with the truth. I suppose one of the very positive things that happened around all of this for me personally has been the massive level of support that we've had from members of the clergy. I was at a function last night and a guy came up and introduced himself as a Dominican priest and just wanted to encourage me to keep going and that happens on a daily basis. We get letters or calls and even from some members of the hierarchy you know – some encouragement.

BK: *Maybe that's a thing that a lot of people possibly don't comprehend either – at the end of the day priests are just people the same as everyone else and there are good ones and bad ones – as there are good and bad people in every profession. Maybe a lot of people can't disassociate the person from the job, as it were?*

CO'G: People don't want to do that because it's too shattering for themselves and their lives and what they've done and how they've lived. Like I said, they bought into the deal. But what if the deal is based on a big fat lie? I can understand why people get so angry but that's about their own fears and their own anxieties and very little to do with what we're doing. Not just do we have many members of the clergy who are supportive of us and encourage us to keep going, we equally have a number of members of the clergy – of both genders – who are clients of the organisation. The whole concept of us working to bring down the Church couldn't possibly be further from the truth! I think the irony of the situation is that the Church has done a very good job of that itself. The reason we're at this point is because when people turned to the Church it wasn't there!

BK: *How did you feel when Cardinal Connell eventually made a sort of apology about what happened?*

CO'G: Cardinal Connell has never apologised for his role. He has never apologised or acknowledged his own negligence and his own failures in this. He's apologised for the fact that children were abused by priests.

BK: *Yes, but it would appear – certainly to me anyway – that the only reason he apologised was because it was found out and was out in the open. If it hadn't been brought out in the open do you think he would ever have apologised?*

CO'G: The greatest sadness for me has always been that the Church is reactive rather than proactive. It doesn't come out and say 'here, look, this is what's going on and this is what we want to do about it – let's talk about it'. It waits for something to come out, it waits for something to be discovered, it waits until it has no choice but to say something and then it says something – usually the wrong thing. It's never proactive.

BK: *Obviously I can't begin to imagine the different emotions that you must go through when you hear different things being said by the likes of Cardinal Connell.*

CO'G: Well, you know, these days I think I'm definitely angry but in a functional rather than a dysfunctional way. Anger is important. I mean, it says 'hang on, what's going on here, this isn't ok . . . what are we going to do about this?' I think it's really important to be in touch with that – it doesn't shock or surprise me. I've been working around this issue professionally now for six years and in terms of how organisations and institutions deal with this stuff, be it social services and the government and the police and whoever else in the UK, or be it the health boards, the Church and the Gardaí or whoever else in Ireland, there are slight differences but they are essentially the same failures that we see again and again. I'm always shocked but I'm never surprised. If you're not shocked then I think you don't get what's happened.

BK: *When someome comes to you who has been abused, how does it affect you? Do you relate to it in terms of what happened to you?*

CO'G: I don't think so . . . no. I don't think it's possible to work with someone in a supportive way – particularly if you're trying to do it professionally – unless you've dealt with your own stuff or unless, at the very least, you continue to deal with it and you find a way to keep it to one side when you're engaging with someone else and that's a really important part of the training that I took. It was why I was so lucky to be trained by the people I trained with because there was a huge focus on that. I think the fact that on another level I've had to go there myself and address this stuff for myself means that I know it's possible and I'm not afraid to go there.

BK: You know that they can do it as well?

CO'G: Yes and I know the devastation and heartache and I know it's possible to go there and come back again. I know that that means I'm ready and willing and able to go there. Everyone who works in the organisation identifies that they themselves have had that experience – that's all of the therapists and all of the staff. It means that as soon as someone comes in the door there is a level of understanding and acceptance that's palpable – that they can perceive. They might get that in other places but it's about their perception of it and it's what allows people to come forward. I know it makes a difference . . . I know it makes it possible for people to shrug off another level of that fear . . . it doesn't mean that it's all gone or that there's instant trust because there isn't.

We say to people 'you take your time and let yourself not trust'. It does make a difference and it does encourage people to speak out because they know that the person sitting with them, if they say to them 'you can get through this', know they can get through it because they themselves have got through it – and that's valuable. Everybody's experience is completely unique and everybody is a unique individual and that's the way the organisation works. The first time we meet with somebody it's about sitting down and working out what they want and what they need to happen for them and then looking at how we can meet that need – so we're very needs responsive. There isn't a number of boxes that we make people jump into – it's not a 'one size fits all' approach. It's very much about what an individual person needs.

BK: There are obvious effects on you with regard to what happened but do you ever wonder what you would be like if it had never happened? What sort of person do you think you would be now?

CO'G: Oh God! Not anymore but endlessly for years I wondered what I would be like if this hadn't happened. It's something that we all go through at different levels. I was sitting with someone this morning who was saying that and couldn't say anything else for about half an hour and it's real. It's about trying to get away from it . . . I am who I am and I think the road to recovery for me was about trying to find out who I was before, throughout, in, beyond, because of and despite the abuse and in every other experience of my life. The big thing for me was recognising that I wasn't the abuse. For years I thought I was foul and separating those [years] off became very important.

BK: Are you happy with who you are now?

CO'G: Yeah, I'm happy with who I am now and I'm getting better at acknowledging that as well . . . ah! No, I am. I feel good about who I am and what I do . . . I don't think I'm any better than anybody else. It's why I find some of this hero stuff a little bit bizarre and extraordinary because I'm very suspicious of the reasons why people create heroes. I think half the time people create heroes so they don't have to believe in their own capacity to do incredible things and I think we're all capable of doing amazing things. The one thing that my work has taught me is to have a huge respect and admiration for the capacity of the human spirit to be incredible which I believe it is.

I've really had a very positive attitude towards the goodness of humanity emerge over the last several years and that's been an amazing part of it . . . that as you go into that dark place you emerge – or I've emerged – really believing in the goodness of humanity. I like who I am but then I like who we all are.

Appendix 3: Timeline of events

1916–1917 – Preparations in the Vatican for the *Codex Juris Canonici* are completed. The code was promulgated in 1917, became effective in 1918 and was a complete codification of all universal Church law then binding in the Latin Church.

1930s–1990s – Approximately 35,000 Irish children and unmarried mothers were sent to a network of 250 Church-run industrial schools, reformatories, orphanages and hostels.

1942 – Fr Martin Clancy is ordained at St Peter's College, Wexford.

1958 – Fr James Grennan is ordained at St Peter's College.

1963 – Death of Bishop of Ferns James Staunton.
       – Fr Donal Collins joins the teaching staff of St Peter's College.

1964 – Donal Herlihy appointed Bishop of Ferns.

1966 – Fr Collins is sent by Bishop Herlihy to London for two years after abusing boarders.

1969 – Rev. Micheal Ledwith appointed to seminary staff at St Peter's.

1972 – Fr Martin Clancy appointed to Ballindaggin.

1974 – Fr James Doyle is ordained at St Peter's College.

1979 – Fr Seán Fortune is ordained at St Peter's College.
       – Visit of Pope John Paul II to Ireland.

1980 – Brendan Comiskey ordained Auxiliary Bishop of Dublin.

1981 – Bishop Donal Herlihy is made a Freeman of Wexford.
       – Bishop Herlihy has Fr Seán Fortune assessed by a psychologist in Dublin.
       – Gardaí do not investigate rumours about Canon Martin

Clancy because of the absence of a written complaint.

1982   – Bishop Herlihy arranges counselling for Fr James Doyle in Dublin.

1983   – Death of Bishop Donal Herlihy.

    – The second *Codex Juris Canonici* is promulgated by Pope John Paul II.

1984   – Bishop Brendan Comiskey is appointed Bishop of Ferns.

    – Seminarians in St Patrick's Seminary, Maynooth, express their concerns to a Senior Dean regarding the alleged inappropriate behaviour of Micheal Ledwith, then a Vice-President of the College, towards younger students.

1985   – Monsignor Micheal Ledwith appointed President of St Patrick's College, Maynooth.

    – Bishop Comiskey has Fr Seán Fortune assessed at St Patrick's Hospital, Dublin.

1987   – The first set of guidelines on child abuse is published by the State.

    – Bishop Comiskey moves Fr Fortune from Wexford to London.

1988   – Desmond Connell is appointed archbishop of Dublin.

    – Bishop Comiskey has Fr Fortune assessed by another psychiatrist at St Patrick's Hospital and by a psychiatrist in London.

    – South Eastern Health Board investigate allegations of abuse against schoolchildren by Fr James Grennan. Bishop Comiskey encourages Fr Grennan to take a holiday while investigations are ongoing. The Garda file into the affair is mislaid and disappears.

    – Fr Donal Collins is appointed Principal of St Peter's College. Not a single teacher at St Peter's, when asked by the bishop, objects to Collins' candidacy for the position.

1989   – Church & General had informed bishops of the availability of insurance cover: Bishop Comiskey purchases a policy without any risk assessment by the insurer.

1990   – States of Fear broadcast on RTÉ, examining abuse in reformatory and industrial schools.

    – Bishop Brendan Comiskey is made a Freeman of Wexford.

    – Bishop Comiskey grants Fr James Doyle sabbatical leave in August. A month later Doyle enters a plea of guilty to indecently assaulting an eleven-year-old boy, at Wexford

District Court. He is the first priest in Ireland to be charged
with this offence.

– Fifty-four primary school teachers in Wexford publicly object
to media coverage of Fr. Doyle's court case.

– Bishop Comiskey arranges counselling for Fr Doyle in
England.

1991 – Bishop Comiskey moves Fr Clancy from Ballindaggin to a
nearby parish after receiving an allegation of abuse against
him. Left in ministry, Fr Clancy dies in 1993.

1992 – Bishop Eamon Casey is exposed in *The Irish Times* as having
fathered a son eighteen years earlier. He flees the country.

– Gardaí are aware of fresh allegations about Canon Martin
Clancy, but decline to interview him.

1993 – It was revealed that the late Fr Michael Cleary had fathered
two children with his long-time housekeeper, whom the
priest lived with as his common-law wife.

– Bishop Comiskey arranges counselling for Fr Donal Collins
in America.

1994 – Death of Fr James Grennan in Monageer.

– Allegation made to Gardaí that Monsignor Micheal Ledwith
abused a boy in 1981. A settlement is agreed by both parties
with no admission to liability.

– The Brendan Smyth scandal erupts in Ireland after he is
sentenced to four years in prison for abuse of children in
Northern Ireland. In November, the coalition government in
the Republic collapses after divisions emerge between Labour
and Fianna Fáil over the handling of extradition requests for
the priest.

1995 – Bishop Brendan Comiskey takes a sabbatical from Ferns to
receive treatment for alcoholism in America. He returns early
in 1996.

– In November, Fr Seán Fortune is charged with child sexual
abuse in Wexford.

– Natural Justice, a leaflet endorsing Biship Comiskey as
a Church leader, is signed by all of Wexford's Oireachtas
members, including three members of the government.

1996 – Bishop Brendan Comiskey holds press conference in St Peter's
to answer questions about his handling of allegations of abuse
by some of his priests.

Appendix 3

- Monsignor Michael Ledwith retires from Maynooth College.
- Framework document, setting down guidelines for the handling by the 33 bishops in 26 dioceses of abuse allegations, is finalised.
- A Garda inquiry into the 1998 Garda handling of investigation in Monageer finds that the matter was not fully investigated by Gardaí at the time.

1998
- Fr Donal Collins receives four-year sentence at Wexford Circuit Court after pleading guilty to indecently assaulting former pupils.
- The Oireachtas passes The Protections for Persons Reporting Child Abuse Act 1998.
- Seminary at St Peter's College is closed due to falling numbers of vocations.

1999
- Fr Donal Collins is released from prison on health grounds.
- Fr Seán Fortune appears at Wexford Circuit Court on 2 March. He is remanded in custody, applies for and is granted bail, and takes his own life on 13 March.
- Pope John Paul II rejects any link between child sexual abuse and celibacy.

2001
- *Sacramentorum Sanctitatis Tutela* provides that all allegations of child sexual abuse should be directed to the Congregation for the Doctrine of the Faith in the Vatican.
- Sex Offenders Act 2001 requires a person convicted of certain sex offences to furnish their name and address to police.

2002
- 19 March: the BBC broadcasts *Suing the Pope*, about the abuse perpetrated by Fr Sean Fortune.
- 1 April: Bishop Comiskey resigns from Ferns.
- 2 April: RTÉ broadcasts *Suing The Pope*.
- 6 April: Bishop Eamonn Walsh appointed Apostolic Administrator of the Diocese of Ferns.
- The Irish government agrees to a generous indemnity deal with the religious orders following negotiations by Education Minister Michael Woods. Eighteen orders would agree to contribute a mere €128m of the redress costs of around €1.1bn.
- Denis McCullough SC is commissioned by the Catholic hierarchy to investigate allegations that the bishops had not responded adequately to complaints of apparent sexual

harassment of seminarians at Maynooth College in the early 1980s.

- RTÉ aired a *Prime Time* television documentary, *Cardinal Secrets*, which accused Cardinal Desmond Connell with mishandling the sex abuse scandal.
- Bishop Eamonn Walsh visits Monageer and apologises to anyone abused by Fr Grennan.
- George Birmingham SC presents a preliminary report on child sexual abuse by priests in Ferns to the Minister for Health and Children, who establishes a non-statutory inquiry under the chairmanship of Justice Francis Murphy.

2003   - Diarmuid Martin is appointed Archbishop of Dublin

2004   - Fr Donal Collins and Fr James Doyle are defrocked.

2005   - Monsignor Micheal Ledwith is defrocked.

- Publication of *The Ferns Report*. The Ferns Inquiry was an official Irish government inquiry into the allegations of clerical sexual abuse in the diocese. The report recorded its revulsion at the extent, severity and duration of the child sexual abuse perpetrated on children by priests acting under the aegis of the Diocese of Ferns. One hundred allegations were made against twenty-one priests between 1962 and 2002.
- The McCullough Inquiry finds that concerns of apparent propensities by Monsignor Ledwith rather than accusations of actual crime or specific offences have been communicated to the bishops by the Senior Dean of Maynooth College.
- The Diocese of Ferns pays out €2,792,118 in compensation to victims of clerical abuse.
- Joseph Ratzinger elected Pope Benedict XVI.

2006   - Denis Brennan appointed Bishop of Ferns.

2007   - An eight-year enquiry and report into the Brothers of Charity Congregation's Holy Family School in Galway investigates allegations of the abuse of 121 intellectually disabled children in residential care in the period 1965–1998.

- First civil action taken against an Irish diocese (Ferns) in the High Court for damages arising from clerical abuse allegations.

2008   - The Archdiocese of Dublin initially refuses the Murphy Commission access to thousands of church documents, claiming they are confidential.

2009   – March: Bishop John Magee of Cloyne removes himself from his duties after it is disclosed he did not follow proper child protection guidelines.

     – May: the report of the Commission to Inquire into Child Abuse (*The Ryan Report*) details cases of emotional, physical and sexual abuse of thousands of Irish children over 70 years who attended more than 200 Catholic-run schools from the 1930s until the 1990s.

     – November: *The Murphy Report* is published. It concludes that the Archdiocese of Dublin's preoccupations in dealing with cases of child sexual abuse, at least until the mid-1990s, were the maintenance of secrecy, the avoidance of scandal, the protection of the reputation of the Church, and the preservation of its assets. All other considerations, including the welfare of children and justice for victims, were subordinated to these priorities. Bishops Donal Murray and James Moriarty resign.

2010   – 5 March: The Diocese of Ferns asks the laity to help pay their outstanding bills arising from compensation claims.

     – 20 March: Pope Benedict in a letter addressed to the Catholics of Ireland, says he is 'truly sorry' for the harm done to Catholics who suffered 'sinful and criminal' abuse at the hands of priests, brothers and nuns.

     – April: death of Donal Collins in Wexford.

     – December: Chapter 19 of *The Murphy Report* is published. Fr Tony Walsh was free to abuse children from 1978, when complaints were first made, until 1996.

2011   – St Peter's College celebrates its bicentenary.

Bibliography

Books

The Boston Globe, *Betrayal, The Crisis in the Catholic Church* (Little, Brown and Company, 2002)

Brady, Conor, *Up With The Times* (Gill & Macmillan, 2005)

Coogan, Tim Pat, *De Valera, Long Fellow, Long Shadow* (Hutchinson, 1993)

Conway, Vicky, Daly, Yvonne & Schweppe, Jennifer, *Irish Criminal Justice* (Clarus Press, 2010)

Conway, Eamonn, Duffy, Eugene & Shields, Attracta, *The Church and Child Sexual Abuse* (Columba, 1999)

Cooney, John, *John Charles McQuaid* (O'Brien Press, 1991)

Culleton, Edward, *Celtic and Early Christian Wexford* (Four Courts Press, 1991)

Downing, John, *Bertie Ahern* (Blackwater Press, 2004)

Dwyer, T. Ryle, *Éamon de Valera* (Poolbeg Press Ltd, 1991)

Ferriter, Diarmid, *Occasions of Sin* (Profile Books, 2009)

FitzGerald, Garret, *All in a Life* (Gill & Macmillan, 1991)

Forde, Rev. Walter, *Church, Communication and Change* (Kara Publications, 1995)

Forde, Rev. Walter, *Memory & Mission, Christianity in Wexford, 600 to 2000 AD* (Diocese of Ferns History & Archive Committee, 1999)

Furlong, Nicky, *A History of Co. Wexford* (Gill & Macmillan, 2003)

Flannery, Tom, *From The Inside* (Mercier, 1999)

Fortune, Fr Seán, *Ballymurn, 1847–1993, A Pictorial History* (1993)

Gahan, John V., *The Secular Priests of the Diocese of Ferns* (Éditions du Signe, 2000)

Hayden, Jackie, *In Their Own Words* (Hot Press Books, 2003)

Hickey, D. J. and Doherty, J. E., *A New Dictionary of Irish History* (Gill & Macmillan 2003)

Hoban, Brendan, *Change or Decay, Irish Catholicism in Crisis* (Banley House, 2004)

Hussey, Gemma, *Ireland Today* (Viking, 1993)

Keogh Dermot, *Ireland and the Vatican: The Politics and Diplomacy of Church State Relations, 1922–1960* (Cork University Press, 1995)

Kinealy, Christine, *A New History of Ireland* (Sutton Publishing, 2004)

Littleton, John & Maher, Eamon (eds.), *The Dublin Murphy Report* (Columba, 2010)

Littleton, John & Maher, Eamon, *What Being Catholic Means To Me* (Columba, 2009)

O'Connor, Alison, *A Message from Heaven: The Life and Crimes of Father Sean Fortune* (Brandon, 2000)

O'Connor, Garry, *Pope John Paul II* (Bloomsbury, 2005)

O'Gorman, Colm, *Beyond Belief* (Hodder & Stoughton, 2009)

Raftery, Mary & O'Sullivan, Eoin, *Suffer the Little Children* (New Island Books, 1999)

Reck, Padge, *Wexford – A Municipal History* (Mulgannon Publications, 1987)

Ridge, Martin, *Breaking The Silence* (Gill & Macmillan, 2008)

Richardson, John E., *Analysing Newspapers* (Palgrave Macmillan, 2007)

Robertson QC, Geoffrey, *The Case of the Pope* (Penguin, 2010)

Scallan, Eithne (ed.), *The Twin Churches Book, Wexford, 1858–2008* (Carraig Mor House, 2008)

Terruwe, Dr Anna & Baars, Dr Conrad W., *Loving and Curing the Neurotic* (Arlington House, 1972)

Tóibín, Colm, *The Empty Family* (Penguin Viking, 2010)

Tóibín, Colm, *Mothers and Sons* (Picador, 2006)

Twomey, Dr Vincent, *The Church and Child Sexual Abuse* (Columba, 1999)

Twomey, Dr Vincent, *The End of Irish Catholicism?* (Veritas, 2003)

Yallop, David, *The Power and the Glory* (Carroll & Graf, 2007)

Reports, inquiries and press releases

Baars, Dr Conrad W., and Terruwe, Dr Anna, *The Role of the Church in the Causation, Treatment and Prevention of the Crisis in the Priesthood* (1971)

Comiskey, Bishop Brendan, *The Church and State. Their Relationship in Ireland* (1986)

Child Protection Guidelines for Post-Primary Schools (2004)

Child Sexual Abuse: Framework for a Church Response (1996)

Doyle, Fr Thomas, *The 1922 Instruction and the 1962 Instruction Crimen Sollicitationis* (www.richardsipe.com, 2008)

The Ferns Report, published by The Minister for Health, 2005

Investigation into Child Sex Abuse in Monageer in 1988 (Department of Justice

1996)

The Report of the Commission to Inquire into Child Abuse (2009)

Kennedy, Margaret, 'Christianity and Child Sex Abuse', *Child Abuse Review* (2000)

Murphy, Sarah. Thesis. 'An understanding of the first State investigation in clerical child sex abuse in the form of The Ferns Report' (2007)

Morris, Fintan, 'St Peter's College in the 20th Century' (www.spcppu.com)

McCullough SC, Denis, 'Inquiry Into Certain Matters Relating to Maynooth College' (2005)

Porteous, Prof. Julian, *The Essence and Mission of Priesthood in Pastores Dabo Vobis* (www.victorclaveau.com)

Report by Commission of Investigation into Catholic Archdiocese of Dublin (2009)

Royal College of Surgeons, Ireland, 'Suing The Pope and Scandalising the People: Irish Attitudes to Sexual Abuse by Clergy Pre and Post Screening of a Critical Documentary' (2009)

Royal College of Surgeons, Ireland, 'Time to Listen, Confronting Child Sexual Abuse by Catholic Clergy in Ireland' (2003)

Sipe, Richard, *Priests, Celibacy and Sexuality* (2009) and an interview with Richard Sipe (www.richardsipe.com, 2009)

Savage, Robert & Smith, James, 'The Church in the 21st Century From Crisis to Renewal' (2002)

Newspapers and journals

Bloomberg Businessweek
County Wexford Press (2001)
Daily Star
Irish Examiner
Irish Independent
Journals of The Wexford Historical Society (2003–2009)
Law Society Gazette (2004)
London Review of Books
National Catholic Reporter
Studies: An Irish Quarterly Review (2000)
Sunday Independent
The Curate's Diary (1995–1998)
The Dublin Review (2006)
The Financial Times
The Forum (1999)
The Furrow (2006)

BIBLIOGRAPHY

The Irish Catholic (2005)
The People Newspaper Group, archives.
The Free Press, archives.
The Irish Times
The Sunday Times
The Wexford Echo Group, archives.

Organisations and websites
Department of Education and Science (2001)
Department of Health and Children (1996 and 1999)
The Catholic Communications Office
The Catholic News Agency
The Church of Ireland Press Office
The Diocese of Ferns Communications Office

www.abusewatch.net
www.bishop-accountability.org
www.catholica.com.au
www.catholicapologetics.info
www.cbsnews.com
www.childabusecommission.ie
www.clerus.org
www.consumerclassactionsmasstorts.com
www.ferns.ie
www.oneinfour.org
www.richardsipe.com
www.studiesirishreview.ie
www.vatican.va
www.victorclaveau.com

Acknowledgements

The author would like to thank his many colleagues in the newsroom in *The Wexford Echo* since he became editor in 1996 who put the loyalty of their readers first in their coverage of the remarkable events in the Diocese of Ferns in the past twenty years. Many people helped in the preparation of this book but it would be remiss for the author not to thank the subediting skills of Helen Ashdown and the advice of Sarah Murphy. A project of this undertaking should be a labour of love, but it wasn't. The book came about through the prism of others' pain, which will continue until their dying day.